# THE ECONOMICS OF MUSIC

## The Economics of Big Business

This series of books provides short, accessible introductions to the economics of major business sectors. Each book focuses on one particular global industry and examines its business model, economic strategy, the determinants of profitability as well as the unique issues facing its economic future. More general cross-sector challenges, which may be ethical, technological or environmental, as well as wider questions raised by the concentration of economic power, are also explored. The series offers rigorous presentations of the fundamental economics underpinning key industries suitable for both course use and a professional readership.

### Published

*The Economics of Music*
Peter Tschmuck

*The Economics of Arms*
Keith Hartley

*The Economics of Airlines*
Volodymyr Bilotkach

# THE ECONOMICS OF MUSIC

PETER TSCHMUCK

**agenda**
publishing

First published in 2017 by Agenda Publishing

Agenda Publishing Limited
The Core
Science Central
Bath Lane
Newcastle upon Tyne
NE4 5TF
www.agendapub.com

ISBN 978-1-911116-07-3 (hardcover)
ISBN 978-1-911116-08-0 (paperback)

**British Library Cataloguing-in-Publication Data**
A catalogue record for this book is available from the British Library

Printed and bound in the UK by CPI Group (UK) Ltd, Croydon, CR0 4YY

# CONTENTS

# ACKNOWLEDGEMENTS

When Steven Gerrard at Agenda Publishing invited me to write a book on the economics of the music business, he preached to the choir, as I had already outlined such a topic. His inquiry, then, was just the trigger I had been waiting for to start writing *The Economics of Music*, a long overdue project. Digitization has revolutionized the music business in unprecedented ways. New business models have emerged, whereas old ones have disappeared. New economic principles have emerged as a result of the structural changes undergone by the industry. Digitization has revealed that music is a public good with positive externalities and incentives to free-ride. The relation between the different music industry sectors – recording, publishing and the live music business – has changed and new players have entered the markets. Whereas the recorded music industry has suffered severely from the digital paradigm shift, music publishing and the live music sector have benefitted from new business opportunities. The economic relevance of secondary music markets such as digital media, branding, sponsorship and merchandising have increased, providing additional revenue sources for labels, publishers and musicians. However, the artistic labour market has also been reconfigured, forcing musicians to search for new revenue streams owing to the decline of the recorded music industry. The relevant literature has so far not accounted for these large-scale changes affecting the industry as it transitions from a physical to a digital world. By explaining the economic rules driving the digital music business today, this book aims to fill this gap.

Such a book project is always a challenge and demands support from different sides. I would like to thank Steven Gerrard for providing a perfect publishing platform. As in the years before, Marco Abel has helped to improve my English by proofreading the manuscript and suggesting valuable ideas for improvement. To focus on writing a book one also needs a laid-back environment. Thus, I would like to thank my wife, Magdaléna, and my daughter, Cornelia, for having been considerate of my writing process and for supporting me in overcoming difficulties. I dedicate this book to them with love.

Peter Tschmuck

# INTRODUCTION

**Music industry, music economy, music business**

If you google the term "music industry" the following Wikipedia entry tops the search list:

> The music industry consists of the companies and individuals that make money by creating and selling live music performances, sound recordings and music videos of songs and instrumental pieces. Among the many individuals and organizations that operate in the industry are: the songwriters and composers who create new music; the singers, musicians, conductors and bandleaders who perform the music; the companies and professionals who create and sell recorded music and/or sheet music (e.g., music publishers, producers, recording studios, engineers, record labels, retail and online music stores, performance rights organizations); and those that help organize and present live music performances (booking agents, promoters, music venues, road crew).[1]

This definition is a list of music industry actors. However, this listing does not tell us anything about the processes and structures of the music industry. The Oxford Music Online entry provides a more general and process-oriented definition of the music industry: "The music industry consists of a network involving the production, distribution, dissemination and consumption of music in a variety of forms, as well as the promotion of live music performances."[2]

In combining both definitions we can identify three closely linked sectors of the music industry: (1) the phonographic/recording industry, (2) music publishing and (3) the live music sector. Some definitions, however, speak about music industries instead of a single music industry, since music recording, music publishing and organizing live music follow different production, distribution and consumption logics. Yet recording, publishing and the concert business are closely linked. A recorded music company usually unites a recording and music publishing branch, since the former relies on the copyrights of

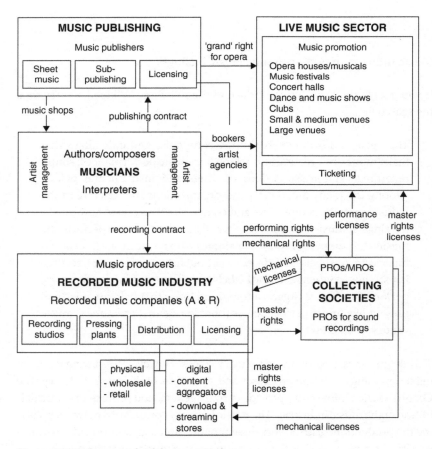

**Figure 0.1** A framework of the music industry

the latter. The concert business is not just the most important revenue source for musicians, but it also helps to sell recorded music. Economic studies prove that the recorded music and the concert markets are complementary goods. For all these reasons, I prefer the notion of three different but interlinked sectors within the music industry establishing "a network involving the production, distribution, dissemination and consumption of music".[3]

In addition to the three core industry sectors, the (music) collecting societies are also integral to the music industry. They form an institutional link between the musicians and the sectors as well as between the sectors. As collective music licensing bodies, they administer the rights of authors and composers (performance and mechanical rights) as well as the publishing rights of music publishers. The main task of performance rights organizations (PROs) and mechanical rights organizations (MROs) is to license the use of music by live music promoters, media companies and other (commercial) music users. In addition, recorded music companies assign the rights of their master recordings to special performance rights organizations that license them for broadcasting (radio, television, online) and other public reproductions of recordings (in clubs, bars, restaurants, shops, hotels, etc.). However, recorded music companies also directly license their master rights to digital music providers (e.g. download and streaming services) and for use in television films, movies, games and commercials. Likewise, music publishers directly license the so-called synchronization rights to advertising agencies and games developers, as well as to movie and television production companies.[4]

However, those commercial music users are not part of the core music industry; they instead provide secondary music markets for further exploitation of music copyrights. Other secondary music markets are linked to the live music business, such as musical instrument manufacturers and traders, ancillary music services (technical equipment, sound engineering, video production, lighting, logistics and transportation, accommodation, costume design and wardrobe, stage design and event conceptualization, pyrotechnics, security, cleaning, etc.), as well as the manufacturing and trade of merchandise. Branding and sponsoring partners of artists and live music promoters provide an additional and fast-growing secondary market in which the brand value of artists and music events are transferred to consumer products, and vice versa. The music industry and the secondary music markets are embedded in the music economy, which additionally includes music education,

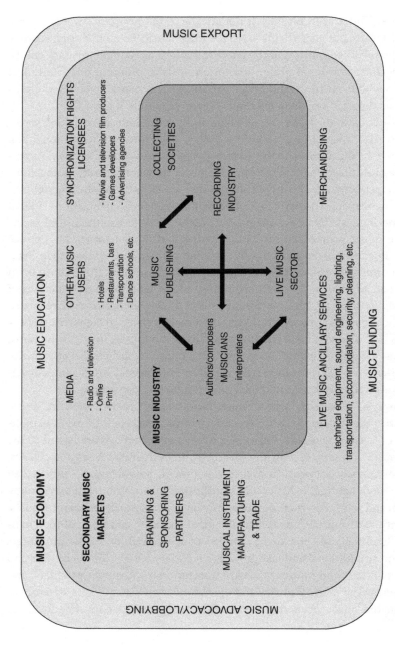

**Figure 0.2** A framework of the music economy

music advocacy/lobbying groups, music export services, and private as well as public music funding bodies.

Although music funding, music export, music education and music advocacy/lobbying also imply economic aspects, they do not directly establish a primary or secondary music market. Hence, this book is not about the music economy in the broadest sense; instead, it focuses on the music industry and the related secondary music markets – except the musical instruments sector.[5] I will highlight the organizational setting of the different sectors and markets and analyse from an economic perspective the role contracts and licensing agreements play, and how copyright regimes and rules of competition affect the practices defining the music industry. Therefore, the book explains the structures, practices and institutional settings of creation/production, dissemination/distribution and reception/consumption of the cultural good music, which together constitute the music business.

## The economic relevance of the music economy

According to the United Nations Conference on Trade and Development (UNCTAD) *Creative Economy Report 2010* (2010: 7), music is at the core of the cultural/creative/copyright industries, regardless of the model used.[6] In Europe, the cultural and creative sector contributed between 0.2 per cent (Malta) and 3.4 per cent (France) of value added to the gross national product (GNP) in 2008 (UNCTAD 2010: 29). In the Creative Industries Economic Estimates of the Department for Culture, Media and Sport (DCMS), a gross value added of £76,900 million was reported for the creative industries in the UK for 2013. The creative industries accounted for 5 per cent of the UK economy (DCMS 2015: 7). Grouping music together with performing and visual arts, the DCMS reports that this sector contributed 245,000 jobs and £5,450 million value added to the UK's GDP in 2013 (DCMS 2015: 14, 19).[7] The sector accounted for 0.79 per cent of total employment in the UK and 14.4 per cent of employment in the creative industries. The sector contributed a gross value added of 0.36 per cent to the total UK economy and accounted for 7.1 per cent of the value added by the creative industries (DCMS 2015). Between 1997 and 2013 "music, performing and visual arts" more than doubled their gross value added from £2,670 million to £5,450 million (DCMS 2015: 25).

The DCMS reports, however, do not exactly cover the music industry, since the statistical classification framework is broader than just music. To offer more precise data, UK for Music published the *Measuring Music* reports, which are collaboratively developed with the DCMS and the Office for National Statistics (ONS). According to the 2015 report, over 117,000 people were employed in the UK music industry and the sector contributed a gross value added of £4,100 million to the overall economy in 2014 (UK for Music 2015: 2). The UK music industry thus accounted for 0.38 per cent of total employment and for 0.08 per cent of the UK's GDP in 2014. According to the report's definition, the music industry consists of the creatives (musicians, composers, songwriters and lyricists), live music, recorded music, music publishing, music producers, recording studios and music representatives.[8] The creatives contribute £1,900 million (46.9 per cent) of value added, the live music sector £924 million (22.8 per cent), the recorded music industry £615 million (15.2 per cent), music publishing £410 million (10.1 per cent), music producers and recording studios £116 million (2.9 per cent) and music representatives £89 million (2.2 per cent). Most of the people – 69,300 (59.1 per cent) – working in the UK music industry are single artists (musicians, composers, songwriters and lyricists). The live music sector also employs a considerable number of people: 25,100 (21.4 per cent). In addition, 10,900 people (9.3 per cent) are music producers or work for recording studios and another 8,520 (7.3 per cent) are employed by recorded music companies. There are 2,300 (2 per cent) music representatives. The music publishers employ the remaining 1,200 (1 per cent) people.

Another recent study on the music industry's economic contribution to a national economy was conducted in Germany for 2014. According to this study (Seufert *et al.* 2015), the music industry contributed a gross value added of €3,900 million to the German economy and it employs 127,600 people. Unlike the UK for Music report, the German study also included the music instrument sector, music collecting societies and private music education (but not public music education and the publicly funded live music sector such as music theatres, concert halls and orchestras). Thus, the German study is broader than the UK study and highlights aspects of the broader music

**Table 0.1** The economic relevance of the UK music industry

| Music industry sector | Gross value added in £m | in % of total | Employment | in % of total |
|---|---|---|---|---|
| Creatives | 1,900 | 46.9 | 69,300 | 59.1 |
| Live music | 924 | 22.8 | 25,100 | 21.4 |
| Recorded music | 615 | 15.2 | 8,520 | 7.3 |
| Music publishing | 410 | 10.1 | 1,200 | 1.0 |
| Producers and recording studios | 116 | 2.9 | 10,900 | 9.3 |
| Music representatives | 89 | 2.2 | 2,300 | 2.0 |
| Total | 4,054 | 100 | 117,320 | 100 |

Source: After UK for Music (2015: 3–4)

**Table 0.2** The economic relevance of the German music industry/economy

| Music industry sector | Gross value added (in million €) | in % of total | Employment | in % of total |
|---|---|---|---|---|
| Live music | 1,040 | 26.6 | 32,629 | 25.6 |
| Recorded music | 880 | 22.5 | 19,866 | 15.6 |
| Musical instruments | 764 | 19.5 | 14,795 | 11.6 |
| Creatives | 573 | 14.6 | 27,895 | 21.9 |
| Private music education | 384 | 9.8 | 28,506 | 22.3 |
| Music publishing | 190 | 4.9 | 2,855 | 2.2 |
| Collecting societies | 85 | 2.2 | 1,070 | 0.8 |
| Total | 3,916 | 100 | 127,616 | 100 |

Source: After Seufert *et al.* (2015: 14–15)

economy. In Germany, the largest music sector was live music with a gross value added of €1,040 million (26.6 per cent) in 2014. Ranked second was the recorded music industry with value added of €880 million (22.5 per cent), which also included music producers and recording studios. The musical instruments sector (manufacturing and trade) contributed a value added of €764 million (19.5 per cent), which is significantly more than the creatives, who generated a value added of €573 million (14.6 per cent). Private music education, which is not part of the core music industry, contributed a value added of €384 million (9.8 per cent), which is twice as much as music publishing with €190 million (4.9 per cent). The smallest sector of the German music industry/economy in 2014 was the collecting societies with a value added of €85 million (2.2 per cent).

Despite using different frameworks and definitions, these studies help us to understand the economic relevance of the music industry/economy for the national GDP. The UK for Music study shows that the core music industry is rather small compared to other industries (e.g. oil and gas industry, financial services industry, automotive industry); but if the focus is widened to the broader music economy, the music-related value added becomes significant. In Germany, the music economy (without the public sector) ranked third behind the press sector and television broadcasting, but is larger than the movie industry, book publishing and radio broadcasting (Seufert *et al.* 2015: 10). If we also include the public music sector (music schools, music universities/conservatories and administrative bodies), we can see that the music economy forms an important part of Germany's overall economy.

## Notes

1. Wikipedia entry "Music Industry", https://en.wikipedia.org/wiki/Music_industry (retrieved 15 August 2016).
2. Oxford Music Online entry "Music Industry", www.oxfordmusiconline.com/subscriber/article/grove/music/A2262804 (retrieved 15 August 2016).
3. *Ibid.*
4. I discuss collecting societies in Chapter 4 (licensing of copyrights) and Chapter 5 (licensing of neighbouring/related rights).
5. Musical instrument manufacturing and trade are very specific economic sectors that follow a different logic of production, distribution and consumption. An in-depth analysis would go beyond the scope of this book.
6. UNCTAD identifies four different mapping models: (1) the UK model of the Department for Culture, Media and Sport (DCMS); (2) the symbolic texts model; (3) the concentric circles model; and (4) the copyright model of the World Intellectual Property Rights Organization (WIPO).
7. The sector *music, performing and visual arts* includes the standard industrial classification codes – 59.20: sound recording and music publishing activities; 85.52: cultural education; 90.01: performing arts; 90.02: support activities to performing arts; 90.03: artistic creation; and 90.04: operation of arts facilities. Employment includes the standard occupational classification for artists (3411), actors, entertainers and presenters (3413), dancers and choreographers (3414) and musicians (3415).
8. Whereas music representatives are included, collecting societies are absent from the music industry definition.

# 1

# A SHORT ECONOMIC HISTORY OF THE MUSIC BUSINESS

The invention of the phonograph by Thomas Alva Edison (1847–1931) in 1877 marked the outset of the modern music industry with mass production of phonograms and the emergence of a global distribution network for music cylinders and records. Music, however, was an economic good before the advent of the recorded music industry. Antique sources prove that musical products were already traded in the centuries BCE. It is reported that the Greek poet Pindar sent 470 lyrics from his hometown Thebes to the tyrant Hieron in Sicily in the fifth century BCE (Baierle 2009: 51). Pindar himself was not just a writer but also a kind of early music entrepreneur. Since lyric verses were usually accompanied by music performances and dance, Pindar also choreographed the dances for his odes. He was commissioned to stage performances in all parts of ancient Greece and was an ancient "impresario" in high demand (Carey 2007). Pindar was an early example of an artist who was commissioned by wealthy and powerful patrons.

We can usefully divide the economic history of music into five periods:

1. The era of music patronage from ancient times until the late eighteenth century;
2. The era of music publishing from the late eighteenth century until the 1920s;
3. The era of broadcasting from the 1920s to the 1950s;
4. The era of the recorded music industry from the 1950s until c.2000;
5. The era of the digital music economy since 2000.

## The era of music patronage

### From the Middle Ages to the Renaissance

The era of early music patronage covers the ancient period until the medieval age when the Catholic Church became the main patron for the arts, especially for music. Music was an integral part of liturgy and the term *cappella* still refers to practising music in chapels and churches. Music schools in monasteries (e.g. the Abbey in St Gall/Switzerland) and at the medieval cathedrals (e.g. Notre Dame in Paris) were centres of music education and almost all famous medieval composers of sacred music received their musical training there.[1] Profane musicians such as Minnesingers in the Holy Roman German Empire and troubadours in France and Spain were high-ranking members of medieval society (e.g. Guillaume IX of Aquitaine (1071–1126) and Oswald von Wolkenstein (*c.*1376–1445)) practising their art at court festivals. Some of them, however, also had to earn their living from performing at village fairs and other festivities, and a few, such as Walther von der Vogelweide (*c.*1170–*c.*1230) managed to climb up the social ladder because of their art.[2]

Whereas sacred music was taught in monasteries and cathedrals, profane music education was not organized until the thirteenth century when municipal music guilds began to regulate music composition. At this time, writing music was seen as a craft rather than an art form. During the Renaissance period, music functioned either in a religious or military context. Singers were trained in court chapels, whereas instrumentalists – mainly trumpeters and drummers – served as court musicians (Tschmuck 2001).

During the Renaissance, the royal courts took over the patronage of music from the clergy. The emergence of centralized states with absolute rulers established a courtly society in the seventeenth and eighteenth centuries (see Elias 1983), and music became an integral part of the self-manifestation of baroque sovereigns and an important tool for representation. The Habsburg Emperor Leopold I, a gifted composer himself, employed more than one hundred musicians, including performers and composers. When he married Margherita of Spain in 1666, he commissioned the Italian composer Antonio Cesti to write the opera *Il pomo d'oro*. It was staged over the course of two days, becoming an integral part of the marriage celebrations that continued for a period of two years.[3] Opera at this time was not viewed as an autonomous art form; instead, it was an integral part of festivities and spectacular events.

## The opera business

During the same period, however, a market-oriented opera business began to develop. The first public opera house – San Cassiano in Venice – was established in 1637 when the first commercial opera *Andromeda* by Benedetto Ferrari and Francesca Manelli was staged during the carnival season. It was the first time that an opera production was not financed by noble patrons but by "the artists themselves who took on the risks and obligations of production" (Piperno 1984: 9).

Court opera and commercial opera existed side by side until the late eighteenth century. Whereas court opera had a representative function and was organized by the courts' bureaucracies, commercial opera adopted the impresario model that spread rapidly from Italy to the rest of Europe. The impresario was a profit-oriented entrepreneur who bore all the financial risks. He raised the money for an opera production, commissioned the composers and librettists, negotiated with the singers and gathered together a suitable orchestra of musicians. Such opera productions were then sent on tour throughout Europe, and at the end of the seventeenth century a tight network of opera houses existed in the European cities that competed for the most popular opera productions. Competition for the best singers by rival impresarios resulted in astronomical fees and established an early business of "stars". "Top castrati such as Farinelli, Caffarelli and Senesino earned season fees of £1,000 to £1,500 per season in the best-paying London market – at the lower bound, 35 times the annual earnings of English building craftsmen" (Scherer 2004: 97). Librettists and composers also benefited from the booming opera business in the eighteenth century.

George Frideric Handel, who started his musical career in Hamburg, moved to London permanently in 1712 to freelance as an opera composer. In 1719 he was named musical director of the newly established Royal Academy of Music, a privately financed music company for Italian operas. Handel's obligations included not just writing operas but also recruiting singers and instrumentalists as well as overseeing the entire opera productions. When the wealthy noblemen withdraw their financial support, the Royal Academy of Music collapsed. Handel, however, invested part of the wealth he had acquired from composing and speculation into a new opera company in partnership with the Swiss John Jacob Heidegger. This new venture fluctuated between profit and loss and survived only by receiving subsidies from the royal family. When, in 1733, a competing opera company – the Opera of the Nobility – was established, which brought the celebrated Farinelli to London and lured the best singers away from Handel and Heidegger, Heidegger ended the partnership. Handel started a new venture as a principal impresario to stage oratorios. After several setbacks, the "oratorio business" eventually rescued Handel from financial ruin and he died a wealthy man (Scherer 2004: 4, 62). Handel is a good example of an eighteenth-century composer who benefited from the newly commercial opera business. Originally a municipal and, later, court employee, he succeeded as a freelance composer, turned into a paid musical director and ended up as a successful entrepreneur.

Such a career, however, was only possible in the booming opera business. Most composers and musicians depended on courts and noble patrons financially. When Joseph Haydn was engaged by Prince Paul Anton Esterhazy as an assistant to the aged kapellmeister Gregor Joseph Werner, the employment contract stated that Haydn had to compose a wide range of ordinary court music. Clause 4 in his employment contract pointed out:

> The said Vice-Chapel-Master shall be under permanent obligation to compose such pieces of music as his Serene Princely Highness may command and neither to communicate such new compositions to anyone, nor to allow them to be copied, but to retain them wholly for the exclusive use of his Highness; nor shall he compose for any other person without the knowledge and gracious permission [of his Highness].
>
> (Somfai 1989: 272)

Haydn's employment contract was typical of those of the era of aristocratic court orchestras. Clause 4 in the contract was just as common as clause 5, which stated that Haydn had to wait daily in the Prince's antechamber to get his musical orders for the day.

Nevertheless, the business model of commercial opera production was transferred to instrumental music performances in the second half of the eighteenth century. Although paid admission concerts were already being organized before 1750 – think of Telemann's and Johann Sebastian Bach's concert series in Zimmermann's coffee house in Leipzig, Hickford's Soho Square Room concerts in London and the Concerts Spirituel in Paris – the origins of the commercial live music business was the concert series organized by the composers Carl Friedrich Abel and Johann Christian Bach in the Carlisle House in London from 1765 to 1783. The "Bach–Abel Concerts" were financed by subscriptions and the organizers bore all financial risks. Although the concert series ended with financial ruin for Abel and Bach, it became the blueprint for other concert ventures outside London and an important forerunner of bourgeois concert life in the nineteenth century (McVeigh 1993: 167–75).

## The era of music publishing

The spread of commercial concerts increased the demand for printed music and transformed the craft of music printing into an industry. Music was first printed shortly after Johannes Gutenberg had invented the technology of moveable type printing in the mid-1450s. Music printing, however, was a time-consuming process and only a few printers, such as Ottaviano Petrucci in Venice and John Rastell in London, were able to produce a considerable number of copies (Scherer 2004: 158). To avoid cheap reproductions of original prints, sovereigns granted monopolistic privileges to the printers. In the German Empire, for instance, only the Emperor could guarantee intellectual property rights. In the sixteenth and seventeenth centuries, more than one thousand imperial music publishing rights were granted (Pohlmann 1962: 1168). The imperial act protected authors from unauthorized reprints by confiscating the pirated editions and by penalizing the publisher.

With the enactment of the Statute of Anne (Copyright Act of 1709) by the British Parliament in 1710, the first modern copyright legislation made London the centre of the early music publishing industry. Walsh & Hare produced the first high-quality music prints around 1730 and Longman & Broderip were the first music publishers to seek protection under the Statute of Anne by submitting their printed musical works to the Stationers' Hall – the London-based book-binders' and booksellers' guild. Other music publishers emerged and the number of music printing shops increased considerably (Baierle 2009: 64).

In continental Europe, however, a music publishing industry was unable to develop before the late 1770s, since composers were under contract to work exclusively for aristocratic courts and were not allowed to publish their work without the consent of the sovereign. With the rise of the concert business and the economic crises of aristocratic households, demand for printed music expanded in the course of the first wave of industrialization and a modern music publishing business emerged in the musical hotspots of Vienna, Paris and Leipzig. While in the years between 1700 and 1778 less than sixty music compositions were published in Vienna, the number of publications dramati-cally increased after 1778, when the Parisian engraver Antoine Huberty and many other printers established their printing shops there (Tschmuck 2002: 213). Similarly, Leipzig became a European centre of music publishing after Bernhard Christoph Breitkopf established a printing company in 1754. In 1795 Gottfried Christoph Härtel joined the venture and Breitkopf & Härtel became the powerhouse for printing the works of all famous German-speak-ing composers such as Haydn, Mozart, Beethoven, Schubert, Mendelssohn-Bartholdy, Schumann and Wagner (Baierle 2009: 71–2).

The innovation of lithography by the Bavarian author and actor Alois Senefelder in 1796 enabled the cheap reproduction of theatrical as well as musical works. Whereas engraving was limited to a maximum of 100 copies, lithography allowed for an unlimited reproduction of music prints. Senefelder's invention was adopted by all relevant music publishers in Europe and served as the basis for the mass production of sheet music (Wicke 1998: 16–17).


## Professionalization and commercialization of the music occupation

With the rise of the bourgeoisie, the music occupation became increasingly professionalized and commercialized during the course of the nineteenth cen-tury. This development was driven by the spread of aristocratic and bourgeois salons where house music was an integral part. The rising demand for pri-vate music education fuelled musical instrument manufacturing, especially of pianos, which evolved from the eighteenth-century cembalos, harpsichords and clavichords. Manufacturers such as Erard (since 1785) and Pleyel (since 1807) in Paris and Bösendorfer (since 1828) in Vienna improved the technology of the piano. Around 1850 the larger manufacturers were producing approximately 800 pianos per year (Ehrlich 1990: 110).

However, a professional concert business could not be run with dilettante and amateur musicians. The professionalization of concert organization came with the emancipation of composers and musicians from the courts in the aftermath of the French Revolution. Most of the court orchestras were dissolved at the end of the eighteenth century. Musicians therefore searched for new opportunities to perform and composers wanted to expose their works to the public.

Pioneering regular public concerts was the Leipziger Gewandhaus, which turned into a concert venue in 1780/81 when the Leipzig philharmonic society Großes Concert started to stage concert series. In 1781 the Gewandhaus became home to one of the first permanent professional orchestras – the Gewandhaus Orchestra (Döhring 1990: 149–51).

With the end of aristocratic music patronage, the Chapelle Royale in Paris was shut down and the Concert Spirituel came to an end in 1791. The Paris Conservatoire, which was initially founded as the École Royale de Chant et de Déclamation (Royal School of Singing and Declamation) under the *Ancien Régime* in 1784, was reorganized in 1793 and began regularly to present instrumental concerts for the public (Locke 1990: 61).

In 1812 the Gesellschaft der Musikfreunde in Wien (Society of the Friends of Music in Vienna) was established to organize charity concerts in representative venues in the Hofburg – the inner city palace of the Emperor – and in Vienna's opera houses. It was thirty years before Otto Nicolai started the first series of philharmonic concerts with admission fees and regular concert programmes (Wiesmann 1990: 93).

In January 1813 a group of musicians, composers and publishers met to establish the Philharmonic Society, which began to organize series of orchestral performances. Although the first concerts were only open to members and their families, the society later allowed wealthy subscribers to visit the concerts. In the third season – 1815 – the society's orchestra turned into a full professional symphony orchestra dependent on box office income (Sachs 1990: 210–14).

The philharmonic societies not only provided platforms for concerts but also initiated professional music education outside the courts. The Gesellschaft der Musikfreunde in Wien laid down in its statutes of 1814 the intention to establish a music conservatory that was eventually founded four years later as the Conservatorium der Gesellschaft der Musikfreunde with hofkapellmeister Antonio Salieri as its first director (Wiesmann 1990: 99). In London, the Philharmonic Society lobbied for a conservatory that was established with financial support by the king as the Royal Academy of Music in 1823 (Sachs 1990: 216–17). In Leipzig, the artistic head of the Gewandhaus Orchestra, Felix Mendelssohn-Bartholdy, founded the Leipzig Conservatory in cooperation with the Gewandhaus Society in 1843 (Döhring 1990: 153).

The rise of commercial concert life

Along with commercial opera, the concert business underpinned the high-brow music life of the emerging bourgeois society of the nineteenth century. The network of concert venues and opera houses also served as platforms for the early touring businesses of virtuosos such as Nicolò Paganini, Franz Liszt and Sigismond Thalberg. The philharmonic concerts, however, were visited by a wealthy audience who could afford the high entrance fees. Professional concert organizers did not meet the demand for cheap concerts. Low-cost music events were mainly offered by coffee houses, restaurants and other entertainment venues, but the most popular way to consume music was dancing. Although the waltz was danced in Vienna before 1800, the Congress of Vienna (1814–15) made it popular all over Europe. The number of ballrooms in Vienna exploded in the post-Napoleonic years (Fantel 1971: 36), with Joseph Lanner (1801–43) and Johann Strauss Sr becoming the masters of the waltz universe. It is reported that Johann Strauss Sr served multiple ballrooms in the same night by conducting several orchestras (Scherer 2004: 47).

The emergence of dance music for a growing urban population who could not afford concert and opera tickets was a precursor of the split between high-brow "classical" music and low-brow "popular" music that later dominated the nineteenth and twentieth centuries. Two different business models had emerged: a publicly funded concert and opera scene on the one hand and a market-based popular music business on the other.

## Music publishing as the core of the music industry

The emergence of the public concert life improved the economic position of the composers. They self-confidently started to claim copyright in their works, but were frustrated by the music publishers' practice of unauthorized reprinting of their works (Tschmuck 2002: 217). Publishers would alter the compositions to make them more marketable for dilettante musicians, and since music fashions immediately changed in the late eighteenth and early nineteenth centuries, publishers were not interested in long-term protection of the compositions (Hunter 1986). Therefore, composers searched for greater protection of their moral rights.

The increasing relevance of the composer to the music publishers' business model led to more author-centred copyright legislation. Following the French Literary and Artistic Property Act of 1793,[4] the Baden Civil Code of 1809[5] acknowledged for the first time the author's rather than the publisher's property in his works. The Prussian Copyright Act of 1837[6] was the first modern copyright act that protected the author of an artistic work. It protected not just a physical good but also an abstract good. Furthermore, copyright was extended to adaptations as well as to performances of dramatic and musical works. Similar copyright acts were also introduced in the Kingdom of Saxony in 1844[7] and in the Austrian Empire in 1846.[8] In 1871 the unified German Empire adopted the copyright legislation of the North German Confederation of 1870, which relied on the Prussian Copyright Act.[9]

Although the authors' and composers' copyrights (especially the moral rights) became protected during the course of the nineteenth century, it was nearly impossible to enforce these copyrights in respect of public performances. When in 1847 the French composer Ernest Bourget heard his music being played by an orchestra at the restaurant Les Ambassadeurs in Paris, he refused to pay his bill, arguing that the restaurant profited from playing his music. Bourget succeeded in the lawsuit that followed. The French courts recognized for the first time the legitimate right of a composer to be paid by a music promoter. With two other fellow composers, in 1850 Bourget founded a provisional union of authors, composers and publishers of music to collect performance fees, which were divided among the union's members. A year later, the union was turned into the world's first collecting society – the SACEM (Société des Auteurs,

Compositeurs et Éditeurs de Musique) (Society of Authors, Composers and Music Publishers), which still exists today.[10]

Copyright legislation and the growing influence of composers strengthened the link between live music performances and music publishing in the second half of the nineteenth century. The music business increasingly became based on the division of labour. A value-added chain emerged, with composers and authors providing the input for a music publishing industry that sold sheet music to a mass audience. The music was promoted by live performances that shaped the musical taste of the growing population of industrialized cities. Therefore, promoters of live music performances became allies of the music publishers.

The perfect incarnation of the modern music industry was New York City's Tin Pan Alley, located around Union Square and its neighbouring streets, where large music publishers ran their offices. A journalist coined the name to describe the tin-like sound of the ill-tuned pianos that could be heard from the offices of the music publishers. The Tin Pan Alley production system "turned song-writing and music publishing into specialized and standardized occupations" (Suisman 2009: pos. 20). The growing demand from vaudeville and minstrel shows fostered the commercialization of music publishing in the 1880s, and music publishing in New York soon became big business. The songwriter Charles K. Harris, who established a publishing company in 1891, had a smash hit with the song "After the Ball", which sold more than one million copies between 1892 and 1895 (Suisman 2009: pos. 330). Harris was able to build a business empire that employed songwriters and composers, song-pluggers, as well as travelling performers touring all over the US. Other music publishers such as Isidore Witmark & Sons, Harry von Tilzer, Edward B. Marks and Leo Feist joined the market and made a fortune selling popular sheet music. Popular songs such as "All By Myself" and "Nobody Knows" sold 2.4 million and 2 million copies, respectively, in 75 weeks (Goldberg 1930: 218).

## The emergence of the recorded music industry

In 1877 Edison invented the phonograph as a by-product of the emerging telephone industry. After unsuccessful attempts to market the phonograph as a Dictaphone (see Gelatt 1955: 33), it soon turned out to be a perfect device for recording and reproducing music. After experiments with precursors of jukeboxes – so-called "coin-in-the-slot-machines" located in public places such as restaurants and train stations that replayed music from music cylinders, which could not be copied (Tschmuck 2012: 14–17) – the invention of the record by the German immigrant Emile Berliner in 1887 was the breakthrough moment of the phonographic industry: records could now be pressed by matrices for mass production (Tschmuck 2012: 18–19).

The 1890s saw the Columbia Phonograph and Victor Talking Machine, which grew out of Berliner's ventures founded in the US, and they soon established branches in Europe and later in other parts of the world. In the US the number of phonographic companies grew from 3 in 1913 to 73 in 1916, when most of the phonograph patents expired (Tschmuck 2012: 34).

Music publishers had a problem with the booming recording industry, however. The record companies used their music without paying for it. Publishers also feared that records would substitute sheet music sales. Therefore, the publishers lobbied for a revision of copyright, demanding levies on mechanical reproduction. Backed by the large publishing houses, in 1909 the bandleader and recording pioneer John Philip Sousa joined with successful songwriter Victor Herbert to campaign for a revision of copyright. The US Copyright Act of 1909 was in large part a direct consequence of those lobbying activities. It stipulated a fee of 2 cents for each music cylinder, record and piano roll sold to be paid to the publishers (Tschmuck 2012: 43). To monetize the new provision in the copyright law, Sousa and Herbert founded the American Society of Composers, Authors and Publishers (ASCAP), which was obliged to collect money for the use of its members' artistic works (Kornfeld 2011: pos. 289–92).

In other countries, copyright legislation was also extended to the new technological possibilities. In 1911, after the new Copyright Act was introduced in the UK, the Mechanical-Copyright Protection Society (MCPS) was also founded to collect fees from the mechanical reproduction of music. The MCPS merged with the Performing Rights Society (PRS) in 1924.[11] In Germany, the Society for Musical Performing and Mechanical Reproduction Rights (later renamed Gesellschaft für musikalische Aufführungs- und mechanische Vervielfältigungsrechte – GEMA) was established after the old copyright regime was replaced in 1901. One of the main promoters of the initially named Anstalt für musikalisches Aufführungsrecht (Institute for the Musical Performing Right) was the German composer Richard Strauss.

The new copyright legislation that went hand-in-hand with the establishment of collecting societies led to a new value-added network in which the economic interests of music publishers, live music promoters and record companies were inextricably interwoven. Thus, the modern music industry emerged in the first decade of the twentieth century.

## The era of broadcasting

### Consolidation of the recorded music industry

In Europe, the First World War put an end to the growth of the recorded music industry. The subsidiaries of foreign companies were seized and nationalized by the authorities and the major companies lost their markets in what were now enemy territories. After the war, the main European markets were controlled by a handful of record companies: Lindström and Polyphon (with Deutsche Grammophon – a former subsidiary of the British Gramophone Co.) in Germany, Pathé Frères in France, and the Gramophone Company as well as Columbia Graphophone in Great Britain (Tschmuck 2012: 34–5).

Until 1913, when the main recording patents expired, the US market was dominated by Edison Phonograph Co., which produced mainly cylinders, Columbia Phonograph Co. (which produced both cylinders and records) and Victor Talking Machine (producing only records). The record emerged as the standard format, whereas the music cylinder disappeared from the market when Edison Phonograph ceased to exist in 1929 (Tschmuck 2012: 31–3).

After 1913 the number of record companies in the US rose quickly from 3 in 1913 to 166 in 1919 (Gelatt 1955: 190–1). New players such as the Sonora Company, Aeolian-Vocalion, Gennett Records, Brunswick-Balke and Collender, Paramount Records and OKeh Records entered the market. In 1921 record sales in the US reached a historic high of $106 million (Tschmuck 2012: 49). However, the recorded music market in the US was to lose 44.3 per cent of its sales revenue in the next four years as a result of overproduction, the hesitant acceptance of new music styles such as jazz and blues, and the emergence of commercial radio broadcasting. Smaller labels went bankrupt or were bought by the majors (Tschmuck 2012: 50–1).

However, even the majors ran into financial problems. Columbia Phonograph had to file for bankruptcy in 1923 and was re-established by its main creditors (Gelatt 1955: 209). The British Gramophone Company also had financial problems and was saved by Victor Talking Machine, which acquired a 50 per cent stake in the company in 1920 (Tschmuck 2012: 52). The British Gramophone Company's main competitor in Europe, Columbia Graphophone, did better. When Bell Laboratories introduced electrical recording technology in 1924, US Columbia Phonograph acquired the patents for electrical recording after Victor Talking Machine had rejected the offer by Bell Laboratories. However, US Columbia Phonograph was unable to exploit the patents because of ongoing financial problems. Therefore, Columbia's former British subsidiary, Columbia Graphophone, stepped in by buying a 60 per cent stake of US Columbia Phonograph along with access to the electrical recording patents. The introduction of electrical recording stabilized Columbia's business and both companies were united under the roof of Columbia International Ltd. A year later the financially suffering German Lindström conglomerate with subsidiaries all around Europe and in Latin America was acquired and integrated into the holding company of Columbia Graphophone (Tschmuck 2012: 54–5).

Electrical recording also revolutionized the film industry, which became interlinked from now on with the music business. The new technology was adopted by Western Electric – the parent company of Bell Laboratories – to synchronize silent movies under the Vitaphone trademark. Warner Bros. licensed the Vitaphone system to produce the first sound film ("talkie") – *The Jazz Singer* starring Broadway star Al Jolson – in 1926. Since *The Jazz Singer* was such a great commercial success, Warner Bros. produced further talkies, and to this end acquired a dozen New York music publishing houses to get access to the compositions for the popular film musicals. Other large Hollywood film studios followed into the music business and also bought music publishing houses (Tschmuck 2012: 77–8). Ryan (1985: 77) has calculated that music publishers affiliated with film studios earned 65 per cent of all payouts by ASCAP in 1937. The film studios did not just buy music publishers; they also entered the recorded music market. Warner Bros. acquired the record division of Brunswick-Balke-Collender in 1930 and, a year later, established the Brunswick Record Corporation, which was eventually sold to Consolidated Film Industries Inc. Consolidated Film still owned a portfolio of record companies that had been organized into the American Record Corporation (ARC) since 1929. Thus, Brunswick became a subsidiary of ARC in 1931 (Tschmuck 2012: 69).

## The music industry as radio industry

However, the structural shift in the music industry happened earlier, which brought the booming broadcasting networks into the centre of the business. In 1926 the owner of Victor Talking Machine, Eldridge Johnson, sold his stake to two New York banking houses who, not really interested in the recorded music business, sold Victor Talking Machine to the Radio Corporation of America (RCA) in 1929. RCA, however, was interested less in producing records than in owning Victor's production facilities and distribution networks. Instead of manufacturing phonographs, which it treated merely as a side-product, RCA-Victor focused on producing radios (Sanjek & Sanjek 1991: 23).

When the Great Depression shook the world economy a few months later, revenue from record sales in the US decreased to an all-time low of $6 million in 1933 – down 92 per cent since 1929. The record companies faced serious financial problems. In the UK, the Gramophone Co. and Columbia Graphophone Co. were forced to merge and created Electrical and Musical Industries Ltd. (EMI) in 1931 (Martland 1997: 136). However, the merger had been approved by the US antitrust authority with the requirement that EMI sell its stake in US Columbia Phonograph to a bank consortium, which went bankrupt in 1934, prompting Columbia Phonograph to be purchased by ARC. ARC, however, could not run the record business profitably. Thus, Consolidated Film sold its phonographic branch to Columbia Broadcasting System (CBS) in 1938 (Tschmuck 2012: 70).

After a period of mergers and acquisitions, by the end of the 1930s the US recorded music industry was under the control of the large broadcasting networks RCA and CBS – except Decca Records, which had been founded with the financial support of British Decca in 1934 (Tschmuck 2012: 69). The networks further strengthened their market dominance by establishing Broadcast Music Incorporated (BMI) as a new performing rights licensing organization in the course of a royalty dispute with ASCAP (Ryan 1985).

In Europe, the record companies also regarded radio as competition for record sales. Several German record companies boycotted the booming Reichsrundfunk by withdrawing their records from the local radio stations. The boycott ended up in a compromise with the Reichsrundfunk allowed to play records for only 60 minutes – instead of 120 minutes – each day in each broadcasting district (Schulz-Köhn 1940: 138). This suggests that the record companies did not believe in the promotional effect of radio, for they would have otherwise increased rather than decreased the on-air exposure of their records.

When the National Socialists seized power in Germany in 1933, the Ministry of Propaganda ordered the now nationalized Reichsrundfunk to stop payment of royalties to the record companies, which violated the Rome Agreement of 1928. Since radio stations in other European countries also refused to pay performing royalties to the labels, the International Federation of the Phonographic Industry (IFPI) was founded in 1933. In the name of IFPI, the German lawyer Alfred Baum sued the Reichsrundfunk. Although the lawsuit was turned down in the first two instances, the Court of Appeals in Leipzig ruled against the Reichsrundfunk and ordered it to pay a severe fine (Riess 1966: 277). The Minister of Propaganda, Joseph Goebbels, fiercely polemicized against the ruling and the "record monopoly" that was controlled by "foreign Jewish capital". The ruling was a Pyrrhic victory for the record companies. The recording of music composed or performed by Jews was prohibited and the record companies were ordered to destroy all records and matrices of recordings by Jewish musicians and composers, including the music of Gustav Mahler, Felix Mendelssohn-Bartholdy, Jacques Offenbach, Irving Berlin and many others (Fetthauer 2000: 34–6). In addition, the Deutsche Grammophon Gesellschaft was liquidated in 1937 and re-founded as a subsidiary of Telefunken GmbH – a joint venture of AEG and Siemens. This was meant to be an intermediate step in unifying the German recorded music industry in the Uniphongesellschaft in 1942, but this never happened (Elste 1984: 111). Nevertheless, the German case highlights that the recorded music companies were also subordinated to the logic of broadcasting, albeit not as a result of market forces but rather of political pressure.

When the Second World War ended, the music industry was dominated by broadcasting networks and their subsidiary record labels. The radio business model in the US was based on ad-sponsored live performances of big bands, whose sound fitted perfectly with the demands of radio broadcasts.

## The era of the recorded music industry

### The rock 'n' roll revolution

Once the war restrictions were lifted in the US, record sales grew from $109 million in 1945 to $218 million in the following year (Tschmuck 2012: 101). However, after 1946 the recorded music market stagnated at this level until 1954. An oligopoly of four major companies – two of them owned by broadcasting networks – controlled the entire value-added network from A & R ("Artists and Repertoire"), music publishing, disc manufacturing to distribution, marketing and radio airplay (Peterson & Berger 1975: 160).

In contrast to the pre-war years, radio airplay of records was recognized as an important promotional tool, and with the liberalization of the US broadcasting market by the Federal Communications Commission (FCC), disc jockeys became the key promoters of music in the late 1940s. Before 1947, the FCC granted only 3–5 broadcasting licenses for each US state – mainly to the large networks. With the advent of FM radio, numerous local radio stations were granted broadcasting licences. Since they could not afford to broadcast live music shows like the large network stations, these local broadcasters relied on the airplay of rhythm and blues records (Peterson 1990). The R & B record companies welcomed the free promotion of their records, since the networks had prohibited their labels from recording R & B music. As a result, the number of record companies increased from 11 in 1949 to almost 200 in 1954 (Tschmuck 2012: 104–11). So-called "independent" record labels such as Atlantic, Imperial, Chess, Mercury and Sun Records entered into a fiercely competitive market, which forced them to find a unique selling proposition by experimenting with and adopting innovative music styles. Thus, R & B was blended with country music, the traditional Southern blues was electrified, and the result was rock 'n' roll. As a result, the US became a music laboratory that also influenced Europe.

After the Second World War, EMI and Decca – both located in London – were the only record majors to compete with the US companies (RCA-Victor, CBS-Columbia, US Decca and Capitol Records). In 1950 the Dutch lighting manufacturer Philips acquired the Dutch and French subsidiaries of British Decca and grew to become an important player on the European recorded music market (Chapple & Garofalo 1977: 194–5). In 1951 CBS-Columbia ceased its traditional collaboration with EMI and switched to Philips. When EMI lost its distribution network along with Columbia's economically important pop repertoire to Philips, the British record major purchased Capitol Records in 1955 (Tschmuck 2012: 130).

RCA-Victor, concerned about this acquisition, also ceased its cooperation with EMI. EMI, having lost half of its music catalogue, compensated for this by entering into distribution deals with several US independent record labels, and as a result the latest rock 'n' roll titles became available in the UK, where they immediately conquered the charts.

British bands were heavily influenced by US artists and blended their local styles with rock 'n' roll from overseas, and in the process created a new, distinct popular music style. In the early 1960s British bands, headed by The Beatles, "invaded" the US market, making EMI and Decca very influential in the US and serious competition for the US majors.


The oligopolization of the recorded music industry in the 1960s and 1970s

The growing market also provided room for new companies: in the US Warner Bros. re-entered the music business by launching Warner Bros. Records in 1958. Five years later Warner Bros. purchased two thirds of Frank Sinatra's Reprise label and entered the popular music business. It was a surprise when New York-based film production firm Seven Arts bought Warner-Reprise in 1967. Seven Arts also purchased Atlantic Records in the same year. It sold the Warner-Reprise-Atlantic conglomerate to Kinney Corporation only two years later. Kinney established Warner Communications, which bought the entire Warner Bros. Corporation including the film studios, then in 1970 bought Elektra Records from Jac Holzman (who was very successful with The Doors), and Asylum Records from David Geffen three years later. Warner-Reprise, Elektra-Asylum and Atlantic Records initially were more or less autonomous label groups, but in the course of the 1970s, Warner centralized not just the distribution network but also the label business and established WEA (W for Warner, E for Elektra and A for Atlantic) (Tschmuck 2012: 134–5).

Besides Warner, two other record majors emerged in the US in the 1960s. The Music Corporation of America (MCA), which was originally founded as an artist agency in Chicago in 1924, bought a controlling interest in US-Decca in 1962. MCA then bought Kapp Records and launched Uni Records. The three labels remained relatively autonomous, but they were merged into the MCA label in 1972 after years of stagnation and decreasing profits. MCA regained success by signing the British rock band The Who in 1970 and Elton John in 1972 (Tschmuck 2012: 132).

The third new US record major – ABC Records – was founded by the American Broadcasting Company (ABC) in 1955 to exploit the film music of ABC's subsidiary Paramount Pictures. Additional record labels were bought and ABC Records became such a huge commercial success that the oil company Gulf + Western bought a majority stake and provided fresh capital to buy Stax, Paramount Records, Duke/Peacock and Dunhill Records to form ABC-Dunhill. ABC Records signings included Ray Charles and The Mamas & The Papas. In 1974 ABC bought back the shares from Gulf + Western and was again the sole owner of the label conglomerate and Paramount Pictures (Sanjek & Sanjek 1991: 133, 156).

The European record majors also expanded their business in the 1960s. In 1962 Philips entered into a joint venture with the German company Siemens AG, the owner of Deutsche Grammophon. After integrating their record businesses in 1966, the label conglomerate was transformed into PolyGram Holding in 1972 (Tschmuck 2012: 149).

EMI and its US branch Capitol Records also benefited from the popular music business, especially by signing the Beach Boys. When Beatlemania began to decline in the early 1970s, EMI incurred losses and diversified by moving into different entertainment fields. Despite EMI's financial problems, the company remained an influential player in the international music industry through its control of nearly 80 per cent of all music copyrights worldwide. In 1979 EMI bought ABC-Dunhill and United Artists Records, which had bought the Liberty/Blue Note label group (Martland 1997: 254–60).

At the end of the 1970s the recorded music industry was an oligopoly controlled by US and European major companies. Only a few economically relevant independent record labels such as Motown, A&M Records, Island and Virgin Records were able to survive the market concentration process of the 1970s.

## The era of the digital music industry

### The rise of the compact disc and the superstar business

Before the compact disc (CD) was introduced, recorded music sales were in decline in almost all important markets because of the introduction of the music cassette and a lack of innovation. Even the large music conglomerates suffered from the crisis. EMI was hit hardest, and was only saved from bankruptcy by being bought by the electronic company Thorn (Martland 1997: 254–60). The other major companies were all forced to cut costs, downsize their portfolio of artists and reduce their personnel (Garofalo 1997: 354).

However, the market introduction of the CD by Philips and Sony in 1982/83 revived the recorded music market. Despite a hesitant start, CD sales grew year on year until the end of the 1980s. Whereas in 1986 CDs accounted for just 10 per cent of US record sales, two years later they surpassed those of records for the first time (Sanjek & Sanjek 1991: 256–8). Significant to the booming recorded music market was the emergence of music television. In 1981 two subsidiaries of Warner Communications launched a music video channel in collaboration with RCA's Communications Satellite Corporation and IT&T called Music Television (MTV). Although the US record majors hesitated to cooperate, the increasing number of viewers and the inflow of advertising revenue convinced them to license their catalogues to MTV in 1983 (Denisoff 1988).

MTV was the perfect vehicle through which to promote superstar pop. Even though music videos increased production costs, they facilitated the exploitation of copyrights across all media and markets. The market segmentation strategy of the 1970s that sought to meet the demand of specific consumer groups became obsolete. Instead the majors invested in only a few star acts, such as Michael Jackson, Prince, Whitney Houston, U2 and Bruce Springsteen, who were capable of generating disproportionately high revenue (Garofalo 1997: 372–3).

## Merger mania in the recorded music industry

CD sales fuelled growth in the recorded music industry – in the US overall sales increased by 110 per cent to $7,500 million from 1982 to 1990 (Tschmuck 2012: 164) – and with fresh capital record companies were able to expand again. In 1986 the German Bertelsmann AG acquired RCA-Victor after it had entered the US market by buying Arista in 1979. The Japanese Sony Corporation purchased CBS-Columbia in 1988 along with Columbia Pictures film studios. Another Japanese conglomerate, Matsushita, bought MCA and its Universal film studios after MCA had previously acquired Motown, Geffen and GRP Records. The year 1989 was in fact the year of mergers and acquisitions in the recorded music industry: PolyGram bought Island Records and A&M Records after Siemens had sold its share to Philips, EMI purchased a 50 per cent stake in Chrysalis Records and Warner Communications merged with Time-Life to bring in its Warner-Elektra-Atlantic (WEA) label group (Tschmuck 2012: 175–7).

When the growth of CD sales continued into the 1990s, reaching a worldwide all-time high of $26,900 million (in trade value) in 1999 (IFPI 2001: 17), the recorded music market became further concentrated. The Canadian conglomerate Seagram bought MCA from Matsushita in 1995 and merged the MCA Music Entertainment Group with Universal Film Studios Inc. to form Universal Music Group. When Seagram also bought Philip's PolyGram from Philips three years later, Universal became the world's largest music company. Universal owner Edgar J. Bronfman Jr later merged the entertainment conglomerate with the French utilities company Vivendi in 2000 (Tschmuck 2012: 179).

## The digital revolution in the music industry

When the German Fraunhofer Institut für Integrierte Schaltungen developed the MP3 (Moving Picture Expert Group/layer 3), it was supposed to be a format for synchronizing film music. However, a beta version of the software spread throughout the Internet as a tool to exchange ripped music files from CDs. In 1999 Shawn Fanning released software called Napster that allowed internet users to search music files directly on the hard discs of other computers. Napster was a huge success and attracted more than one million registered users just a few months later. The Recording Industry Association of America (RIAA) sued Napster for copyright infringement in December 1999. After a three-year battle before the court, RIAA succeeded and Napster was shut down, although it was bought by Bertelsmann AG – the owner of Bertelsmann Music Group. However, Bertelsmann failed to commercialize the peer-to-peer file-sharing system and Napster went bankrupt in November 2002.

However, this was not the end of file sharing. Napster was succeeded by decentralized file-sharing applications (e.g. KaZaA, Limewire, BearShare and Torrent-based clients such as The Pirate Bay) that did not use a central server like Napster. The music industry's bodies around the world declared war on internet "piracy" and systematically sued providers of file-sharing software. In 2003 the RIAA began to sue individual file-sharers. National IFPI branches and collecting societies followed. Nevertheless, the level of peer-to-peer (P2P) file sharing remained high, which prompted some countries' legislative bodies to introduce graduated response measures to dam up the unauthorized use of copyrighted material.

In addition, the recorded music majors licensed Apple's download music service iTunes, which also became accessible to non-Apple users in 2003. Apple's iTunes soon controlled more than 80 per cent of the emerging digital music market (Tschmuck 2012: 191). To avoid market dominance by just one digital music provider, the majors changed their strategy when music-streaming services such as Spotify and Deezer surfaced around 2010. The streaming companies were forced to pay two-digit million-dollar advances, recoupable with the streaming revenue, to the majors. Since the usually under-capitalized streaming companies could not afford to pay such advances, the majors as well as the indies' licensing agency MERLIN took minority stakes that could be monetized in the case of a flotation or initial public offer (IPO).

Thus, recorded music companies could stabilize their business and become profitable after a painful process of consolidation. CD-pressing plants and physical distribution networks were sourced out and the number of employees dramatically reduced. The structural change was accompanied by a change of ownership. Universal's founder Bronfman, together with an investor group, acquired Warner Music Group from Time-Warner in 2004. In the same year, Sony Corporation and Bertelsmann AG merged their recording businesses, but eventually Bertelsmann sold its share to Sony in 2008. In 2007 the EMI Group was sold to the private equity firm Terra Firma. Since Terra Firma could not meet all its liabilities in 2010, it lost EMI to its financial backer Citigroup. The bank giant sold EMI's recording branch to Universal Music Group and the publishing arm to Sony/ATV publishing in 2011. In the same year, Bronfman's investors group sold Warner Music Group to Access Industries, a holding group controlled by the Russian businessman Len Blavatnik (Tschmuck 2012: 180). In 2016 the international recorded music industry was controlled by an oligopoly of three major companies: Universal Music Group (owned by Vivendi Group), Sony Music Entertainment (owned by Sony Corporation) and Warner Music Group (owned by Access Industries).

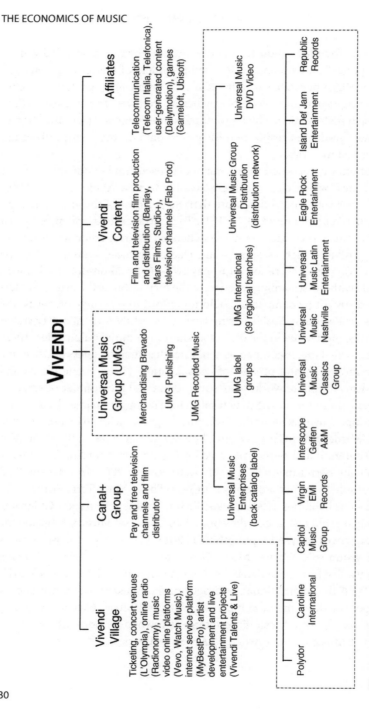

**Figure 1.1** Organizational structure of Universal Music Group, March 2016
Source: After Vivendi (2016b)

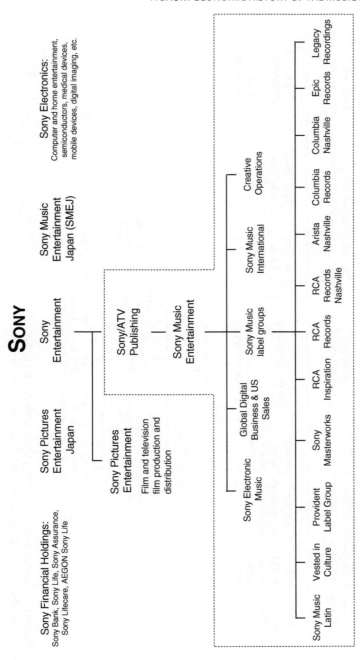

**Figure 1.2** Organizational structure of Sony Music Entertainment, 2016
Source: After Sony Corporation (2016, n.d.)

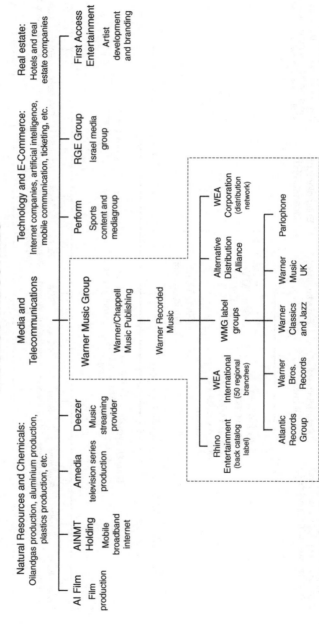

**Figure 1.3** Organizational structure of Warner Music Group, 2016
Source: After Warner Music Group (2015) and Access Industries (n.d.)

Whereas the music download market remains dominated by Apple/ iTunes, the music-streaming market is much more competitive with hundreds of streaming companies having entered the market and fighting for market share. However, internet giants such as online retailer Amazon and micro-advertising company Google, which bought the user-generated platform YouTube in 2007, as well as Apple with Apple Music, have entered the music-streaming market to control the digital distribution of music.

The growing importance of the live music business in the music industry

Back in the early 1990s the concert business was very fragmented and dominated by regional promoters. Touring was seen by the record labels as a promotional tool to sell CDs. The first major challenge to the established system of fragmented local live music markets was Elvis Presley's national tour deal with the Concerts West promotion agency in 1970. Concerts West paid Elvis's management $1 million to acquire the right to book a national tour. To do so, they had to cut out the various middlemen and contracted directly with the venues (Budnick & Baron 2011: 201). In response, various disgruntled promoters encouraged impresario Bill Graham to start a competing model of national touring that relied on a network of local promoters. Although the first national stadium tour of Bob Dylan with The Band ended up in a fiasco, it showed that national tours could be profitable if they were organized by a single promoter who cuts out the middlemen (Budnick & Baron 2011: 203). Toronto-based Concerts Productions International (CPI), founded by Michael Cohl, eventually perfected the national touring concept and succeeded in organizing Michael Jackson's *Victory* stadium tour in 1984 (Budnick & Baron 2011: 204–6). In 1989 CPI bought out the Rolling Stones from Bill Graham Presents promotion agency for a guaranteed sum of $65 million for fifty dates of the *Steel Wheels* tour. This was only affordable because rather than approaching each of the fifty concerts separately, the entire tour was seen as one package, thus enabling the cross-collateralization of the individual shows. This meant that the local promoters and venues were only getting flat fees after costs and expenses (Budnick & Baron 2011: 211). Since this tour was a great success, CPI promoted three more tours of the Rolling Stones, making them the top touring act of the

1990s, grossing more than $750 million from 333 shows (Budnick & Baron 2011: 214). Cohl's new model of national touring attracted other superstars such as Pink Floyd, Crosby, Stills, Nash & Young and David Bowie (Budnick & Baron 2011: 214).

In 1998 Michael Cohl sold the conglomerate to SFX Entertainment (Budnick & Baron 2011: 163). By acquiring nearly all important local concert promoters in North America, SFX Entertainment became the main force in the music promotion business (Budnick & Baron 2011: 166–9). In March 2000 SFX founder Robert F. X. Sillerman sold the company to what was at the time the world's largest radio broadcaster, Clear Channel Communications, for $4,400 million (Budnick & Baron 2011: 192). Despite the expected synergies to Clear Channel's radio and advertising business, SFX Entertainment could not be run at a profit and was spun off into a separately traded company named Live Nation in spring 2005 (Budnick & Baron 2011: 225). In 2009 Live Nation merged in a $2,500 million deal with the world's largest ticketing company, Ticketmaster, which had acquired one of the world's largest artist agencies, Front Line Management, two years earlier (Budnick & Baron 2011: 314). In 2011 Live Nation announced its cooperation with Universal Music Group. Thus, a new and very powerful player emerged in the music industry, which controls nearly all parts of the industry's value-added network.

Whereas the recorded music industry was in decline after 2000, the live music industry prospered. In Germany, the revenue from concert ticket sales increased by more than 10 per cent from 1995 to 2013 to €2,700 million. In the same period, the relatively robust recorded music market in Germany lost half of its volume – from €2,650 to €1,350 million. Thus, concert ticket sales accounted for 67 per cent of the joint revenue in 2013, compared to 48 per cent in 1995 (GfK 2014: 6). The live music business thus emerged as the main revenue source for musicians. The Billboard Money Makers List 2015 indicates that, on average, top artists of the US music business earned more than 77 per cent of their income from touring in 2014.[12]

The recorded music market lost its dominance in the digital music economy to the live music entertainment market. Whereas it was the record that was at the centre of the value-added network from the 1950s, in the age of digital music it is now the musicians who have become the main revenue source for the industry.

## Notes

1. For an analysis of medieval music life, see Page's entry "Medieval" in *Grove Music Online*.
2. For "Troubadours" and "Minnesingers", see Milsom's entries in the *Oxford Companion to Music Online* (2015).
3. See Schmidt's article "Il pomo d'oro" in *The New Grove Dictionary of Opera Online*.
4. See original text and commentary on the French Literary and Artistic Property Act of 1793 in Primary Sources on Copyright (1450–1900): www.copyrighthistory.org/cam/tools/request/showRecord.php?id=record_f_1793 (retrieved 21 February 2017).
5. See original text and commentary on the Baden Civil Code of 1809 in Primary Sources on Copyright (1450–1900): www.copyrighthistory.org/cam/tools/request/showRecord.php?id=record_d_1809 (retrieved 21 February 2017).
6. See original text and commentary on the Prussian Copyright Act of 1837 in Primary Sources on Copyright (1450–1900): www.copyrighthistory.org/cam/tools/request/showRecord.php?id=record_d_1837a (retrieved 21 February 2017).
7. Saxon Copyright Act of 1844 in Primary Sources of Copyright (1450–1900): www.copyrighthistory.org/cam/tools/request/showRecord.php?id=record_d_1844 (retrieved 21 February 2017).
8. Austrian Copyright Act of 1846 in Primary Sources of Copyright (1450–1900): www.copyrighthistory.org/cam/tools/request/showRecord.php?id=record_d_1846b (retrieved 21 February 2017).
9. Copyright Act for the North German Confederation 1870 and the German Empire 1871 in Primary Sources of Copyright (1450–1900): www.copyrighthistory.org/cam/tools/request/showRecord.php?id=record_d_1870 (retrieved 21 February 2017).
10. See https://societe.sacem.fr/en/history (retrieved 19 February 2017).
11. For a short history of MCPS and PRS for Music see: www.prsformusic.com/aboutus/ourorganisation/ourhistory/Pages/timeline.aspx (retrieved 5 November 2015).
12. See Blog of Music Business Research, "Music Streaming Revisited – The Superstars' Music Streaming Income", 13 July 2015, https://musicbusinessresearch.wordpress.com/2015/07/13/music-streaming-revisited-the-superstars-music-streaming-income/ (retrieved 5 November 2015).

## 2

# MICROECONOMICS OF MUSIC: MUSIC AS AN ECONOMIC GOOD

### The fundamentals of the music market economy

Music as an economic good is traded on different markets – for example the market for recorded music and the market for concerts. Before analysing music as an economic good, we have to understand how music markets work.

The father of modern economics Adam Smith (1723–90) explained that the market allocates scarce resources like an "invisible hand" (Smith [1776] 1811 III: 181). In the first book of *The Wealth of Nations*, Smith ([1776] 1811 I: 21) states: "It is not from the benevolence of the butcher, the brewer or the baker that we expect our dinner, but from their regard to their own interest." Thus, if individuals are driven by their self-interest, the result is a free market economy that efficiently allocates scarce resources. The market, therefore, is a metaphorical place where demand meets supply (see Figure 2.1).

Demand and supply are represented by curves. The demand curve (D) describes the consumer's willingness to purchase a quantity of a good at a given price, whereas the supply curve (S) represents the producer's willingness to sell a unit of a good at a given price. The market price of a good is represented by the point where the demand curve crosses the supply curve. At the market price, the supplied quantity of a good is entirely taken up by the buyers demanding the good. The market price remains in an equilibrium as long as all external factors are stable.[1] Such a situation is called Pareto efficiency. According to the Italian economist and sociologist Vilfredo Pareto, efficiency (or optimality) is a state of allocation of goods in which one individual cannot be made better off without making another individual worse off. Thus, the market provides Pareto-efficient results (see Varian 2010: 15–16).

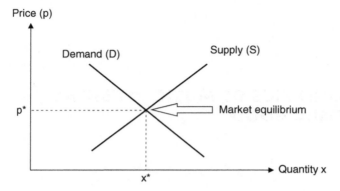

**Figure 2.1** The fundamental market model

In our model, a new price and new Pareto-optimal state emerges if external factors change. Consider a concert by a famous band, for example. If rumour spreads that the concert could be the last one before the band splits, more fans might be inclined to buy a ticket than would otherwise be the case. Since the number of tickets is limited by the capacity of the concert venue, such additional demand would cause a rise in ticket prices. The additional demand for concert tickets shifts the original demand curve (D) outward to a new demand curve (D'). This results in a higher market price (p') (see Figure 2.2a).

Let us assume that the concert promoter decides to stage an additional concert by the band the following day. This results in an additional supply of tickets that shifts the supply curve from S to S', resulting in a lower price p" (see Figure 2.2b).

The market price mechanism, therefore, reflects the degree of scarcity on a market. If scarcity is reduced by either additional supply or lower demand, the price decreases; in turn, it rises when scarcity is increased by additional demand or lower supply of a good.

What this shows is that there is a negative relationship between price and demand. The impact demand has on price changes can be measured with the help of the concept of price elasticity. The demand for concert tickets is elastic if an increase in prices by 1 per cent results in a decrease in demand of more than 1 per cent. If the demand decreases by less than 1 per cent when the price rises by 1 per cent, we speak of an inelastic demand.

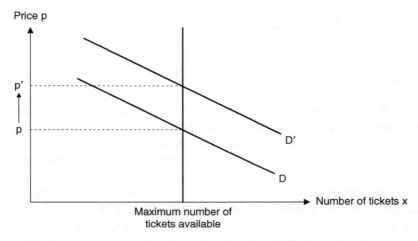

**Figure 2.2a** The effect of an additional demand for concert tickets

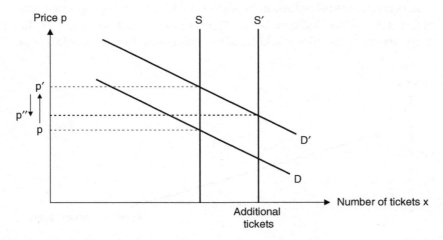

**Figure 2.2b** The effect of an additional supply of concert tickets

$$\frac{\text{Percentage change in demand}}{\text{Percentage change in price}} < -1 \dots \text{inelastic demand}$$

$$\frac{\text{Percentage change in demand}}{\text{Percentage change in price}} > -1 \dots \text{elastic demand}$$

We know that hardcore fans of a band are less price-sensitive than occasional concert goers. Price elasticity of demand is reflected, therefore, in the slope of the demand curve. A flat demand curve implies elastic demand (see Figure 2.3a), whereas a steep slope in the curve implies inelastic demand (see Figure 2.3b).

Understanding price elasticity of demand is important when deciding on price policy. We can assume that entertainment products such as music are highly price-elastic. Thus, even modest price increases for CDs, music downloads, music-streaming subscriptions and concert tickets would cause a disproportionately high decrease in demand, which in turn would result in a revenue decline (see Figure 2.4).

In contrast, a small reduction in prices would lead to a disproportionately higher demand and higher revenue. Since a price reduction by one of the major record companies would force the others also to reduce prices, this

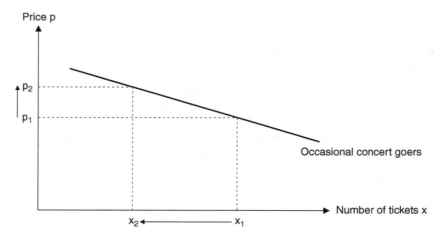

**Figure 2.3a** The price elasticity of demand for occasional concert goers

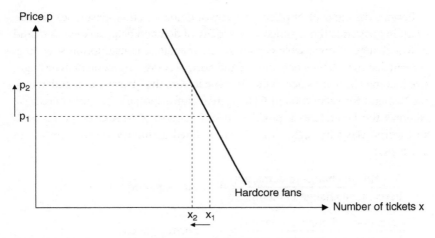

**Figure 2.3b** The price elasticity of demand for hardcore fans

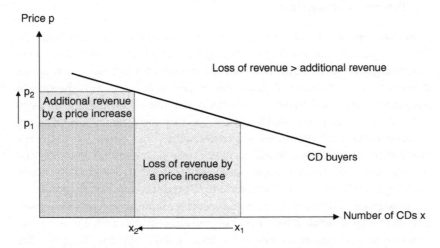

**Figure 2.4** The impact of a price increase in the case of elastic demand

could lead to a negative price spiral resulting in a loss of revenue for all companies. Therefore, the providers of music products and services want to avoid a change in prices. This explains why the price of CDs, music downloads and music subscriptions remain relatively stable over time.

Besides the concept of price elasticity of demand, other elasticities are relevant in economic theory. Income elasticity of demand helps us to understand how a change of disposable consumer income alters consumption spending. We can distinguish between inferior and normal goods: the former have a negative income elasticity since higher income lowers the quantity demanded (e.g. the demand for second-hand CDs decreases if disposable income increases), whereas the latter have a positive income elasticity. Moreover, goods with an income elasticity higher than 1 are defined as luxury goods (see Varian 2010: 285).

$$\frac{\text{Percentage change in demand}}{\text{Percentage change in income}} < 0 \ldots \text{inferior good}$$

$$\frac{\text{Percentage change in demand}}{\text{Percentage change in income}} > 0 \ldots \text{normal goods}$$

$$\frac{\text{Percentage change in demand}}{\text{Percentage change in income}} > 1 \ldots \text{luxury goods}$$

Most entertainment goods – including music – are in that sense luxury goods. Thus, a higher income results in a disproportionally higher demand in entertainment goods. Conversely, however, the demand for entertainment goods disproportionally decreases if disposable income is reduced, as is the case in economic crises. It was therefore no surprise that the recorded music industry suffered severely from the Wall Street crash in October 1929 and the following world economic crisis. Recorded music sales in the US decreased by 92 per cent from $75 million in 1929 to $6 million in 1933 (see Tschmuck 2012: 49–50). The US recorded music market literally disappeared owing to a shift of consumer spending from "non-essential" entertainment products to necessary goods.

Cross-price elasticity is another important economic concept. "The cross-price elasticity of demand measures how the quantity demanded of one good responds to a change in the price of another good" (Mankiw 2014: 98). We can distinguish two cases:

1. Negative cross-price elasticity: A rise in the price of one good decreases the demand in the other good – the two goods are substitutes;

$$\frac{\text{Percentage change in demand in good 1}}{\text{Percentage change in the price of good 2}} < 0 \ldots \text{substitutes}$$

2. Positive cross-price elasticity: A rise in the price of one good increases the demand in the other good – the two goods are complements.

$$\frac{\text{Percentage change in demand in good 1}}{\text{Percentage change in the price of good 2}} > 0 \dots \text{complements}$$

### The rise of concert ticket prices: are CDs and concert tickets complements?

In "The Economics of Real Superstars", the economist Alan Krueger (2005) analysed ticket prices of rock concerts in the US, which rose by 82 per cent in the period 1996 to 2003; this was considerably higher than the increase in the consumer price index of 17 per cent in the same period (see Figure 2.5).

Krueger (2005: 25) hypothesizes "that concert prices have soared because recording artists have seen a large decline in their income from record sales, a complementary product to concerts." In the past, when the main income source for artists was to sell records, they had an incentive "to price their tickets below the profit-maximizing price for concerts alone" (Krueger 2005: 25).

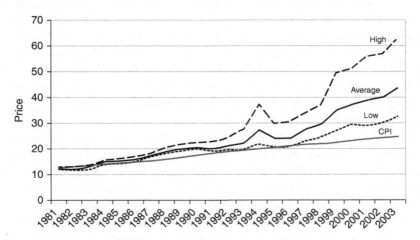

**Figure 2.5** Average price per ticket for high- and low-price tickets and consumer price index (CPI), 1981–2003
Source: Krueger (2005: 7)

Concert tickets were complementary goods to records. Due to the negative cross-price elasticity, an increase in the price of concert tickets would have caused a decline in the demand for records. Since records were the main income source for artists, artists did not favour a rise in concert ticket prices. However, when the link between records and concert tickets sales weakened in the course of digitization, both goods became less complementary. A rise in the price of concert tickets, now the main income source for artists, no longer severely hurts the demand for records.

## Is file sharing a substitute for recorded music sales?

Krueger's hypothesis is based on the assumption that file sharing has caused a decline in recorded music sales (Krueger 2005: 26). This implies that music file sharing and recorded music sales are substitutes. The most prominent exponent of the substitution hypothesis is Stan J. Liebowitz. He argues that the substitution effect of file sharing on recorded music sales dominates other effects such as a positive sampling/exposure effect and network effects. "The copy is treated as a substitute for the original. If the copy is identical or close in quality and if the cost of making the copy is low, the copy for a price of zero dominates the original at its positive price" (Liebowitz 2004: 9). In other words: "[U]nauthorized downloading of a copyrighted file can be a substitute for the purchase of that copyrighted work. The substitution of a downloaded copy for the purchased original obviously has a negative effect impact on sales" (Liebowitz 2006: 17). In an empirical study, Liebowitz (2008: 15) highlighted that "file-sharing is responsible for a reduction in sales that is larger than the sales decline that occurred and that file-sharing aborted what otherwise would have been a growth in sales."

In contrast, other economists provided empirical evidence that the sampling effect of file sharing renders the substitution effect. The sampling hypothesis argues that file sharing lowers sampling costs and that therefore more consumers become familiar with heretofore unknown music/artists. Hence, more consumers buy music from legitimate distribution channels. Felix Oberholzer-Gee and Koleman Strumpf tested the hypothesis that P2P file sharing has a negative impact on album sales, but rejected it on empirical grounds. They concluded "that the impact could not have been larger than

6.0 million albums. While file sharers downloaded billions of files in 2002, the consequences for the industry amounted to no more than 0.7% of sales." To sum up: "there is no statistically significant effect of file sharing on sales" (Oberholzer-Gee & Strumpf 2007: 39).

Since the empirical evidence for the substitution hypothesis is contradictory, the question whether or not file sharing has caused the drop in recorded music sales remains unresolved.

## Music and market failures

### Music as a public good with positive externalities

In the model of a perfect market economy, the market efficiently solves all allocation problems and there is no need for state intervention and regulation. Nevertheless, economists have discovered different forms of market failure, which describe a situation in which goods are inefficiently allocated by the market mechanism; as a result, the market is not Pareto-efficient. "In cases of market failure, the individual pursuit of self-interest found in markets makes society worse off – that is, the market outcome" (Krugman & Wells 2012: 16).

A form of market failure is caused by public goods. The concept of public goods was introduced for the first time by the economist Paul Samuelson in his article "The Pure Theory of Public Expenditure" (1954). In contrast to private goods, public goods are neither excludable nor rivals in consumption. Excludability means that individuals who do not want to pay the market price are excluded from the consumption of a private good. Rivalry in consumption means that an individual appropriates the entire benefit from a private good by paying the market price.

In contrast, public goods are non-excludable and non-rival in consumption. "That is, people cannot be prevented from using a public good and one person's use of a public good does not reduce another person's ability to use it" (Mankiw 2014: 216). Therefore, public goods are freely available. An additional consumer of a public good thus has a marginal benefit at zero marginal costs, thereby increasing the overall social welfare. Therefore, public goods are socially desirable. Due to free-riding, however, public goods are not supplied by a private party – which is why a public good must be financed and supplied by a public body.

Music is a public good. Think of an open-air concert at a health resort. It is not effectively possible to exclude people from listening to the music and there is no rivalry in consumption, since the individual enjoyment from music is not curtailed by the presence of other music listeners. Controlling access to the concert is undesirable, since all music lovers should enjoy the concert to increase social welfare.

Nevertheless, the problem of free-riding still exists. If anyone is enjoying music for free, no money can be collected to pay the musicians. To solve the payment problem, the audience can be asked to make a donation for the concert, or the health resort has to pay the musicians, or local authorities can subsidize the concert with public money. All these "solutions" replace the absent price mechanism and compensate for market failure.

The increase in social welfare from public goods is a form of positive externality. An externality arises when a person engages in an activity that influences the well-being of a bystander but that person neither pays nor receives compensation for that effect. If the impact on the bystander is adverse, it is called a negative externality. If it is beneficial, it is called a positive externality (Mankiw 2014: 196).

Since a market equilibrium is not Pareto-efficient when there are externalities, non-market solutions are needed to internalize externalities. The usual way to internalize a positive externality is to subsidize the production of a public good (see Figure 2.6).

If a positive externality exists ($S_{ext}$), the price of an externality ($p_{ext}$) equals the subsidy to the producers of a public good. The subsidy thus lowers the producers' costs, which results in the supply of more quantities ($x_{sub}$) of the public good at a lower price ($p_{sub}$). The new price reflects a Pareto-efficient market equilibrium.

However, it is questionable whether or not music has positive externalities. Opera and classical music are often perceived as educational goods with positive externalities. In these cases, however, the market price is too high and the output too low. Therefore, a subsidy is needed to internalize the externality. Alternatively, one could argue that classical music is just an entertainment good without educational impact. In this case, the subsidization of concert halls and opera houses cannot be justified by the externality argument.

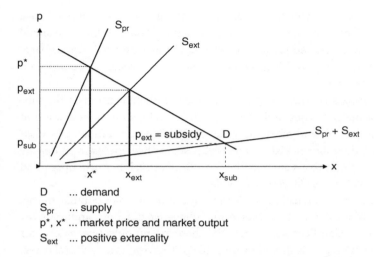

**Figure 2.6** The internalization of a positive externality by subsidization

Another problem arises from valuing externalities. Since we do not know the magnitude of an externality, the correct level of subsidization cannot be defined. A method for assessing the additional social demand for a public good with a positive externality is contingent valuation. It is a survey-based technique valuing non-market resources. In the case of public goods, people are asked to unveil their willingness-to-pay (WTP). The WTP, then, is the measure for a tax that can be used to subsidize the production of a public good. Although several economists question the concept of contingent valuation (Diamond & Hausman 1994), it is a widely accepted method for assessing the WTP for cultural goods (Noonan 2002).

## Music as a merit good

Whereas the market failure of public goods emerges on the supply side because of the lack of a price mechanism, Richard Musgrave (1957) highlighted a market failure on the demand side using the concept of merit goods. A merit good makes a person better off, but the person does not realize the benefit of consuming the merit good. Since a person does not unveil her/his preferences for a merit good, the good is not supplied by a private party. Thus, the state has to provide a merit good to increase social welfare. Medical care, education, as well as the arts and culture are supposed to be merit goods. Thus, consumer sovereignty should be replaced by social preferences.

In most European countries, the merit good argument legitimizes the subsidization of opera houses and concert halls as well as music education at public music schools and music universities. Public radio stations play classical music and public television stations broadcast live operas from heavily subsidized music festivals such as the Salzburg Festival, because opera and classical concerts are seen as merit goods.

This implies that classical music is more meritorious than popular music, which is rarely subsidized. However, critics challenge the merit argument for classical music. Alan Peacock argues that there are no objective criteria for why and how merit goods should be subsidized. This results in "cultural paternalism, which might be justified on the grounds that the community does not know what is good for it" (Peacock 1994: 151). Even Richard Musgrave relativizes the merit good argument: "The concept of merit or demerit goods, to be sure, must be viewed with caution because it may serve as a vehicle for totalitarian rule" (Musgrave & Musgrave 1989: 58).

## Music as a club good

An exclusion mechanism turns public goods into so-called club goods or toll goods. The economist James Buchanan described them for the first time in his 1965 article "An Economic Theory of Clubs". With his club good theory, he fills the gap between the purely public and purely private goods. When introducing a price mechanism – think of a toll road – a club good becomes excludable in consumption, but it is still non-rival.

All music events with an access system – for example concerts and opera houses as well as music festivals – can therefore be defined as club/toll goods. The ticket price makes them excludable in consumption, but listening to the performances is still non-rival. In a concert, an individual appropriates the entire benefit from listening to the music despite the presence of other music lovers.

However, there are large fixed costs to build a concert hall or opera house and to organize music festivals, but the marginal cost of an additional concert goer is more or less negligible. Thus, the average total cost of a concert visit (the total cost divided by the number of visits) falls as the number of visits rises. Hence, a concert can be interpreted as a natural monopoly.

"An industry is a natural monopoly when a single firm can supply a good or service to an entire market at a lower cost than could two or more firms. A natural monopoly arises when there are economies of scale over the relevant range of output" (Mankiw 2014: 302). A natural monopoly is a market failure. Since the average total costs fall with additional output, a single supplier of a club good can produce any amount of output at the least cost. If an additional supplier enters the market, the output per producer decreases owing to higher average costs (Mankiw 2014). Thus, a natural monopoly is not Pareto-efficient (see Figure 2.7).

If a natural monopolist supplies a club good at the market price ($p_S$), she/he cannot cover the average price and, thus, incurs a loss. Therefore, the natural monopolist has to produce an output ($x_{AC}$) where price equals average cost ($p_{AC}$). She/he then covers her/his costs but will produce too little output relative to the efficient amount.

To solve the problem of a natural monopoly, an authority could run the business by itself, bearing the loss of a lower market price. Alternatively, the

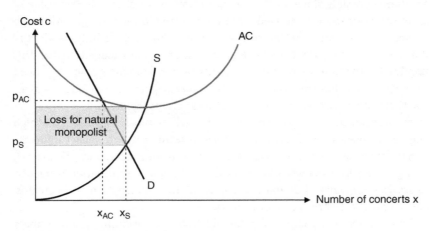

**Figure 2.7** The inefficiency of a natural monopoly
Source: After Varian (2015: 452)

authority could also pay a lump sum to a private supplier of a club good that would allow the supplier to break even. Another solution is to regulate the natural monopoly through a reasonable price policy. In this case, a regulator sets a price that allows the natural monopolist to avoid a loss. This explains why it is nearly impossible for concert halls and opera houses to supply their performances at a price that covers their average costs. Therefore, opera houses are often subsidized (in Europe) or supported by wealthy patrons (in the US). In non-regulated music markets – such as the market for pop and rock concerts – ticket prices are often cross-subsidized by branding and sponsoring arrangements. Since the touring and international concert business seems to be a natural monopoly, just a few large promoters such as Live Nation and AEG dominate the market.

## Music as an information good with network externalities

As highlighted before, music is not just a private good, but it also appears as a public/merit good and a club good. Furthermore, music can be transformed from a pure public good (free open-air concert) into a club good (paid music performance in a concert hall) as well as into a pure private good (record, CD, etc.) by technological means. The transformation from one category into another is possible since music is an information good. The market value of an information good is derived from the information it contains. Although no standard definition of "information" exists, almost all definitions identify it as a carrier of meaning and as a precondition of knowledge transfer. This implies that the value of information goods derives from their usage. You need to experience an information good (CD, concert, opera, etc.) to judge its quality. Therefore, information goods are also experience goods.

The consumption of experience goods such as music is linked to a high degree of uncertainty. Therefore, a music consumer has to collect information before experiencing the good, for example from concert and CD reviews, ratings, chart information and word-of-mouth. Since information is needed to assess the quality of an information good, this information cycle creates, alters, and also destroys economic value.

This economic dynamic can be illustrated by examining the impact technological change has had in the music economy. Originally, music was a public good (non-excludable and non-rival) in public music ceremonies (e.g. as music in the liturgy and as a court entertainment), but later – at the end of the eighteenth century – impresarios turned music into a club good by staging operas and concerts and collecting entrance fees. Music printing and later – at the end of the nineteenth century – sound recording transformed music into a private good with a price mechanism constituting excludability and rivalry in consumption. Together with the emergence of copyright, technological means provide the basis for the modern music industry. However, in the 1920s commercial broadcasting again unveiled the public good characteristics. Music consumption on the radio was free, but it was financed by either commercials (private radio) or fees (public radio). In the course of digitization, the public good characteristics of music became even more relevant. Since digital music can be copied without a loss in quality at zero marginal costs, free-riding in the form of P2P file sharing became a widespread phenomenon. Although the impact of file sharing on music sales is still disputed, the Internet unveils two additional effects of music as an information good: (1) the network effect and (2) positive feedback.

"When the value of a product to one user depends on how many other users there are, economists say that this product exhibits network externalities or network effects" (Shapiro & Varian 1998: 13). The network effect is linked to demand-sided economies of scale. The more users that are part of a network, the more valuable the network becomes. This is true for communication networks – telephone, the Internet, social media applications and so on – but also for virtual networks such as the users of a specific music format. Owing to network effects, records prevailed over music cylinders and CDs replaced vinyl records; and when internet users adopted MP3 technology to transfer digital music files over the Internet, network effects were also at work.

The value of networks follows Metcalfe's law, which is more a rule of thumb than a law. According to the Ethernet inventor Robert Metcalfe, the value of a network rises with the square of the number of users: $n \times (n - 1) = n^2 - n$. If the network size is 100 and each user of the network values the network at $1, then the value of the entire network is $90. If the network's size increases to 1 million, the network value explodes to $999,999,000,000 (approx. $100 billion) (Shapiro & Varian 1998: 184).

Since it is more attractive to join a larger network than a smaller one, a large network grows faster than smaller networks because of positive feedback. Positive feedback explains why some internet applications such as Facebook, Twitter, YouTube and Spotify became dominant by superseding competitors that are less attractive and have a smaller user base. Another example is Apple Inc. Apple turned from a small and irrelevant computer manufacturer in the 1980s to one of the world's largest corporations in the 2000s by providing a virtual network of devices and services (Mac, iPod, iPhone, iPad, iCloud, iTunes) to store information goods such as music, film, texts and so on. The network was so attractive for consumers to join that other initially powerful computer and software firms such as IBM and Microsoft lost ground and market shares. IBM eventually sold its personal computer business to Chinese consumer electronics conglomerate Lenovo in 2005. In contrast to Apple, IBM was a very bureaucratic company with large overheads and fixed costs. Such a company needs a large and growing market to benefit from economies of scale. However, if market growth comes to an end, market share can only be gained by mergers and acquisitions. If new consumer behaviour emerges as a result of, say, technological change, large companies tend to remain stuck in their old technological paradigm. They lose ground to smaller companies relying on new market niches that are not attractive for a large corporation. Benefiting from their technological advantage and from positive feedback, the smaller companies grow at the expense of the large companies and eventually replace them. Thus, positive feedback for the winners is negative feedback for the losers.

To sum up, demand-side economies of scale of network effects lead to two different effects (Shapiro & Varian 1998: 173):

1. Positive feedback makes the strong grow stronger and the weak grow weaker.
2. Negative feedback makes the weak grow stronger and the strong grow weaker.

## Music as a common good

Common goods are defined as goods that are non-excludable but rival in consumption. Examples for common goods are natural resources, fish grounds, hunting grounds, but also public parking sites and roads.

The ecologist Garrett Hardin described the main problem of common goods in his *Science* article "The Tragedy of the Commons" in 1968, arguing that if all group members were to use common resources for their own benefit and with no regard for others, all resources would eventually be depleted: acting based on pure self-interest, for example, leads to overfishing the seas and to turning the rainforests into wasteland.

The famous Woodstock music festival of 1969 was a kind of common good. Access to the festival ground was free since the organizers could not complete fences and access gates in time. The unexpected massive inflow of festival visitors caused not only a traffic jam back to New York City but also disastrous sanitary conditions and a water and food shortage. Supplies had to be brought in by army helicopters, which also had to fly in some of the festival acts. Although Woodstock was a financial and organizational disaster, it subsequently became an iconic event signifying freedom, peace and an alternative lifestyle (Rosenman *et al.* 1999; Lang 2009).

However, Elinor Ostrom has highlighted that the "Tragedy of the Commons" is not an inescapable fate. If a social community regulates access to common pool resources (CPR) – as Ostrom calls common goods – the over-use of common goods can be limited and the tragedy of the commons can be avoided. Ostrom (1990: 90) identifies the following design principles that effectively govern the use of common goods:

- clearly defined boundaries;
- congruence between rules of appropriation and provision and local conditions;
- collective-choice arrangements allowing for the participation of most of the appropriators in the decision-making process;
- effective monitoring by monitors who are part of or accountable to the appropriators;
- graduated sanctions for appropriators who do not respect community rules;
- conflict-resolution mechanisms that are cheap and easy to access;
- minimal recognition of rights to organize (e.g., by the government);
- in respect of larger CPRs: organization in the form of multiple layers of nested enterprises with small, local CPRs at their bases.

A special case of common goods are digital commons. Digital commons are defined as "information and knowledge resources that are collectively created and owned or shared between or among a community and that tend to be non-excludable" (Foster Morell 2010: 5). This allows the collective process of music creation in a social community. The production of music by DJs is a good example. A DJ takes already existing pieces of music and compiles them; this is called sampling. It is normal that subsequently other DJs use the derivative music track, so that the result is an endless process of collective recreation.

Since sound recordings are usually protected by copyright, permission is needed to use a piece of music from a recording. However, record companies rarely allow the use of sound recording samples without the payment of a considerable license fee. Therefore, Lawrence Lessig and others developed the concept of creative commons (CC) licences in 2001 to enable the lawful use of works (Lessig 2001). The modular system of CC licensing enables authors to define how people use their works. They may allow others to copy, distribute, display and perform the work and make derivative works as long as authorship is credited, but they can also restrict the use of a work by allowing the distribution of derivative works only under a licence identical to the licence that governs the original work, or by forbidding any commercial use and by disallowing the creation of derivate works.[2] Creative commons licensing regulates the use of digital commons in a way that avoids locking away information goods from the public while ensuring their use according to the wishes of the authors.

Rivalry in consumption

| | Rivalrous | Non-rivalrous | |
|---|---|---|---|
| | **(Digital) Common goods**<br>Copyrighted music tracks | **Public/merit goods**<br>Free accessable music performances | Non-exclud-able |
| | **Private goods**<br>Vinyl records, CDs, music downloads | **Club goods**<br>Music performances in opera houses, concert venues and festivals | Exclud-able |

**Figure 2.8** A typology of music as an economic good

## Conclusion

To sum up, music can appear as different economic goods: (1) It is a public good if access is totally free and if there is no rivalry in consumption (e.g. free open-air concert); (2) it is a club good if access to music is restricted by an access system but with no rivalry consumption (e.g. music performances in concert and festival venues); (3) it is a (digital) commons good if music consumption is non-excludable but rival (e.g. copyright-protected digital music tracks); and (4) it is a purely private good if music is excludable and rival in consumption (e.g. vinyl records, CDs and paid music downloads) (see Figure 2.8).

## Notes

1. A more detailed explanation of the market/price mechanism can be found in textbooks on microeconomics, for example Varian (2010) and Mankiw (2014).
2. For a detailed explanation of the concept of creative commons licensing, see Wikipedia, "Creative Commons License", https://en.wikipedia.org/wiki/Creative_Commons_license (retrieved 2 December 2015).

# 3
# THE ECONOMICS OF MUSIC COPYRIGHT

## The justifications for a music copyright

As we have seen, music has public good characteristics. Without any restrictions, music would be in the public domain and could be used without permission at zero cost. Thus, there is no incentive to produce music for economic ends. The introduction of property rights therefore allows composers and authors to control their intellectual property. According to Landes and Posner, the possession of an intellectual property right "enables people to reap where they have sown" (Landes & Posner 2003: 13). The benefit from appropriating the returns from intellectual property has to be compared with the cost incurred in doing so. The costs of property rights are manifold. Landes and Posner (2003: 16–21) identify (1) the cost of transferring intellectual property rights, (2) the cost of obtaining such rights and (3) the cost of protection. From an economic point of view, the introduction of an intellectual property rights regime makes sense if its benefits exceed the cost involved in applying it.

The most important intellectual property rights in the field of music are copyrights. There are two different sets of justifications for a copyright of musical works: moral justifications and justifications based on non-alienable exploitation rights. The first – and important – moral justification of copyright is that a composer and author has the right to the fruits of her/his works. The second is the Kantian assumption that a work is an extension of a person's personality. And the third moral justification is that society has an obligation to recognize the contributions from creators because these contributions increase social welfare (see O'Hagan 1998: 78–9). The moral justifications, especially the Kantian argument, play an important role in continental Europe copyright legislations. The three most common moral rights that are granted in European copyright laws – according to O' Hagan (1998: 84) – are: (1) the right to be identified as the creator of a work that protects against plagiarism (paternity right); (2) the right to be protected against alterations to one's work (integrity right); and (3) the right to publish a work, but also to prohibit the publication of one's work (publication right).

However, European copyright legislations also protect the economic interests of authors by granting non-alienable exploitation rights such as performing rights, reproduction rights, broadcasting rights, dissemination rights and making available rights (the so-called internet rights).[1] These economic rights can be licensed to a third party (e.g. a music publisher) for further exploitation. Whereas European copyright covers the moral and economic interests of authors, the US Copyright Act is mainly based on economic justifications for a copyright. The main theoretical argument for the introduction of a copyright is closely related to property rights theory: "The public good represented by composers' and authors' work in a market without copyright would presumably be undersupplied, since society would have no mechanism with which to signal creators of the true collective value placed on their work."[2] According to this argument, composers have no incentive to write music in the absence of a copyright. However, it is evident that music is also produced when no copyright exists, which was the case for centuries. Thus, copyright – in the sense of authors' rights – is not the ultimate reason for creativity and musical innovation.

## Copyright and the music industry structure

### The monopoly

Copyright grants a temporary monopoly that is an incentive for publishers to copy and disseminate musical works. They and other intermediaries such as record companies need copyright protection as part of their business models. The production of a CD is a costly matter, which is why record companies feel they have to be able to recoup their cost by exploiting a temporary monopoly

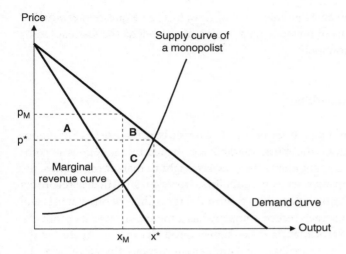

**Figure 3.1** The inefficiency of a monopoly

for the recording granted by copyright. These related or so-called neighbouring rights are no longer connected to the author. In the field of music, they are granted to performers, phonogram producers and broadcasting companies.[3]

A monopoly, however, allocates resources inefficiently (see Figure 3.1). A monopolist maximizes her/his profit when the marginal revenue = marginal cost, which is represented by the monopolist's supply curve. The monopolist thus sets a higher price ($p_M$) than the efficient market price ($p^*$). At the same time, the monopolist supplies a lower output ($x_M$) than the output of a competitive market ($x^*$). Consequently, consumers are worse off in a monopoly than in a competitive market. They have to pay a higher price for fewer supplied goods. Therefore, a monopoly is not Pareto-efficient. In addition, more consumers would buy at the lower market price ($p^*$). This results in a welfare loss that equates to the rectangle C and triangle B, whereas the monopolist earns a profit $P_M = (p_M - p^*) \times x_M$ (= rectangle A).

Hence, there are two opposite effects of copyright. On the one hand, the free-riding effect in the absence of copyright causes an underproduction of cultural goods. By introducing intellectual property rights the production level is increased, which leads to a welfare gain. On the other hand, the temporary monopoly increases prices, which leads to under-consumption and a welfare loss. From an economic point of view, it is just a question of whether the welfare gain from introducing a copyright outweighs the loss caused by the temporary monopoly.


## Monopolistic competition

Neither the recording industry nor the live music business are pure monopolies, however. Rather, the music markets are shaped by monopolistic competition. Since copyright grants the exclusive right to market recordings, the phonograph companies act as monopolists. However, a particular recording of, for example, Beyoncé competes against the recordings of other artists and record labels. Thus, each record company has a monopoly over its products, but many other record labels make similar products that compete for the same consumers. Monopolistically competitive markets therefore have the following characteristics (Mankiw 2014: 331):

- Many sellers: There are many firms competing for the same group of customers.
- Product differentiation: Each firm produces a product that is at least slightly different from those of other firms. Thus, rather than being a price-taker, each firm faces a downward-sloping demand curve.
- Free entry and exit: Firms can enter or exit the market without restriction. Thus, the number of firms in the market adjusts until economic profits are driven to zero.

Firms in a monopolistically competitive market act as monopolists maximizing their profits when marginal costs equal marginal revenue. Nevertheless, firms are in a competitive market where free entry and free exit drive economic profit to zero in the long run. Thus, the price equals total average cost (Figure 3.2).

Compared to a pure competitive market, the price ($p_{MC}$) in a monopolistically competitive market is higher and the market output is lower ($x_{MC}$). Thus, monopolistic competition is not Pareto-efficient and produces the usual welfare loss of monopolistic pricing.

In the end, we can conclude only that monopolistically competitive markets do not have all the desirable welfare properties of perfectly competitive

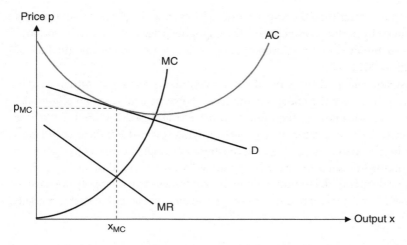

**Figure 3.2** Profit maximization in a monopolistically competitive market in the long run
Source: After Mankiw (2014: 334)

markets. That is, the invisible hand does not ensure that total surplus is maximized under monopolistic competition. Yet because the inefficiencies are subtle, hard to measure and hard to fix, there is no easy way for public policy to improve the market outcome (Mankiw 2014: 337).

The oligopoly

However, the different sectors of the music industry – recording, publishing and the live music business – are shaped by a few large dominant players (the majors) and myriads of small companies (independents). The so-called "indies" operate on a monopolistically competitive market, whereas the majors are in an oligopoly. Thus, the major companies have to act strategically, since the output decision of a major depends on the decisions of the other majors. The oligopolistic majors are better off if they act like a monopolist – setting a single price above marginal cost. Therefore, the large companies have to cooperate when price-setting by forming a price cartel. However, anti-trust laws prohibit any agreements between oligopolists to avoid cartels in any form. Thus, oligopolistic firms pursue their self-interest: "[T]hey produce a quantity of output greater than the level produced by monopoly and less than the level produced by perfect competition. The oligopoly price is less than the monopoly price but greater than the competitive price (which equals marginal cost)" (Mankiw 2014: 352).

Instead, oligopolistic firms do not maximize profits but rather market shares. The larger the company, the more power it has to set an oligopolistic market price near to the monopoly price (Mankiw 2014: 352). Thus, it is attractive for a record major to grow by buying successful indie record labels in order to enlarge its catalogue of master recordings that are copyrighted. It is, therefore, no surprise that all copyrighted industries tend to be oligopolies. To get a deeper understanding of the market forces in an oligopoly, we have to look at the contractual relations between the different actors in such a market.

## Copyright and contractual economics

For a better understanding of the impact of copyright on the music business, it is necessary to go beyond neoclassical microeconomic theory. As we have seen, the sectors of the music industry are shaped by large corporations. Major companies have dominated the recording as well as the music publishing industry since the late nineteenth century. However, the initially highly competitive live music market has also become an oligopoly in recent years with the rise of Live Nation and AEG. Thus, we need to know how large music entertainment conglomerates work and evolve – and copyright plays a crucial role.

Ronald Coase introduced a path-breaking economic concept in his seminal paper *The Nature of the Firm* (1937) for understanding why companies emerge. He based his explanation on the concept of transaction cost. Coase highlights that market transactions are not free of cost. Information costs, bargaining costs, and also policing and contract enforcement costs emerge when obtaining a good or service – the so-called transaction cost. According to Oliver Williamson (1979), the determinants of transaction cost are frequency, specificity and uncertainty of a transaction. The higher the transaction cost incurred, the more likely a transaction is not made on the market but within a hierarchy – which is another word for a company (Williamson 1975).

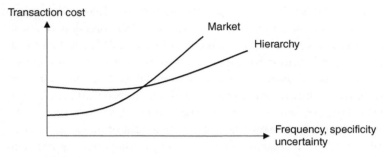

**Figure 3.3** The decision criteria between markets and hierarchies
Source: After Schoppe (1996: 162)

Transaction cost thus plays a crucial role in the establishment of large music corporations. Uncertainty and specificity are prevalent in the music business. According to Richard Caves, the production and dissemination of creative products such as music is highly uncertain because of what he calls the "nobody knows" principle (Caves 2000: 3). A music business rule of thumb says that only 10 per cent of all record releases break even. This means that 10 per cent of recordings have to cross-subsidize the loss made by the remaining 90 per cent of recordings. In addition, as soon as a recording is made, it can only be sold at a given price. There are no other alternative uses of such a recording. Hence, music recordings are highly specific investments. The financial capital embodied in the recording is lost if the record is a flop, which is referred to as a sunk cost (Mankiw 2014: 286). Granting copyrights helps to decrease uncertainty by exploiting a music product for a very long period. Copyright is a kind of long-term insurance against poor business decisions.

However, copyright also functions as a market entry barrier in the music industry. "[T]he only way a competing firm can obtain existing copyrights is by buying them from the owner or acquiring a licence to use them, which the copyright owner may not grant as the new entrant is a competitor" (Towse 2010: 387). Therefore, the history of the music industry manifests a continuous flow of mergers and acquisitions, as we saw in the first chapter.

As an example of this, recording companies do not just buy each other (horizontal integration), but also merge with different companies in the music industry's value-added chain; this is called vertical integration. Thus, the major recording companies are also owners of the world's largest music publishing houses; this is known as upstream integration. The record majors also control downstream activities such as CD and DVD pressing, physical distribution networks and even music retailing (think of EMI's HMV record stores). However, digitization has forced them to disintegrate because of rising transaction costs. Thus, record majors have sold their pressing plants and most of the physical distribution in order to invest in the acquisition of master recordings catalogues; economic theory refers to this as flexible specialization (Storper & Christopherson 1987). With the advent of music streaming, the record majors again integrated downstream by buying minority stakes in some of the emerging music-streaming companies to control the dissemination of digital music.

Control is the most important asset in the uncertain environment of the music industry. The music industry's companies execute their control through contracts. However, no contract is ever complete. Caves highlights that the incompleteness of contracts in the recording industry is even greater than in the rest of the economy (Caves 2000: 61–4). As a result of the "nobody knows" problem, recording companies want to control almost all intellectual property rights linked with music creation. Apart from their dealings with superstars, the recording companies are in the stronger bargaining position. They insist on the *exclusive* transfer of copyright for a recording. This enables record companies to monopolize the commercialization of the authors' and musicians' creative work, which leads to monopolistic competition in the music industry. Since the monopolization of music works creates market entry barriers, in the long run there is a lack of competition and a tendency towards oligopolization of the industry structure. If only a few market actors dominate the market, they will strive for stabilization of their market power by

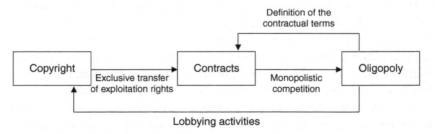

**Figure 3.4** The relation of copyright, contracts and market structure
Source: Tschmuck (2009: 262)

increasing the span of control. Therefore, they dictate the contractual terms with the authors and musicians on the one hand and they lobby legislative bodies for restrictive copyright laws on the other (see Tschmuck 2009: 261).

## Monopoly power and optimal copyright terms

The copyright term is a crucial aspect of copyright protection and monopoly power. Whereas the Statute of Anne (1709/1710) granted to publishers copyright protection of 14 years – a term that was meant to be renewable only once – the copyright term has since been extended to a span of 70 years after the death of the author. The Sonny Bono Copyright Term Extension Act of 1998 extended existing copyright protection for works of corporate authorship in the US to 120 years after creation or 95 years after publication, whichever endpoint is earlier.[4] In the European Union, the copyright term for sound recordings was extended from 50 to 70 years in 2011.[5]

The US as well as the EU copyright extension was criticized by highly regarded IP law professors and economists, including Nobel laureates Sir James Mirrlees and Kenneth Arrow, as both ineffective and unnecessary, so why is a copyright term extension harmful from an economic perspective; and what is the optimal length of copyright protection?

### The economic problems of a copyright term extension

Landes and Posner (2003) modelled the situation of optimal copyright at an aggregate level. This implies that an increasing level of protection increases not just revenue but also cost, since much creative work reuses previous work. Further, there is a competition of works: if the number of works increases, the increased competition reduces the revenue obtained from a given work. In addition, we have to assume a variation in production costs across works as well as a variation in demand (and welfare) across works. Taking these factors into account, we can derive the following propositions:

1. Some production of creative works occurs without any copyright protection;
2. The supply of creative works increases with the introduction of copyright protection;

3. However, there are diminishing returns to protection; and
4. Eventually increasing the level of protection reduces the supply of creative works, since beyond a specific level of protection "the cost of expression to marginal authors will dominate, so that the number of works will begin to fall" (Landes & Posner, 1989: 335).

We can now derive an aggregate welfare function, in which overall welfare depends on the sum of welfare contributed by each work and the total cost of producing works, including administrative and enforcement costs. However, the welfare contributed by each (existing) work diminishes with the level of protection because of the deadweight loss associated with copyright protection. Thus, the overall welfare gain depends on the welfare deriving from new works, the decline in welfare from existing works (because of the deadweight loss) and production and administration costs. Since a term extension would increase the deadweight loss as well as production and administrative costs, it is intuitive that overall welfare has to decline. This intuitive conclusion is supported by Landes and Posner (2003: 220), who state that a retrospective extension of copyright:

> can't affect the incentive to create new works, since a retroactive extension affects only the return on works already in existence .... Retroactive extensions do not enhance incentives to create expressive works, so if those incentives are the only benefits from copyright, such extensions will increase transaction and access costs without generating any offsetting value.

Hence, we can conclude that a copyright term extension has two negative effects: (1) at best, the number of works that will be produced does not change, but it is in fact expected to diminish; and (2) the cost of production and administration increase, since the size of the public domain decreases. Therefore, we have to expect a decrease in social welfare from a copyright term extension.

## The optimal length of copyright protection

Pollock (2009) derived a model from empirical parameters (probability density function or PDF) that suggests a substantially shorter copyright term than

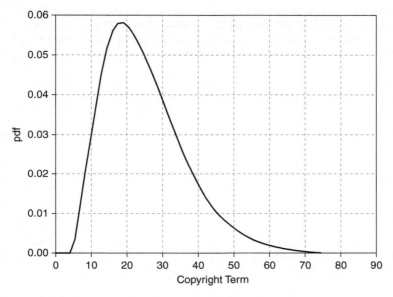

**Figure 3.5** The optimal length of copyright protection
Source: Pollock (2009: 42)

any current existing ones: "Using existing data on recordings and books we obtain a point estimate of around 15 years for optimal copyright term with a 99% confidence interval extending up to 38 years" (Pollock 2009: 24).

The model suggests that a copyright term of about 15 years would raise social welfare to an optimum – measured in works produced – with a revenue for copyright holders that equals production cost in the long run. Therefore, copyright terms of 70 years and more are much too long from an economic perspective.

## Notes

1. See Directive 2001/29/EC of the European Parliament and of the Council of 22 May 2001 on the harmonisation of certain aspects of copyright and related rights in the information society.
2. Cited in O'Hagan (1998).
3. See International Convention for the Protection of Performers, Producers of Phonograms and Broadcasting Organizations ("Rome Convention" of 26 October 1961).

4. Sonny Bono Copyright Term Extension Act, Sonny Bono Act 1998, Pub.L. 105–298.
5. European Commission, 2008, Proposal for a European Parliament and Council directive amending Directive 2006/116/EC of the European Parliament and of the Council on the term of protection of copyright and related rights.

# 4

# MUSIC PUBLISHING

## Music publishing functions

When the music publishers dominated the music industry at the end of the nineteenth century, their main aim was to sell sheet music. As mentioned in Chapter 1, "After the Ball" became the first million-seller song in 1893 and others followed. Today, however, sheet music sales are just a side business for music publishers. The main function of a music publisher in the digital age is the acquisition and exploitation of copyrights.

## Copyright acquisition

The traditional way of obtaining copyrights is to contract a songwriter for a specific song (individual song contract) or for a specific period of time to compose and/or write songs (exclusive songwriter's contract). In an individual song contract, a songwriter assigns all the copyrights of a single song to a publisher in return for a non-returnable advance that is fully cross-collateralized with any royalties earned by the songwriter until the production cost is recouped. Several hundreds of dollars or euros are the usual advances for a single song contract (Hull *et al.* 2011: 122–3). In an exclusive contract, a songwriter agrees to exclusively compose and/or write music for a publisher for a certain period. Such a contract usually lasts a year, but longer contracts – up to seven years – are possible should the publisher wish to develop an artist (developmental deals), especially when the publisher expects the songwriter to become a recording artist. Thus, singer/songwriter Alanis Morissette was initially signed for seven years by MCA Music Publishing before her album debut in 1995 (Hull *et al.* 2011: 121). During the contract period the songwriter receives a weekly or monthly advance that is fully deductible from any royalties received from record sales, sheet music sales, synchronization fees and so on (Brabec & Brabec 2004: 13). In both cases the copyrights can be exploited by the publisher as long as the author is alive and for a period of 70 years after her/his death.

The traditional model of copyright acquisition is typical for small music publishers. Larger companies usually purchase smaller song catalogues from successful songwriters and music producers who run their own publishing companies. Larger music publishers even acquire other publishers to enlarge their catalogues to gain market share; for example, German BMG Rights Management has become the world's fourth largest music publisher – behind the major music publishers Universal Music Publishing (UMP), Sony/ATV Publishing and Warner/Chappell Music – by acquiring several publishing companies since 2010.

## Copyright exploitation

The main task of a music publisher is to license copyrights to music users. The publishers earn their income from a variety of sources:

- public performances and broadcasting (performance fees);
- licensing music for recordings (mechanical license fees);
- licensing music to motion pictures, television films/series, home videos, games, commercials and so on (synchronization fees);
- licensing music to digital music users (ringtones, ring-back tones, music download and streaming services, etc.); and
- print music publishing.

### *Public performance rights*
Since it is impossible to monitor all public performances of their musical repertoire, music publishers teamed up with authors and composers to establish performance rights organizations (PROs). As mentioned in Chapter 1, the world's first PRO was the French SACEM – founded in 1850 – to collect performance fees from all public locations where the compositions of its

members were performed. Other PROs were established in Europe around 1900. In the US, although public performance rights were enacted in 1897, an efficient and comprehensive collection of performance fees was not possible until the foundation of the American Society of Composers, Authors and Publishers (ASCAP) in 1914 (Krasilovsky *et al.* 2007: 145).

Since an ASCAP contract was exclusive, it was nearly impossible for foreign authors and composers to become an ASCAP member. Therefore, the German immigrant Paul Heinecke founded the Society of European Stage Authors and Composers (SESAC) in 1930 to represent European authors and composers in the US and collect performance fees for their works (Krasilovsky *et al.* 2007: 146–7). When ASCAP raised their license fees in 1940, the large US broadcasting networks NBC and CBS refused to pay the higher fees and boycotted the ASCAP repertoire. Instead, the networks set up a competing PRO – Broadcast Music Incorporated (BMI) – to become independent from ASCAP. After ten months of boycott, ASCAP and the broadcasting networks settled their conflict by agreeing to a lower fee, but BMI stayed in business (Ryan 1985). Today in the US, three PROs co-exist, each operating a more or less similar business model. They compete in signing new songwriters and publishers by offering different electronic monitoring systems for radio airplay and live performances.

Unlike in the US, the collecting societies in Europe enjoy a national monopoly for the assigned rights. The German GEMA, for example, has the sole right to collect fees from music performances in its territory. A rights holder is therefore obliged to exclusively sign with a collecting society of her/his home state. However, the European Commission aims at fostering competition among the national collecting societies by allowing rights holders to assign their online rights to a national collecting society of their choice.[1]

The US as well as the European PROs only administer the non-dramatic performance rights ("small rights") for their members. The rights for dramatic performances (operas and other musical theatrical performances) – the so-called "grand rights" – are administered by the publishers themselves or by specialized agencies representing them (Hull *et al.* 2011: 130).

### Mechanical rights
A mechanical licence is "the permission from the copyright owner of a musical composition to manufacture and distribute copies of the composition

embodied in phonorecords intended for sale to the public" (Hull *et al.* 2011: 77). The mechanical right was first introduced when piano rolls, music cylinders and records became a widespread economic success. At first, player piano manufacturers as well as recording companies used the repertoire of music publishers without permission, prompting the music publishers to bring law suits. At the same time, the publishers lobbied for an extension of copyright law to mechanical reproduction of music, which was to result in copyright law reforms in Europe as well as in the US. The US Copyright Act of 1909 introduced a compulsory mechanical licence for phonorecords, which required the rights holders to grant such a licence if the record labels paid a statutory rate of 2 cents per copy to the rights holders. The mechanical right is compulsory because rights holders must give permission for the use of a non-dramatic musical work for mechanical reproduction, and once a mechanical right is granted to a recording company in the US, any other record label can make a cover version of the same song without further permission. The statutory rate of 2 cents remained unchanged until 1972. Since then, the rate has changed several times and is now at 9.1 cents for recordings of a song lasting 5 minutes or less and 1.75 cents per minute or a fraction thereof for those lasting over 5 minutes.[2] Since 2004 a Copyright Royalty Board (CRB) – three judges appointed by the Library of Congress – sets the statutory rate for phonorecords, full and limited downloads, ringtones and interactive music streaming. Since non-interactive streaming services (webcasters) do not deliver a copy to their users, they do not require a mechanical licence. Thus, they are exempted from paying a mechanical licensing fee (Hull *et al.* 2011: 79–80).

However, most mechanical licences in the US are not compulsory since the recording companies seek to negotiate a rate significantly lower than the statutory rate. It is for this reason that the National Music Publishers Association (NMPA) founded the Harry Fox Agency in 1917 to collect mechanical licensing fees for their members. Initially the Harry Fox Agency also administered the publishers' synchronization rights, but it closed its synchronization department in 2002 since most of the publishers had started to license their synchronization rights directly. Today the Harry Fox Agency offers a joint mechanical and synchronization licence (Krasilovsky *et al.* 2007: 65) and several other agencies also handle the licensing of mechanical and synchronization rights, including the American Mechanical Rights Agency (AMRA), established in 1961 (Krasilovsky *et al.* 2007: 167).

Unlike in the US, no compulsory mechanical licensing regime exists in Europe, so specialized Mechanical Rights Organizations (MROs) administer mechanical rights: the Mechanical-Copyright Protection Society (MCPS) in the UK was founded in 1911 in anticipation of the UK Copyright Act of 1911 and later, in 1924, merged with the Performing Rights Society (PRS), which is now the PRS for Music; the Dutch PRO–Buma Association (founded in 1913) established the STEMRA Foundation in 1936 to collect mechanical fees for Dutch composers, authors and music publishers. In Germany, however, no specialized MRO exists, since GEMA[3] also administers mechanical rights, whereas in Austria the AKM[4] administers performance rights and AustroMechana is responsible for collecting mechanical fees.

*Synchronization rights*
Film studios, television companies, home video producers, advertising agencies and video games producers must obtain synchronization rights in order to include music in their products. However, the synchronization rights are not administered by collecting societies but by either the music publishers themselves or contracted synchronization rights agencies. Today's major publishers demand synchronization fees of $50,000 for a significant use of a song in a movie and up to $250,000 if the song is used as the movie soundtrack. A one-year use of a song in an advertising commercial can cost up to $500,000 and video game producers can pay a flat fee of between $1,000 and $6,000 for a lesser-known song (Hull *et al.* 2011: 137).

*Online rights*
As a result of the digitization of the music industry, new forms of music uses have emerged. MROs usually license the making available right, which was introduced in European copyright law to cover music download and streaming services as well as other online music providers. However, larger music publishers seeking to avoid the costly digital rights clearance in each of the EU's member states have teamed up with collecting societies in the larger EU countries. Thus, BMG Rights Management established a joint venture with the German GEMA – called ARESA – to license its Anglo-American repertoire to digital service providers across Europe,[5] and similarly Sony/ATV launched the pan-European licensing venture SOLAR with UK's PRS for Music and the German GEMA.[6] These deals put smaller European collecting societies under

pressure, since the major publishers do not license their digital repertoire through them, resulting in decreasing revenues and economic problems. The pan-European deals also make the system of reciprocal agreements among collecting societies that would allow small collecting societies to license the world's music repertoire obsolete – at least in the digital sphere.

### Print music publishing

Although sheet music sales are a side business for most of the music publishers – they account for less than 10 per cent of total income (Hull *et al.* 2011: 137) – the demand for printed music from schools, music schools, conservatoires and music universities, and also from private individuals, is still considerable. Some music publishers such as Hal Leonard, Music Sales Corp. and Alfred Publishing Company in the US as well as Schott Music in Germany and Universal Edition in Austria specialize in preparing, printing and distributing sheet music, folios and music books. The print publishers act internationally by licensing their popular repertoire to sub-publishers in other countries. In such a sub-publishing deal the licensee agrees to pay a minimum of 10 per cent of the retail price, which is usually divided equally between publisher and songwriter (Krasilovsky *et al.* 2007: 2). The Internet offers new possibilities for print music publishers to market their products. Sheetmusicdirect.com – a joint venture by Hal Leonard and Music Sales – and musicnotes.com – operated by Alfred Publishing – offer their sheet music repertoire as downloads and for mail order.

## The market and industry structure of music publishing

Music industry analyst Will Page calculated a value of $11,340 million for the global music publishing market in 2014, comprising $7,550 million for the collection of performance fees, $1,320 million for mechanical collections and $350 million for private copying collections by CISAC[7] members and $420 million for non-CISAC mechanical collections (e.g. Harry Fox Agency collections). A further $1,700 million of revenue is added for music directly licensed by the publishers ("grand rights" and synchronization rights).

A long-term analysis shows that the global music publishing market nearly doubled from $5,840 million in 1994 to $9,400 million in 2011 (Baierle

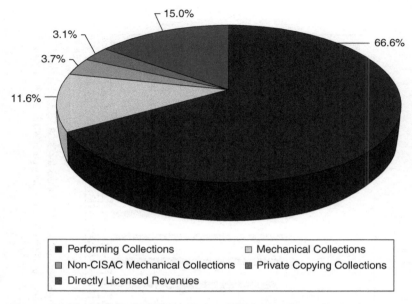

**Figure 4.1** The global value of the music publishing market in 2014
Source: After Music Business Worldwide (2015c)

2009: 215). Though the market data are from different and not fully compara-
ble sources, they nevertheless indicate a robust and growing publishing market, whereas the recording market significantly decreased in the same period.

The Global Collections Reports by CISAC confirm that the music publishing market has been growing since 2008. However, CISAC statistics only
cover the numbers reported by its member collecting societies. Therefore,
data on mechanical collections by Harry Fox Agency and similar US mechanical rights agencies, as well as revenue from the publishers' direct licensing
of rights (e.g. synchronization rights and "grand rights"), are not included in
the CISAC numbers.

CISAC collections for performance and mechanical rights, as well as from
private copying and resale rights, increased by 12.9 per cent from 2008 to
2014, despite the ongoing decrease in the recorded music market. The drivers
of growth are the prospering digital music market and the live music sector,
but also steadily growing revenues from licensing music to television and radio
stations. To sum up, the music publishing market shows no signs of a crisis,

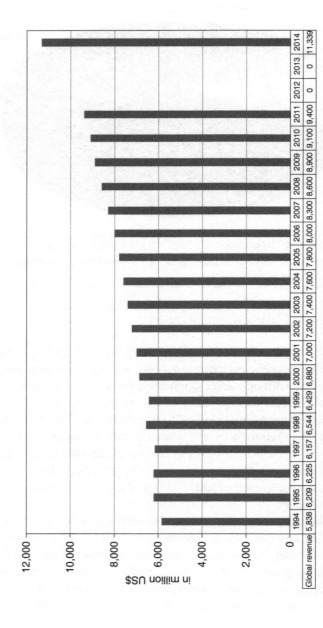

| Global revenue | 1994 | 1995 | 1996 | 1997 | 1998 | 1999 | 2000 | 2001 | 2002 | 2003 | 2004 | 2005 | 2006 | 2007 | 2008 | 2009 | 2010 | 2011 | 2012 | 2013 | 2014 |
|---|---|---|---|---|---|---|---|---|---|---|---|---|---|---|---|---|---|---|---|---|---|
| | 5,838 | 6,209 | 6,225 | 6,157 | 6,544 | 6,429 | 6,880 | 7,000 | 7,200 | 7,400 | 7,600 | 7,800 | 8,000 | 8,300 | 8,600 | 8,900 | 9,100 | 9,400 | 0 | 0 | 11,339 |

**Figure 4.2** The global music publishing revenue, 1994–2014

Sources: 1994–2000: NMPA (2002); 2001–2005: calculation by Baierle (2009: 215); values for 2008–2011: Financial Times Music & Copyright, 344, cited in Baierle (2009:215); values for 2008–2011 are projected; 2012–2013: no data available; 2014: Page (2015)

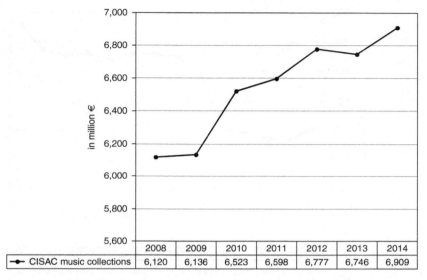

| | 2008 | 2009 | 2010 | 2011 | 2012 | 2013 | 2014 |
|---|---|---|---|---|---|---|---|
| CISAC music collections | 6,120 | 6,136 | 6,523 | 6,598 | 6,777 | 6,746 | 6,909 |

**Figure 4.3** Global CISAC collections for musical works, 2008–2014
Source: After CISAC (2010–2015)

although in some segments – private copying, recording and reprography – revenue has been declining.

The growth of the music publishing market is also reflected in the balance sheets of the major publishers – Universal Music Publishing, Sony/ATV and Warner Chappell. Universal Music Group Publishing's revenue increased by 83.5 per cent from 2002 to 2015. However this growth was mainly driven by the acquisition of BMG Music Publishing in May 2007 for €1,639 million. Nevertheless, music publishing revenue continued to increase in the following years despite the sale of certain music catalogues (Rondor UK, 19 Music, 1 Songs and BBC Catalogue) to CP Masters BV and ABP in 2008 in order to comply with the stipulations by the EU competition authority (Vivendi 2007: 135).

Sony/ATV Music Publishing has also grown over the past few years by acquiring economically significant music catalogues, such as Tony Martin's Baby Mae Music in 2001, the country music publisher Acuff-Rose in 2002 and the catalogue of the famous songwriting duo Jerry Leiber and Mike Stoller in 2007. In 2012 Sony/ATV became the world's largest music publisher

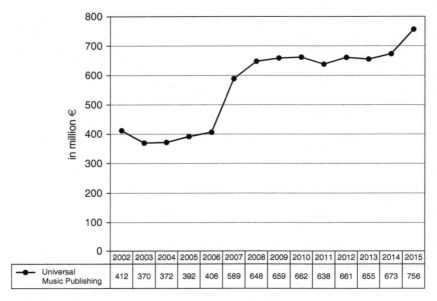

| | 2002 | 2003 | 2004 | 2005 | 2006 | 2007 | 2008 | 2009 | 2010 | 2011 | 2012 | 2013 | 2014 | 2015 |
|---|---|---|---|---|---|---|---|---|---|---|---|---|---|---|
| Universal Music Publishing | 412 | 370 | 372 | 392 | 406 | 589 | 648 | 659 | 662 | 638 | 661 | 655 | 673 | 756 |

**Figure 4.4** The revenue of Universal Music Publishing, 2002–2015
Source: After Vivendi (2002–2015)

by purchasing EMI Music Publishing – a vast catalogue with publishing rights for more than 1.3 million titles (Sony Corporation 2013: F 31–2). Therefore, Sony's 50 per cent stake in Sony/ATV rose in value to $709 million (¥71,300 million) in 2016 (Sony Corporation 2016: F 90). In April 2016 Sony and the Estate of Michael Jackson entered into an agreement whereby Sony obtained full ownership of Sony/ATV by acquiring the 50 per cent interest in Sony/ATV held by the Estate (Sony Corporation 2016: 32).

Warner Music Group's music publishing company Warner/Chappell recorded decreasing revenues from 2008 to 2013, with a slight increase in 2014 and further decrease in 2015. However, a $25 million additional payment of mechanical fees from record companies accrued in prior years is the primary explanation for the all-time high of music publishing revenues in 2009 (Warner Music Group 2009: 64). In the following years, the decreasing music publishing revenue was due mainly to a decline in mechanical fees, reflecting the ongoing recession in the recorded music market, especially the shrinking CD sector. Whereas mechanical fees contributed 43.5 per cent to the total music publishing revenue in 2005, this share decreased to 17.8 per

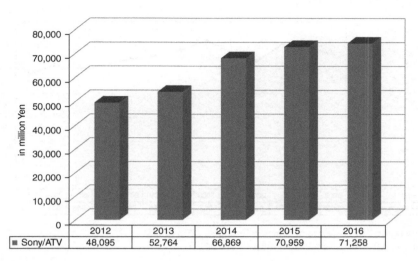

| | 2012 | 2013 | 2014 | 2015 | 2016 |
|---|---|---|---|---|---|
| ■ Sony/ATV | 48,095 | 52,764 | 66,869 | 70,959 | 71,258 |

**Figure 4.5** The revenue of Sony/ATV Music Publishing, 2012–2016
Source: After Sony Corporation (2012–2016)

cent in 2015. The performance revenues from music broadcasts and live performances have become the main income source for Warner/Chappell since
2008 with a share of almost 40 per cent of total publishing revenue in 2015.
The loss of mechanical revenues has been offset by fast-growing digital revenues. The income from licensing music copyrights to online music service
providers and for mobile ringtones increased by 395 per cent from 2005 to
2015. Whereas digital revenue streams accounted for just 3.3 per cent of total
music publishing income, in 2015 they became as important as revenues from
mechanical and synchronization licensing with a share of more than 20 per
cent. The growth of digital revenue was mainly driven by a $12,000 million
increase in music-streaming revenue in 2015 (Warner Music Group 2015:
41). Synchronization revenues as well as other revenues – mainly from sheet
music licensing – have remained more or less stable in the observed period.

This comparison of the three major music publishers highlights that growth
and gaining market share has only been possible by purchasing large music
catalogues such as Sony/ATV's acquisition of EMI Music Publishing in 2012.
When no relevant music catalogues are bought, as in Warner/Chappell's case,
music publishing revenues remain more or less stable. However, the composition of revenue has altered dramatically. Mechanical fees from licensing
sound carriers such as CDs significantly lost ground, whereas revenues from

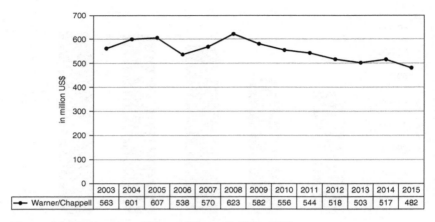

**Figure 4.6** The revenue of Warner/Chappell, 2003–2015
Source: After Warner Music Group (2005–2015)

| | 2003 | 2004 | 2005 | 2006 | 2007 | 2008 | 2009 | 2010 | 2011 | 2012 | 2013 | 2014 | 2015 |
|---|---|---|---|---|---|---|---|---|---|---|---|---|---|
| Warner/Chappell | 563 | 601 | 607 | 538 | 570 | 623 | 582 | 556 | 544 | 518 | 503 | 517 | 482 |

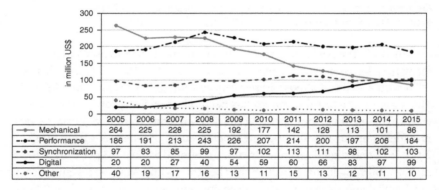

| | 2005 | 2006 | 2007 | 2008 | 2009 | 2010 | 2011 | 2012 | 2013 | 2014 | 2015 |
|---|---|---|---|---|---|---|---|---|---|---|---|---|
| Mechanical | 264 | 225 | 228 | 225 | 192 | 177 | 142 | 128 | 113 | 101 | 86 |
| Performance | 186 | 191 | 213 | 243 | 226 | 207 | 214 | 200 | 197 | 206 | 184 |
| Synchronization | 97 | 83 | 85 | 99 | 97 | 102 | 113 | 111 | 98 | 102 | 103 |
| Digital | 20 | 20 | 27 | 40 | 54 | 59 | 60 | 66 | 83 | 97 | 99 |
| Other | 40 | 19 | 17 | 16 | 13 | 11 | 15 | 13 | 12 | 11 | 10 |

**Figure 4.7** The revenue of Warner/Chappell by segments, 2005–2015
Source: After Warner Music Group (2005–2015)

licensing music performances and especially from online music providers have increased. The growing music publishing market was fuelled primarily by the market entrance of independent music publishers, in particular BMG Rights Management and Kobalt.

After Bertelsmann AG had sold BMG Music Publishing in 2007 to Universal Music Publishing and had withdrawn from the recorded music industry by selling its 50 per cent stake of Sony/BMG to Sony Music Entertainment in 2008, the German media giant established a new music publishing company

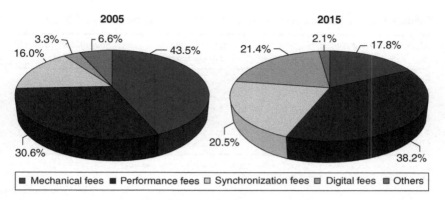

**2005**

3.3%  6.6%
16.0%  43.5%
30.6%

**2015**

2.1%  17.8%
21.4%
20.5%
38.2%

■ Mechanical fees  ■ Performance fees  □ Synchronization fees  ■ Digital fees  ■ Others

**Figure 4.8** The music publishing revenue of Warner/Chappell by segments, 2005 and 2015
Source: After Warner Music Group (2005–2015)

called BMG Rights Management as a joint venture with private equity firm Kohlberg Kravis Roberts & Co. (KKR).[8] BMG Rights Management quickly expanded by purchasing small and medium-sized music publishing companies such as Crosstown Songs, Cherry Lane Music Publishing, Stage Three Music, Evergreen Copyrights, Chrysalis Music Publishing, Bug Music, R2M, Dreyfus Music, Montana, Union Square Music Publishing, USM Songs and Verse Music Group. BMG became the fourth largest music publisher when it acquired Virgin Music Publishing and Famous UK Publishing, which had to be spun-off by Sony/ATV to secure European regulatory approval for its acquisition of EMI Music Publishing in 2012.[9] In 2013 Bertelsmann AG bought out KKR's 51 per cent stake in BMG Rights Management for €300 million. In the same year, BMG again invested in recorded music by purchasing Sanctuary Records from Universal Music Group – a divestment made in compliance with the conditions imposed by the regulatory authorities to allow it to acquire EMI Recorded Music in 2012. However, music publishing remains the main business of BMG Rights Management, which administers about 1.9 million music copyrights.

Another fast-growing entrant in the international music publishing market is Kobalt. Founded in 2000, Kobalt only *administers* copyrights – songwriters retain full ownership and control of their works – and guarantees a revenue share of about 90 per cent for the copyright holders, which is significantly higher than in traditional songwriting contracts. Hence, Kobalt has attracted

**Table 4.1** Music publishing companies, global revenue market share 2013–2015

| Music publishing company | Global revenue market share | Number of administered music copyrights |
|---|---|---|
| Sony/ATV | 29.5% | 3.97 million |
| Universal Music Publishing | 23.0% | 3.20 million |
| Warner/Chappell | 12.5% | 1–2 million |
| BMG Rights Management | 5.4% | 1.9 million |
| Kobalt Music Group | 3.9% | 600,000 |
| Other independent publishers | 25.7% | n/a |

Source: Music & Copyright, "WMG Makes Biggest Recorded Music Market Share Gains of 2015; Indies Cement Publishing Lead", 28 April 2016

prominent musicians and music producers, including Max Martin, 50 Cent, Gotye, Lenny Kravitz, Skrillex, Maroon 5 and Paul McCartney.[10] Kobalt is the only large music publisher that has increased its market share – to 3.9 per cent in 2014 – by organic growth rather than through acquisitions. Kobalt also set up a label service division in 2012, and with American Music Rights Association (AMRA) launched the world's first digital mechanical and performing rights society.[11] Kobalt Music Group increased its revenue from £25.7 million in 2010 to £50.1 million in 2014, but is still making an operative loss of almost £1 million.[12]

Despite new market entrants, the global music publishing market is a tight oligopoly controlled by the publishers of the music majors. In 2015 Sony/ATV, Universal Music Publishing and Warner/Chappell had a combined market share of 64 per cent.

## Notes

1. EU Directive on collective management of copyright 4 February 2014.
2. CRB Decision, 74 F.R. 4529, 26 January 2009.
3. GEMA stands for Gesellschaft für musikalische Aufführungs- und mechanische Vervielfältigungsrechte (Association for Music Performing and Mechanical Reproduction Rights).
4. AKM stands for Autoren, Komponisten und Musikverleger (Authors, Composers and Music Publishers).
5. Billboard.biz, "BMG, GEMA Ink New Pan-European Digital Licensing Deal", 10 June 2015, www.billboard.com/articles/news/6590840/bmg-gema-ink-new-pan-european-digital-licensing-deal (retrieved 15 January 2016).

6.  Billboard.biz, "Sony/ATV Launches Pan-European Licensing Venture SOLAR", 25 September 2014, www.billboard.com/articles/business/6259381/sonyatv-launches-pan-european-licensing-venture-solar (retrieved 15 January 2016).
7.  CISAC is the acronym for the International Confederation of Societies of Authors and Composers and is as a global umbrella association for performing rights organisations.
8.  Reuters, "KKR, Bertelsmann Plan Music Venture", 7 July 2009, www.reuters.com/article/bertelsmann-idUSN0735018520090708 (retrieved 31 January 2016).
9.  The Hollywood Reporter, "BMG Buys Virgin, Famous Music Catalog from Sony/ATV", 21 December 2012, www.hollywoodreporter.com/news/bmg-buys-virgin-famous-music-406080 (retrieved 31 January 2016).
10. See www.kobaltmusic.com (retrieved 19 February 2017).
11. Music Business Worldwide, "Kobalt Launches a Collection Society – and Invites Publishers to Join", 8 June 2015, www.musicbusinessworldwide.com/kobalt-launches-collection-society-invites-publishers-join/ (retrieved 31 January 2016).
12. Company check, "Financial Accounts of Kobalt Music Publishing", https://companycheck.co.uk/company/04089275/KOBALT-MUSIC-PUBLISHING-LIMITED/financial-accounts (retrieved 31 January 2016).

# 5

# SOUND RECORDING

## The function of sound recording

Unlike music publishing, the recording industry was severely hit by digitization. According to the International Federation of the Phonographic Industry (IFPI), the global recording market decreased by 44.2 per cent during the period 1999 to 2015. The record companies had to adjust their business model to the emerging digital music environment and redefine the functions of the sound recording business: artists and repertoire (A & R), production and marketing.

## The A & R function

Talent scouting and the acquisition of repertoire is the main function of a recording company. No record company can afford to rely solely on a back catalogue of master recordings, and must invest in new talent and new repertoire. The A & R person embodies this function in a record company. The traditional role and romantic image of a person scouting for talent in small music venues has changed during the course of digitization. Social media such as Facebook and YouTube have become important means for discovering new talent, such that desktop research and data mining have supplemented and even substituted to some extent the daily visit to clubs, concerts and festivals.

New actors have also appeared on the A & R scene. Instead of sourcing and developing acts over several years, record companies, especially the record majors, have started to outsource the A & R function by contracting freelance A & R people or purchasing master recordings from music producers and A & R teams. Another possibility for avoiding the risk of A & R failures is to acquire successful indie record labels and their artists' rosters (see Klembas 2013: 256–7). Non-traditional A & R platforms have also emerged in the past few years, such as television casting shows – for example *X Factor* and *Pop Idol* – which outsource the process of finding new talent to the audience. Whereas casting shows have a long tradition in the music business, the concept of crowdsourced A & R has become a new practice in the digital age. Internet platforms such as Soundcloud and Bandcamp allow artists to upload, promote and share their music with their fans. Crowdfunding platforms do not just collect money for music projects but also provide a means to assess the popularity of artists. Music crowdfunding platform SliceThePie went a step further by establishing SoundOut in 2009. SoundOut analyses and compiles millions of reviews and ratings made by more than one million paid users of music tracks uploaded to SliceThePie, and by using operating algorithms it gets a representative market panel.[1] Thus, the costly process of assessing master tapes and music tracks is outsourced to a so-called "smart" crowd.

When record companies discover new and promising artists, it is crucial to sign them on an exclusive basis. This is important since most of the costs of record production are up front and sunk at the beginning of the recording process. A major record company invests $500,000 to $2,000,000 in a newly signed recording artist according to IFPI (2014: 13). The numbers might be very optimistic and reflect mainly US figures, but they highlight the risk involved in the recording music business. Nielsen Soundscan reported that in 2011 in the US 1,500 of 76,875 albums released (and which sold at least one copy) accounted for 100 million of 113 million total unit sales. In other words, 1.95 per cent of album releases accounted for 88.5 per cent of sales.[2]

Hence, each contract is a bet on the future success of an artist. In a standard recording contract, therefore, the artist agrees to record a defined number of music titles for a record label and exclusively assigns all rights necessary to make and to disseminate the recordings. In exchange, the record company agrees to release the recordings and pays a non-returnable advance of between $50,000 and $350,000 for international stars (IFPI 2014: 13). However, advances are prepayments that will be deducted from the contracted royalties earned. The labels usually set against advances the recording costs, producer fees, cost of video production and some of the marketing expenses (e.g. promotion costs), such that an artist may receive royalty payments only if the record breaks even (Hull *et al.* 2011: 201–2). Therefore, the record label bears all the costs and risks of the recording project.

In a master recording contract the artist make the recordings by themselves, bearing all the costs, and offers the final master tape to a record label for further exploitation. In return, the record label pays an advance and offers a higher royalty rate than in a standard recording contract (Lyng *et al.* 2011: 290–324). The master recording agreement is the more common type of contract in Europe and is especially preferred by independent labels.

When EMI re-signed Robbie Williams in 2002, the record company offered him an advance of £80 million for four albums and a hit compilation. In return, EMI negotiated a percentage of *all* revenue streams of the artist including record sales, touring, sponsoring and merchandising. This was the first "360 deal" in the music business. Global music promoter Live Nation popularized this model by signing superstar Madonna in 2007. Live Nation paid a signing bonus of $17.5 million, an estimated advance of $50–60 million for three albums and $50 million in cash and shares for the right to promote her concert tours; it also guaranteed a concert tour revenue split of 90 per cent in favour of Madonna as well as a 50/50 split of all income from licensing the artist's image (Pitt 2010: 71). Irish rock band U2, US rapper Jay Z, Nickelback and Shakira also signed similar 360 deals with Live Nation (Pitt 2010: 72) and this type of contract has rapidly spread in the recording music business. Apart from the usual recording agreement, the labels take a share of revenues from touring, merchandising, sponsoring, endorsements, fan club websites, movies and television, and even publishing royalties (Hull *et al.* 2011: 207). Therefore, the major record companies set up artist management divisions to exploit all these income streams.

In all three contract types – artist recording contract, master recording agreement and "360 deal" – the record companies acquire full ownership of the master recordings. Sound recordings are protected by neighbouring rights, which are also called related rights. In the European Union the term of copyright protection for neighbouring rights is 70 years from the end of the year in which the record was made. In the US the situation is more complex. Recordings made before 15 February 1972 are protected by individual US states' laws and will enter into the public domain at the latest in 2067 (US Copyright Act 1976 17 USC. §301(c)). The copyright term for released recordings made between 1972 and 1977 is 95 years from release date (17 USC. §303(a)). The copyright term for released recordings made after 1977 is 70 years after the death of the producer and 95 years if the recording was made for hire (17 USC. §302(a), (c)). Finally, all unreleased recordings made after 15 February 1972 are protected for 70 years after the producer's death and for 120 years if the recording was made for hire (17 USC. §302(a), (c)).

Work for hire is a specific aspect of US copyright law and differs from European provisions. Whereas in Europe copyright as well as related rights cannot be sold (only licensed), the full transfer of copyright ownership in the US is possible if a copyrighted work is made by a salaried employee or commissioned by a record label for the use in motion pictures and other audiovisual works, as well as in compilations and as a supplementary work (e.g. an arrangement of a pre-existing song) (Krasilovsky *et al.* 2007: 185–90). In such cases the record label does not need further consent from a singer/songwriter to exploit the copyrights and related rights.

## The production function

As soon as an artist has signed an exclusive contract with a record label, the production process starts. Hull *et al.* (2011: 214) state that "[i]t is the recording, not a song or music, that is the final product and it is the producer who is at the centre of the creation of that process". Indeed, record producers moved into the centre of music production with the adoption of multi-track recording in the 1960s. Since then it has become possible to manipulate the recording process, allowing music producers to become part of the artistic process. Think of George Martin, who initially signed The Beatles to EMI's Parlophone label and later became The Beatles' main producer and the mastermind of seminal albums such as *Revolver* (1966) and *Sgt. Pepper's Lonely Hearts Club Band* (1967).

In the late 1960s the role of music producers changed. Whereas most of them were salaried employees of record companies in the 1950s and 1960s, they became independent when their input into the artistic process grew more important. Since then, the producers have become the key figures in the recorded music industry, some of them having become superstars in their own right, especially in the hip hop, rap and dance music genres – for example Jay Z, Eminem, David Guetta and Skrillex – fusing the artist and producer functions.

The recording process involves technical, artistic and management skills, so a music producer needs to be multi-talented. Producers might be involved in A & R by finding new talent and suitable material to record, and they could even be songwriters and composers. Producers arrange and supervise recording sessions and hire studios, studio musicians and sound engineers as necessary. The management function comprises budgeting the productions and negotiating contracts with artists on the one side and record labels on the other (Hull *et al.* 2011: 214–15).

In a standard producer contract, the record label pays a non-returnable but fully recoupable advance and guarantees royalty rates from 3 to 6 per cent of the published price to dealers. The label contracts a producer either for a single song or for an entire album. The production process also includes overdubbing, mixing and mastering the tracks as well as remixing the master recording for special occasions such as radio airplay. The producer is obligated to deliver a final master that is commercially and technically acceptable to the label (Hull *et al.* 2011: 216–17).

In the pre-digital era, quality recording could only be secured in a professional recording studio. Some studios became legendary, such as EMI's Abbey Road Studios in London, Decca's Pythian Temple in New York, the Gold Star Studios in Los Angeles and the FAME studio in Muscle Shoals, Alabama. However, digitization has decreased production costs to a fraction of previous costs, and today it is possible to record in one's living room using a good laptop and high-end microphones. Hence, private recording studios of artists and producers became widespread, whereas the number of professional studios dramatically declined. Existing professional studios offer a wide range of services to recording artists, producers, record labels, as well as advertising agencies, television and radio stations, movie companies and video games producers (Hull *et al.* 2011: 221–3).

As with sound recording studios, manufacturing of phonograms in pressing plants has suffered from the decline of recorded music sales in the past. The major record companies reduced capacities by closing down pressing facilities and outsourcing pressing plants. The dissemination of music through digital channels is far more cost-effective than phonogram manufacturing.

Instead of selling CDs, it is much more profitable to license master rights to music download and streaming services. The record companies usually license their master rights directly to digital music providers. Since major record companies own vast back catalogues, it is essential for digital music services to license these recordings. However, smaller independent record companies usually lack the market power to license directly with download and streaming services. Therefore, in 2007 influential indie labels launched Merlin, a global digital rights agency that collectively and globally licenses the master rights of more than 650 member record companies to digital music services.[3]

Apart from digital music licensing, the public performance of recorded music has been administered by specialized not-for-profit collecting societies for decades now. One of the oldest PROs for licensing recorded music is the British PPL (Phonographic Performance Limited) founded by Decca and EMI in 1934 after a successful lawsuit against a coffee shop playing their records without the permission of the rights holders.[4] PPL and other PROs, such as the German GVL and French SCPP, collect licensing fees from recordings played on radio and television, on cable and satellite networks, and also in shops, bars, offices, restaurants, hotels, gyms, and so on.

PPL statistics show that revenue from licensing master rights has increased over the past few years. PPL's licence fee income and distributable revenue increased by 115 per cent and 119 per cent, respectively, between 2004 and 2014. Hence, PPL and other PROs have benefited from digitization (see Figure 5.1).

In the US, no performance right for sound recordings exists yet. Therefore, over-the-air broadcasters play recordings without the consent of and remuneration for the rights holders. In 1995, however, the Digital Performance Right in Sound Recordings Act was passed to clarify the legal situation of webcasters and satellite radios. In 2003 the Recordings Industry Association of America (RIAA) founded a non-profit digital performance rights organization – SoundExchange – to collect licensing fees from non-interactive music-streaming services (webcasters) such as Pandora and iHeartRadio, as well as from satellite transmitters such as Sirius/XM. The US Copyright Royalty Board (CRB) sets the licensing rates and the total sum of collected fees are distributed in a 50/50 split to the record labels and performing artists. Of the performing artists' revenue 45 per cent goes to featured artists, 2.5 per cent to non-featured musicians who are members of the American Federation of Musicians (AFM), and the remaining 2.5 per cent to non-featured vocalists

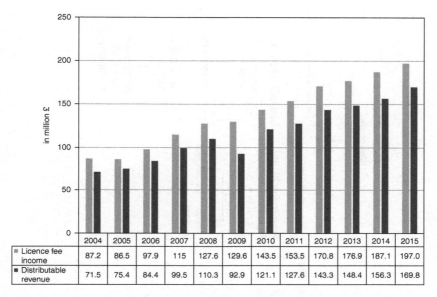

| | 2004 | 2005 | 2006 | 2007 | 2008 | 2009 | 2010 | 2011 | 2012 | 2013 | 2014 | 2015 |
|---|---|---|---|---|---|---|---|---|---|---|---|---|
| ■ Licence fee income | 87.2 | 86.5 | 97.9 | 115 | 127.6 | 129.6 | 143.5 | 153.5 | 170.8 | 176.9 | 187.1 | 197.0 |
| ■ Distributable revenue | 71.5 | 75.4 | 84.4 | 99.5 | 110.3 | 92.9 | 121.1 | 127.6 | 143.3 | 148.4 | 156.3 | 169.8 |

**Figure 5.1** PPL licensing revenue and net distribution to rights holders, 2004–2015
Source: After PPL (2008–2015)

who are members of the American Federation of Television and Radio Artists (AFTRA) (Hull *et al.* 2011: 101–3) (see Figure 5.2).

## The marketing function

According to Philip Kotler (2015), the classical marketing functions are product, price, place and promotion – the so-called "4Ps" of marketing. The 4Ps have to be coordinated in a marketing mix to succeed in the marketplace. The marketing mix is, therefore, rooted in market research to unveil consumer behaviour and their needs. Marketing goals and a marketing strategy are then derived and guide the decisions made in the marketing mix. The following briefly describes the four marketing functions.

### Product policy
The purpose of product policy is to design goods and services to satisfy customers' needs. Traditionally the record was the main object of product policy.

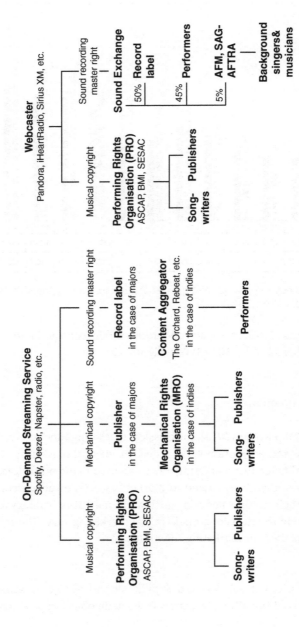

**Figure 5.2** Licensing structure for digital performance rights in the US
Source: After Rethink Music (2015: 11–13)

In the course of digitization, however, it has become obvious that artists are in the centre of the value-added network. Therefore, it is important to create a market-conforming artist brand. A brand is more than a product. Unlike products that may serve utilitarian functions, brands can create uniqueness and can appeal to a personal lifestyle. A good artist brand has strong brand identity and personality. The brand identity is a mix of name, trademark, communication and visual appearance. A successful brand policy can bridge the gap between the brand image that is in the consumers' heads and the brand identity (Neumeier 2004: 20). Successful artists are often successful brands, such as Lady Gaga, Madonna, Bruce Springsteen, the Rolling Stones and the Vienna Philharmonic Orchestra, to name just a few. Those artist brands have developed a brand personality that consists of "a set of human characteristics associated with a brand" (Aaker 1997: 347). Apart from artist brands, music genres (e.g. classical music, jazz, soul, disco, hip hop/rap, electronic dance music (EDM)), record labels (e.g. Atlantic, Chess, Motown, Blue Note, Def Jam), as well as music festivals and even companies (e.g. Live Nation) are brands with a specific identity.

However, music brand management is just one aspect of product policy, which also includes innovation management (closely linked to A & R), quality management and product and service management.

*Price policy*
The price of a CD, a music download track, a monthly streaming subscription or a concert ticket is usually not based on the costs of production. Instead of cost-based pricing, value-based pricing and competition-based pricing are the main concepts of price-setting in the music industry (Hull *et al.* 2011: 251). Value-based pricing is based on the perceived value for a product for consumers. Thus, ticket prices do not reflect the costs of production but the value fans attribute to the live event. Special recording editions including a CD, vinyl record, a download code and some merchandise are also priced higher than the costs would justify.

However, price-setting is not the main factor in competition in an oligopoly. The record business has a long tradition of three-tiered pricing for records and CDs: full price, mid-price and budget price. The price tiers are used to price discriminate among different target groups. The full price aims at fans and early movers who want to be among the first to buy a CD. Re-released recordings and compilations are often mid-price CDs for music-interested consumers who do not want to pay too much for a CD. Finally, budget price CDs are often licensed recordings for occasional consumers who rarely but spontaneously buy CDs, for example in a supermarket (Hull *et al.* 2011: 254–6).

Price discrimination also plays a crucial role in the digital music market. Online music-streaming services offer a "freemium" tier to attract music consumers in order to convert them to premium users. Most of the services offer different monthly subscription price models to meet different consumer needs. However, several streaming services have dispensed with the freemium approach and offer music streams in high sound quality for a higher monthly subscription.

In competition-based pricing, prices are set in comparison to those of competitors. When Apple/iTunes set the standard price for music downloads at $0.99 for a single track and $9.99 for an album, the price did not cover the overall cost. iTunes' price policy, therefore, was a market entry barrier for competitors. Nevertheless, powerful internet giants such as Amazon have tried to compete by offering an even lower price in a "loss-leader" pricing strategy. In music retailing, discount stores such as Wal-Mart and Target in the US and Saturn/Media Market and Tesco in Europe intentionally set the price of CDs below the usual retail price to drive consumers into their stores with the hope of getting them to also buy other products with higher profit margins. Thus, traditional music retailers and discounters that depended upon CD profit margins have suffered financial difficulties, resulting in many chains closing (Hull *et al.* 2011: 257). Amazon adopted loss-leader pricing for CDs and later for music downloads to generate traffic on its website in order to sell other high-profit-margin products. Amazon's price strategy was the last chapter in the revolution of the music retailing landscape.

## *Physical and digital music distribution policy*

Digitization revolutionized the distribution of recorded music with digital channels becoming the main source of music consumption. Whereas digital album sales accounted for 3 per cent of all album sales in the US in 2005, the share was 43 per cent ten years later according to Nielsen SoundScan data. However, in this period, album sales dropped dramatically, with total album unit sales falling by 61 per cent from 618.9 million to 241.4 million (without track and streaming equivalent albums) (see Figures 5.3 and 5.4).

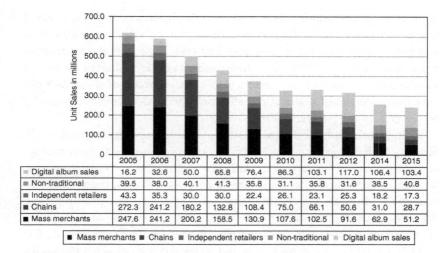

**Figure 5.3** Album unit sales in the US by retailers, 2005–2015
Source: 2005–2012: Nielsen (2005–2012); 2013 no data on distribution channels
share is available; 2014–2015: Nielsen (2014, 2015)

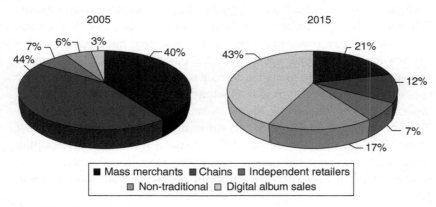

**Figure 5.4** Album unit sales in the US by retailers, 2005 and 2015

Analysis by distribution channels also highlights the fact that mass market outlets (e.g. Wal-Mart) as well as store chains (e.g. Best Buy) lost market share, with physical sales having decreased by 79 per cent and almost 90 per cent, respectively, since 2005. Apart from direct digital music sales (e.g. on iTunes), non-traditional music distributors are the winners from digitization. Non-traditional channels include physical sales on the Internet (e.g. by Amazon), mail order services, direct physical sales (e.g. at concerts) and non-traditional retailers (e.g. rack jobbers). Their sales have remained more or less stable at $40 million. Independent retailers, such as the record shop around the corner, have had a stable market share of about 6–8 per cent in the period of digitization, although their sales have decreased by 60 per cent in the past ten years.

The network of physical music distribution is labour-intensive and costly. Sales agents have to stay in touch with record stores and key account managers have to serve major customers. Although digitization leads to the automatization of ordering services and thus a decrease in costs, much capital is tied up in wholesale warehouses, shelf space and logistics (transport and delivery). Thus, the recorded music majors outsource some of their physical distribution capacities. For example, Warner Music Group sold its CD and DVD manufacturing, packaging and physical distribution operations for $1,010 million to Cinram (Warner Music 2005: 36) in order to focus on the digital music business. In 2015 Warner earned more than 50 per cent of its recorded music sales from digital music distribution.

Digital music channels have emerged as the main way to consume music. When in 2003 Apple Inc. made its iTunes online store also available to non-Apple users, the recorded music majors licensed their music catalogues to the new music download service to curtail P2P file sharing. iTunes' music download service soon gained a dominant market share of about 80 per cent in the digital music market (Tschmuck 2012: 191). The majors had lost control over music distribution, one of the key areas of the music industry. With the advent of music-streaming services in the second half of the 2000s, the majors adopted a different strategy. The majors' streaming business model is not only based on royalties from licensing their music catalogues but it also guarantees upfront payments from the streaming platforms.

It is reported that the three recorded music majors own 18–20 per cent of Spotify (Hardy 2013: 285). Access Industries, the parent company of Warner Music Group, invested $130 million in 2012 and an additional $109 million (with French telecom Orange) in 2015 in the French streaming operator Deezer.[5] In the event of an initial public offering (IPO), a stake in a prospective stock exchange-traded company can be a very profitable investment.

*Promotion*

> Promotion of a recording involves all the activities of informing and
> motivating the buyer, including all types of media coverage, personal
> selling, tour support, promotional incentives for retailers, grassroots
> marketing and new media marketing.
>
> (Hull *et al.* 2011: 263)

The communication of music products to consumers is one of the key elements of music marketing. IFPI (2014: 13) reports $200,000–$700,000 of marketing and promotion spend by a major record company for a newly signed
act. This figure seems to be very high and might reflect the US market in
particular, but it gives an idea how important marketing and promotion is in
the recorded music business. It also reflects the marketing power needed to
break an act internationally.

A record label has several promotional instruments it can use to commu-
nicate with the public. We can roughly distinguish between advertising and
publicity. Advertising is directed to either consumers (consumer advertising)
or intermediaries (trade advertising) and includes paid television and radio
spots, space advertising in newspapers and (trade) magazines, adverts on the
Internet, billboards and posters, as well as flyers and direct mailing campaigns
(Hull *et al.* 2011: 267). Advertising aims to generate attention and to trigger
purchases. Publicity aims at getting exposure within the media to help create
an image of the artist for the public. The target group for publicity are journalists who are provided with press releases and (electronic) press kits including artists' biographies, photos, a discography, video clips and other material,
with the aim of facilitating features on radio and television and interviews in
print and online, and to attract general public attention through press conferences (Hull *et al.* 2011: 264–5).

Radio promotion is a special instrument within the promotional mix, since
airplay remains important for recorded music sales. Record label promotions
people and commissioned independent radio promoters seek to influence
radio programme directors to include songs in their playlists. The history
of radio promotion teaches us that record labels also use illegal promotion
practices – known as payola. With the advent of disc jockeys in the 1950s,
it became a widespread practice by record companies to pay DJs to give
their songs airplay. After investigations by the US Senate, the Legislative

Oversight Subcommittee of the House Committee on Interstate and Foreign Commerce examined in hearings the payola practices adopted by record labels and star disc jockeys such as Alan Freed and Dick Clark in 1959. The hearings unveiled a network of bribes and resulted in court sentences for Alan Freed and record label promoters (Sanjek & Sanjek 1991: 155–95).

With the launch of Music Television (MTV) in 1981, music promotion for television programming became obligatory. The record majors had to invest in music video production, which drastically increased production costs, with budgets for superstar music videos running upwards of $300,000 (Hull *et al.* 2011: 270). When the music television channels started to replace music videos with non-music shows and other content, the high costs of producing a video were questioned. In the internet age, however, music videos for platforms such as YouTube, Vevo and tape.tv are still highly relevant, but the costs of production have decreased significantly.

The Internet provides further important promotional tools, such as "viral" marketing. Viral marketing capitalizes on social media to spread word-of-mouth endorsements electronically. Blogs, messaging services, postings, e-mail listings, shares, likes tweets and so on allow the spread of news, photos, videos and music tracks rapidly among thousands of internet users. Social networking sites such as Facebook, Google+, Twitter and Pinterest are the key platforms for these activities.

Social media and video-sharing webpages such as YouTube have become essential for artists' self-promotion and do-it-yourself (DIY) marketing. The costs of internet promotion are comparatively low, but the potential reach can be tremendously high. Since the entry barriers are extremely low, artists have to struggle for visibility and attention in an ocean of information.

## The market and industry structure of sound recording

### The physical recorded music market

According to IFPI numbers, the global recorded music market has decreased by 44.2 per cent since 1999 to $15,000 million in 2015. This tremendous revenue loss reflects the change from a physical to a digital music market. In 2014 global digital music sales overtook physical sales accounting for a share of 45.8 per cent of total recorded music sales (in trade value).

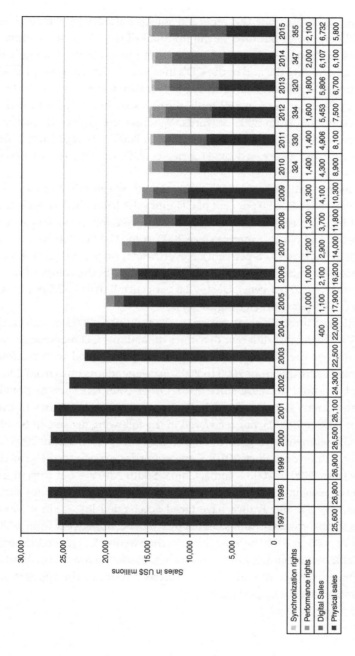

|  | 1997 | 1998 | 1999 | 2000 | 2001 | 2002 | 2003 | 2004 | 2005 | 2006 | 2007 | 2008 | 2009 | 2010 | 2011 | 2012 | 2013 | 2014 | 2015 |
|---|---|---|---|---|---|---|---|---|---|---|---|---|---|---|---|---|---|---|---|
| Synchronization rights |  |  |  |  |  |  |  |  |  |  |  |  |  | 324 | 330 | 334 | 320 | 347 | 355 |
| Performance rights |  |  |  |  |  |  |  |  | 1,000 | 1,000 | 1,200 | 1,300 | 1,300 | 1,400 | 1,400 | 1,600 | 1,800 | 2,000 | 2,100 |
| Digital Sales |  |  |  |  |  |  |  | 400 | 1,100 | 2,100 | 2,900 | 3,700 | 4,100 | 4,300 | 4,906 | 5,453 | 5,806 | 6,107 | 6,732 |
| Physical sales | 25,600 | 26,800 | 26,900 | 26,500 | 26,100 | 24,300 | 22,500 | 22,000 | 17,900 | 16,200 | 14,000 | 11,800 | 10,300 | 8,900 | 8,100 | 7,500 | 6,700 | 6,100 | 5,800 |

Sales in US$ millions

**Figure 5.5** The global recorded music market (in million $ trade value), 1997–2015
Source: After IFPI (1998–2013, 2014b, 2015b, 2016)

Decreasing CD sales put the recorded music industry into recession. Whereas CD unit sales boomed in the first half of the 1990s with annual growth rates of about 20 per cent, growth slowed down in the second half of the 1990s, heralding the end of the CD's lifespan. CD album sales peaked in 2000 with 2,400 million copies sold, but since then the CD market has decreased by 74.2 per cent to 569 million units sold in 2015. This downturn had accelerated from 2005 onwards. Whereas the global CD market volume decreased by 20.6 per cent from 2000 to 2005, it halved from 2005 to 2010 and further decreased by 41.3 per cent from 2010 to 2015 (see Figure 5.6).

A closer look at national recorded music markets reveals different dynamics. Whereas Sweden lost 90 per cent of CD unit sales from 2000 to 2015, the decrease of 59.3 per cent in Germany was less severe for the same period. Outside Europe and North America since 2000, some CD markets have even grown, such as India (+137.8 per cent). Nevertheless, since 2000 CD sales in the large recorded music markets have been decimated in the course of digitization: France (−70.0 per cent), UK (−72.6 per cent), Brazil (−82.5 per cent) and the US (−87.3 per cent) (see Figure 5.7).

Examination of three different periods − 2000 to 2005, 2005 to 2010 and 2005 to 2015 − highlights different dynamics on national CD markets. Some countries, such as the US and Spain, follow the global trend with modest annual average decreases from 2000 to 2005, accelerated loss rates from 2005 to 2010 and a slowed decrease since 2010. Other countries such as Brazil, Germany and South Korea suffered from the most severe decreases in the period from 2000 and 2005, but recovered in the following decade. In South Korea, the CD segment even grew by an average of 1.7 per cent from 2005 to 2010 and by 1.1 per cent since 2010. Some countries experienced a growth of CD sales from 2000 to 2005 − India, China, South Africa − but with more or less severe losses in the following decade. However, most countries such as Australia, the UK and France have faced accelerated losses since 2000. Sweden is a special case. CD unit sales fell by 9.8 per cent per year from 2000 to 2005. From 2005 to 2010 the annual loss in the Swedish CD market slowed to 1.7 per cent. In the following five years the CD market in Sweden collapsed with an annual decrease rate of 27.5 per cent as a result of the widespread success of music streaming (see Figure 5.8).

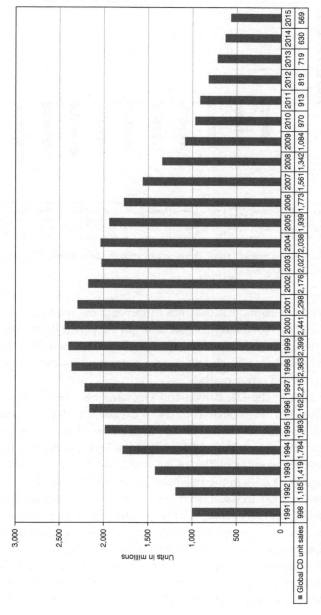

| | 1991 | 1992 | 1993 | 1994 | 1995 | 1996 | 1997 | 1998 | 1999 | 2000 | 2001 | 2002 | 2003 | 2004 | 2005 | 2006 | 2007 | 2008 | 2009 | 2010 | 2011 | 2012 | 2013 | 2014 | 2015 |
|---|---|---|---|---|---|---|---|---|---|---|---|---|---|---|---|---|---|---|---|---|---|---|---|---|---|
| ■ Global CD unit sales | 998 | 1,185 | 1,419 | 1,784 | 1,983 | 2,162 | 2,215 | 2,363 | 2,399 | 2,441 | 2,298 | 2,176 | 2,027 | 2,038 | 1,939 | 1,773 | 1,561 | 1,342 | 1,084 | 970 | 913 | 819 | 719 | 630 | 569 |

**Figure 5.6** The global CD market segment from 1991 to 2015 (unit sales in millions)
Source: After IFPI (1992–2013, 2014b, 2015b, 2016)

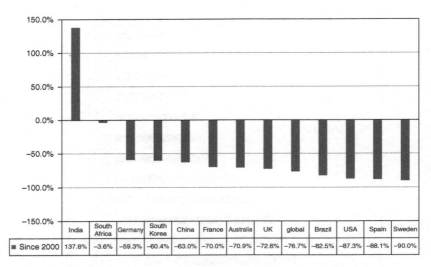

| | India | South Africa | Germany | South Korea | China | France | Australia | UK | global | Brazil | USA | Spain | Sweden |
|---|---|---|---|---|---|---|---|---|---|---|---|---|---|
| Since 2000 | 137.8% | −3.6% | −59.3% | −60.4% | −63.0% | −70.0% | −70.9% | −72.6% | −76.7% | −82.5% | −87.3% | −88.1% | −90.0% |

**Figure 5.7** The change rates of the CD market in selected countries, 2000–2015
Source: After IFPI (2000, 2016)

This analysis highlights that specifics of the national markets – such as availability of CD players, internet and smartphone penetration, consumer behaviour, demographics and cultural characteristics – caused different market dynamics, and that there was no simple explanation for the recession of the physical recorded music market.

Since CD sales in the US, Britain and Germany have been falling since 1999–2000, it might seem obvious to try to explain this decrease with the appearance of Napster, which had already attracted millions of users by late 1999. However, the figures also highlight that the Japanese market, the second largest sound recording market in the world, had already suffered an 8.2 per cent drop in CD sales in the two years prior to 1999 and that it was up by 7.9 per cent in 2000. In Japan, sales were in decline even before the onset of Napster, which industry representatives might explain by pointing to the emerging practice of "ripping" and "burning" CDs. For the French market no such simple explanations work. In 2001 a historic high in CD sales was recorded before the recession started in 2002, when the hype around Napster was already history. Since it is not very realistic to assume that French music consumers had been unaware of how to obtain music for free over the Internet

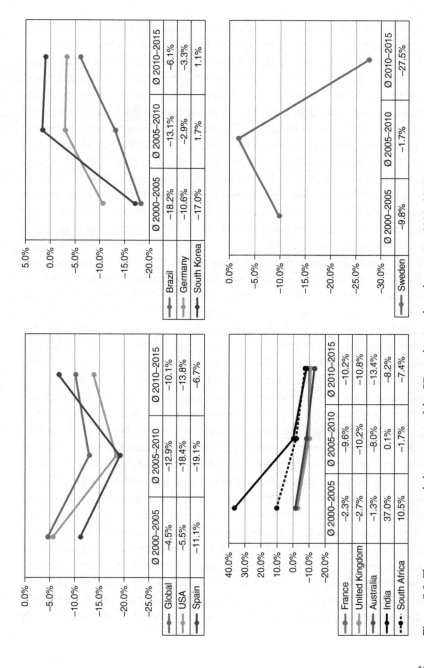

**Figure 5.8** The average annual change rates of the CD market in selected countries, 2000–2015
Source: After IFPI (2000–2013, 2014b, 2015b, 2016)

until 2002, we can assume they used Napster as avidly as consumers in other countries. Similarly, it cannot be explained why the UK market – after a drop of 17.7 per cent from 2000 to 2001 – was able to hold its sales level in subsequent years, despite the emergence of new P2P file-sharing systems. Indeed, from 2003 to 2004 one could even observe an increase of 4.4 per cent. The first strong sales slump in the UK took place only in 2007. These empirical anomalies put the "file-sharing thesis" into question. Serious research findings on file-sharing behaviour (Blackburn 2004; Tanaka 2004; Andersen & Frenz 2007, 2010; Oberholzer-Gee & Strumpf 2007; Huygens *et al.* 2009; McKenzie 2009; Hammond 2012) have also shown that file sharing does not necessarily have a negative impact on physical and digital sales. However, other studies have identified the more or less negative effect of file sharing on the recorded music market (Peitz & Waelbroeck 2004; Michel 2006; Rob & Waldfogel 2006; Zentner 2006; Liebowitz 2008).

If we accept, however, the most negative scenario of a substitution rate of file sharing on recorded music sales of 30 per cent (Zentner 2006), we need a model to explain the remaining 70 per cent of sales losses. We have to go back to the preceding decades. A comparison of recorded music sales by format from 1973 to 2014 highlights that the music cassette dominated the period from 1984 to 1994, while in the same period the vinyl record fell into economic irrelevance. Long-play vinyl formats reached their peak in 1981 with 1,100 million sold worldwide. In 1984 the same number of vinyl LPs and music cassettes – 800 million units – were sold. At this point – in the second year after its launch – the CD accounted for only 20 million copies worldwide. In the following years, however, the CD segment began to grow; thus in 1989 more CDs were sold worldwide (600 million) than LPs (400 million). However, the music cassette remained the market leader with a historical high of 1,500 million units sold in 1989. It was not until 1993 that the CD (1,420 million units) outperformed cassettes (1,380 million units) and became almost the sole source of sales in the market (see Figure 5.9).

If we add sales of single formats to this picture, a process of transformation that started in the first half of the 1980s is also revealed. In 1983, after years of stagnation, 27.5 per cent more singles were sold than in the previous year – namely 800 million units, which was a historic high. In the subsequent years, sales of singles sharply declined, despite the introduction of the CD single. In 1993, after the CD had taken the leadership position in the market, only

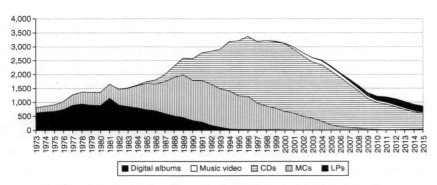

**Figure 5.9** The long-play format change on the global recorded music market, 1973–2015
Source: After IFPI (1973–2013, 2014b, 2015b, 2016)

410 million singles were sold and the single market had almost halved. The bottom of the decline for the single format had still not been reached. Ten years later, in 2003, just over 233 million units sold were singles – a decrease of 70.9 per cent compared to 1983. What happened?

The overall market for recorded music had become a market for long-play formats. This reflects a business strategy that had been pursued since the late 1960s mainly by the majors, who turned the single into a way to test the market for unknown, non-established artists. Only after the first and perhaps also the second single sold quite well would an album be offered to music consumers, because of the better price–performance ratio compared to the single. For established acts in particular, singles sales played virtually no role anymore. The album had become – economically and artistically – the format of choice. However, even though many concept albums were released, the long-play album format had the disadvantage for many consumers that it contained only two or three tracks that were ultimately of interest to the buyer, with the rest considered as dispensable filler. The industry also developed the hit compilation album, which increased the flood of albums further.

The shift from single- to long-play formats went hand in hand with a strategic reorientation that had its roots in the second half of the 1960s, prompted by changes in market segmentation. Previously, only three or four market segments existed, such as, for example, "white" pop charts, "black" R & B charts and the classical music charts in the US. The labels and especially the majors had realized that they could increase profits by applying a supply policy targeted at specific groups. New market segments such as country and western, folk and many varieties of rock music – hard rock, psychedelic rock, art rock, jazz rock, heavy metal, and so on – were established. This segmentation strategy certainly complemented a landscape of differentiated musical tastes and music consumers welcomed this.

However, the segmentation strategy took on a life of its own in the 1970s. Carried on by indie labels, new, innovative music genres such as punk, disco, hip hop/rap and various forms of electronic music emerged. Market segments became increasingly smaller and with them the profit margins shrank. What was originally conceived as a profit-maximizing instrument for the majors now worked against them. The result of this has already been seen in the declining sales figures in the late 1970s. The majors embarked on a new strategy of severely reducing their artist rosters, and instead of serving all market segments, they committed to the superstar principle. Thus, the 1980s saw pop superstars such as Michael Jackson, Prince, Madonna, Elton John, George Michael, Lionel Ritchie and Bruce Springsteen dominating the market.

In parallel, the recorded music market was booming because of the CD. The sharp rise in sales and revenue figures, however, masked the basic problem of a highly differentiated genre landscape, which had been further fragmented by innovations by the independent labels. This further fragmentation did not matter as long as the established album business model worked. But the ability to offer music tracks online over the Internet rendered this business model obsolete. The figures show that in recent years the album market has turned back into a singles market. While in 2015 global CD sales had already declined below the level of the 1990s, singles sales prospered with the explosion in digital track downloads, while sales of digital albums grew only slowly. Since 2004, when digital sales were reported for the first time, single sales have nearly quintupled to 1,700 million units in 2015, whereas the number of albums sold in the same year was 850 million units (see Figure 5.10).

Clearly one cannot earn the same revenue from the sale of the same number of single units as long-play units. Therefore, the drop in sales has been a consequence of the conversion of an album market to a singles market. File sharing can be interpreted in this context not as a cause but as a symptom of the digital revolution in the music industry.

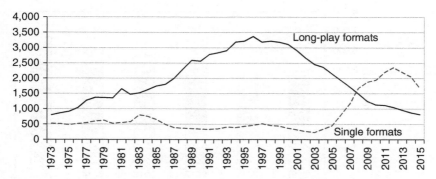

**Figure 5.10** The development of long-play and single formats in comparison, 1973–2015
Source: After IFPI (1973–2013, 2014b, 2015b, 2016)

## The digital recorded music market

Since 2004 the global digital music market has grown from $400 million to $6,700 million in 2015. The digital music market, however, has transformed several times since it first emerged (see Figures 5.11 and 5.12).

Mobile phone personalization (ringtones and ring-back tones) was a significant segment of the digital music market from 2005 to 2010. In the US sales of ringtones peaked in 2008, accounting for 33.6 per cent of all digital music sales. The US figures show, however, that the mobile music segment has decreased dramatically since then and accounted for just 1.1 per cent of the digital music sales in 2015.

Unlike the CD, the music download segment has prospered since 2005 with increasing growth rates. In the US, however, download music sales peaked in 2013 with $1,200 million for digital album sales and $1,600 million for single-track sales. Revenues from advert-supported streaming and subscription services, which were more or less on a constant level of about $200 million annually until 2010, then took off. Streaming and subscription revenues have increased by 555 per cent or $1,400 million since 2012. If we also consider the payouts from SoundExchange, which collects licensing fees from internet and satellite radios in the US and Canada, streaming revenue grew by 1,033 per cent or $2,200 million (see Figure 5.13).

On a global scale, revenues from subscription and streaming supported by advertising outperformed single-track sales for the first time in 2014, with

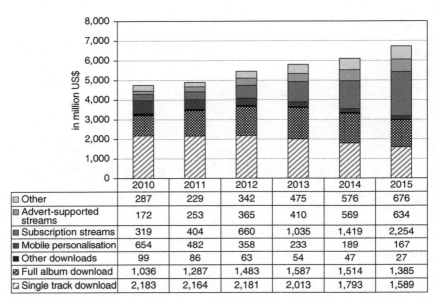

| | 2010 | 2011 | 2012 | 2013 | 2014 | 2015 |
|---|---|---|---|---|---|---|
| ☐ Other | 287 | 229 | 342 | 475 | 576 | 676 |
| ■ Advert-supported streams | 172 | 253 | 365 | 410 | 569 | 634 |
| ■ Subscription streams | 319 | 404 | 660 | 1,035 | 1,419 | 2,254 |
| ■ Mobile personalisation | 654 | 482 | 358 | 233 | 189 | 167 |
| ■ Other downloads | 99 | 86 | 63 | 54 | 47 | 27 |
| ⊠ Full album download | 1,036 | 1,287 | 1,483 | 1,587 | 1,514 | 1,385 |
| ▱ Single track download | 2,183 | 2,164 | 2,181 | 2,013 | 1,793 | 1,589 |

**Figure 5.11** The global digital music market, 2010–2015
Source: After IFPI (2015b: 9; 2016: 49)

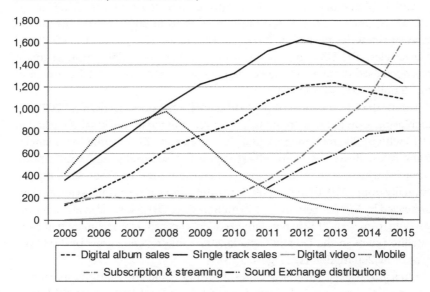

**Figure 5.12** The US digital music market, 2005–2015
Source: After RIAA (2005–2015)

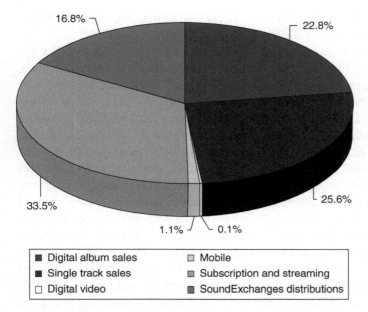

16.8%

22.8%

33.5%

1.1%  0.1%

25.6%

■ Digital album sales    ▢ Mobile
■ Single track sales     ▤ Subscription and streaming
□ Digital video          ■ SoundExchanges distributions

**Figure 5.13** The US digital music market by format, 2015
Source: After RIAA (2015)

a digital music market share of almost a third. Thus, in 2015 revenue from subscription streams and advert-supported streams were the largest segment (33.5 per cent), followed by single-track download sales (25.6 per cent) and digital album downloads (22.8 per cent).

These trends suggest that the music-streaming business is the future of the recorded music industry. In 2015 the global music-streaming market (advert-supported as well as subscription) had a sales volume of $2,250 million, which is even larger than the single-track download market ($1,600 million) (IFPI 2016: 49). However, the market share of music streaming differs between countries. Whereas in Sweden music streaming is 66.5 per cent of the overall recorded music market, in Germany just 11.4 per cent of recorded music revenue comes from music-streaming sources. Japan, the world's second-largest recorded music market, lags behind with 4.6 per cent.

In absolute figures, the US is by far the world's largest music-streaming market with a trade value of $788.3 million. Nearly two thirds of global streaming revenue is generated in the US. The UK ranks second with a market volume of $262.4 million, followed by South Korea ($161.9 million), Germany ($149.5 million), France ($131.1 million) and Sweden ($121 million).

However, in terms of the market share of music streaming, we get a different picture. The third most developed music-streaming market is China, where 55 per cent ($93.3 million) of all (legal) recorded music income comes from music streaming. The leading digital music providers in China are not Apple's iTunes or Spotify, but China Mobile, China Telecom, IQIYI and above all Tencent with China's most popular music-streaming site QQ Music.[6] In Sweden, the home base of Spotify, and in Norway, from where TIDAL originates, the music-streaming market accounts for, respectively, 66.5 per cent and 59.5 per cent of the recorded music market. The fourth member of the top streaming markets is South Korea, with a music-streaming market share of 57.5 per cent. Denmark (47.9 per cent), Columbia (43.8 per cent), the Caribbean states (including Barbados, Costa Rica, Dominican Republic, El Salvador, Guatemala, Jamaica and Panama) (48.9 per cent), Taiwan (42.3 per cent), Singapore (41.6 per cent) and the US (including SoundExchange payouts) also have an overall market share of more than 40 per cent (see Figure 5.14).

If we compare the digital market share with the share of music-streaming revenue of overall recorded music sales, we can identify five different market types:

1. Music-streaming markets: China, Sweden, Norway, Denmark, South Korea, Columbia, Singapore, Taiwan and the Caribbean states. Neither the physical market nor download sales are relevant.
2. Mixed digital music markets: USA, Peru, Mexico, Ireland, Singapore, Thailand, Philippines, New Zealand and India. The revenue from digital download sales is still relevant, but in decline.
3. Download music markets: Australia, Canada and Indonesia. The digital download market is still essential.
4. Physical music markets with a significant streaming market share – low digital market share and medium music-streaming share: Finland, Hong Kong, the Netherlands, Spain, Ecuador, Brazil, Turkey, Taiwan and Chile. Both physical sales and digital download sales are still relevant.
5. Physical music markets – low digital market share and low music-streaming share: since 19 markets are included in this category, we can usefully further distinguish them. There are those countries with a digital market share higher than 25 per cent with a relatively well-established streaming market (streaming market share higher than 10 per cent but lower than

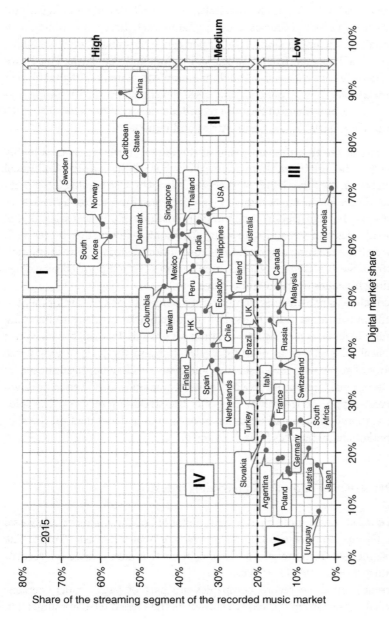

**Figure 5.14** A typology of international music-streaming markets in 2015
Source: After IFPI Global Music Report 2016

20 per cent): UK, France, Russia, Italy, Germany, Switzerland, Greece and Malaysia. In other countries a low digital market share corresponds with a medium streaming share (10–20 per cent): Slovakia, Czech Republic, Argentina, Hungary, Poland, Bulgaria, Belgium and Venezuela. Finally, we can identify countries with a still dominant physical market (digital market share is lower than 30 per cent) and a less developed music-streaming segment (streaming share of the total recorded music market is lower than 10 per cent): Austria, Japan, South Africa and Uruguay.

Thus, we can see that the landscape of the digital music markets is highly diverse. On the one hand, there are markets that still have a strong physical market, but on the other hand, markets also exist where streaming is the main revenue source for the music industry – and between these two extremes there are markets characterized by different combinations of physical sales, digital download sales and streaming revenue. The complexity further increases if we divide the streaming market into a subscription sector (i.e. streaming revenues from Spotify, Deezer, Napster, etc.) and an advert-supported sector (i.e. streaming revenues from YouTube, Vevo, etc.).

To conclude, since music streaming is at a different stage of development in different international music markets, a uniform market strategy for fostering streaming revenue is not the best solution for growth. Instead, the relevance of physical sales as well as download sales, but also the level of piracy, the relevance of advert-supported services and even the GDP per head should be taken into consideration if recorded music companies intend to shut down the advert-supported freemium tiers of music-streaming services. The solution lies, therefore, in a market differentiation that is dependent on the specific market characteristics in each country.

## Industry structure of the sound recording industry

The recorded music industry is a tight oligopoly of three majors: Universal Music Group, Sony Music Entertainment and Warner Music Group. The majors emerged from mergers and acquisitions that have shaped the recording industry since 1985 (see Chapter 1).

Currently, all three record companies are part of larger conglomerates: Universal Music Group (UMG) is a subsidy of the French telecommunication and entertainment concern Vivendi. Japanese electronics giant Sony owns Sony Music Entertainment and Access Industries has bought Warner Music Group. Together the three majors accounted for a recorded music market share of at least 73 per cent in 2015: Universal Music Group (33.5 per cent), Sony Music Entertainment (22.6 per cent) and Warner Music Group (17.1 per cent) (Warner Music Group 2014: 12). The remaining 26.8 per cent is divided among myriads of indie record labels (Music & Copyright 2016). However, there are a few independents that are economically relevant, such as Concord Records, Epitaph Records, Curb and Big Machine (Taylor Swift's label) in the US, Naïve in France, Edel/Kontor and MCP in Germany, Ministry of Sound, Cooking Vinyl, PIAS and the Beggars Group (with Rough Trade Records, Matador Records and XL Recordings) in the UK, Avex Music Group and Nippon Columbia in Japan, and the classical music label NAXOS.

Digitization has forced majors as well as indies to reconfigure their business models. Instead of focusing on record production and distribution alone, the companies of the recording industry entered the licensing business, artist management and even in the live music business, merchandising and branding. Although revenues have declined considerably since 2000, the revenue basis has broadened. Hence, Universal Music Group and Warner Music Group now report revenues from artist services, merchandising and licensing separately from physical and digital music sales. However, selling recorded music is still the majors' core business, with recorded music sales accounting for two thirds of UMG's and Warner Music's revenue (see Figure 5.15).

The revenue mix has changed significantly, however. Universal's physical sales have declined from €5,900 million in 2002 to €1,400 million in 2015 – a decrease of 76 per cent. Digital sales, reported for the first time in 2005, grew by 662.5 per cent to €2,000 million in 2015. Digital sales outperformed physical sales for the first time in 2013. In 2015, however, income from music streaming accounted for 48.3 per cent of digital sales and 28.2 per cent of overall recorded music sales. Income from licensing master rights is the third pillar of UMG's business model. Licensing revenue increased by 58.6 per cent to €728 million during the period 2007 to 2015 (Vivendi 2016: 14) (see Figure 5.16).

When UMG bought the Sanctuary Group in 2007, the deal also included the acquisition of an artist management and live music agency that "provide[s] a springboard for UMG's expansion into music related businesses" (Vivendi 2007: 17). Following this, UMG established an artist management and event

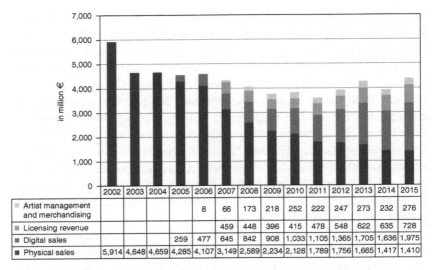

| | 2002 | 2003 | 2004 | 2005 | 2006 | 2007 | 2008 | 2009 | 2010 | 2011 | 2012 | 2013 | 2014 | 2015 |
|---|---|---|---|---|---|---|---|---|---|---|---|---|---|---|
| Artist management and merchandising | | | | | | 8 | 66 | 173 | 218 | 252 | 222 | 247 | 273 | 232 | 276 |
| Licensing revenue | | | | | | 459 | 448 | 396 | 415 | 478 | 548 | 622 | 635 | 728 |
| Digital sales | | | | 259 | 477 | 645 | 842 | 908 | 1,033 | 1,105 | 1,365 | 1,705 | 1,636 | 1,975 |
| Physical sales | 5,914 | 4,648 | 4,659 | 4,285 | 4,107 | 3,149 | 2,589 | 2,234 | 2,128 | 1,789 | 1,756 | 1,665 | 1,417 | 1,410 |

**Figure 5.15** The revenue mix (excluding publishing) of Universal Music Group, 2002–2015
Source: After Vivendi (2002–2015)

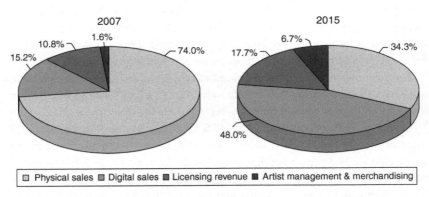

**Figure 5.16** The revenue mix (excluding publishing) of Universal Music Group, 2007 and 2015
Source: After Vivendi (2007, 2015)

management unit including Twenty First Artists and the Trinifold agency for pop music stars, as well as Universal Classical Management and Productions (UCMP) for classical music stars (Vivendi 2008: 28). In 2011 UMG launched

Berlin- and London-based Centre Stage Artist Management (CSAM) to include the top stars of the UCMP roster. The acquisition of the Sanctuary Group also brought them a merchandising business that was set up as a separate unit under the Bravado label. Bravado produces and sells artist-branded and other branded products in fashion shops, at concerts and on the Internet (Vivendi 2012: 23). UMG also established Universal Music & Brand to license the brands of artists managed by UMG in partnership with manufacturers of branded goods (Vivendi 2014: 19). The combined revenue from artist management and merchandising increased from €66 million in 2007 to €276 million in 2015.

In 2010 UMG's parent company Vivendi also entered the ticketing market by acquiring Digitick, and then See Tickets a year later, to form Vivendi Ticketing. Vivendi Ticketing organizes the ticketing of the Glastonbury music festival in the UK and also tickets for the Eiffel Tower and the palace of Versailles (Vivendi 2014: 28).

UMG is no longer a music recording and music publishing company; it has diversified into artist and brand management as well as merchandising and live music; it collaborates with Vivendi Ticketing and holds considerable stakes in music-streaming services such as Spotify, Soundcloud and Vevo.

Warner Music Group (WMG) has diversified its business in a similar way. Digital sales overtook physical sales for the first time in 2013 and increased by 736 per cent from $137 million in 2005 to $1,100 million in 2015. In the same period, physical sales decreased by 70.3 per cent from $2,600 million to $767 million. Licensing revenue, which rose from $202 million in 2005 to $288 million in 2015 (+42.6 per cent), and revenue from artist services and merchandising, confined the overall revenue loss to 7.4 per cent in the period from 2001 and 2015 (see Figures 5.17 and 5.18).

Since 2005, Warner Music Group has been offering so-called expanded rights deals to new recording artists "to capitalize on ancillary revenues, from merchandising, fan clubs, sponsorship, concert promotion and artist management, among other areas" (Warner Music Group 2014: 4). WMG has therefore built a network of concert promoters and artist agencies to provide tour support, merchandising sales, sponsorship, brand partnerships and fan club support (Warner Music Group 2015: 8–9).

WMG's diversification into artist management was accompanied by an expansion of the label and music catalogue. In 2003 WMG bought a 50 per cent share in Puff Daddy's Bad Boy Records, and in 2004 expanded its share in

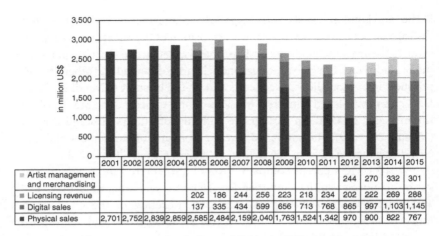

| | 2001 | 2002 | 2003 | 2004 | 2005 | 2006 | 2007 | 2008 | 2009 | 2010 | 2011 | 2012 | 2013 | 2014 | 2015 |
|---|---|---|---|---|---|---|---|---|---|---|---|---|---|---|---|
| Artist management and merchandising | | | | | | | | | | | | 244 | 270 | 332 | 301 |
| Licensing revenue | | | | | 202 | 186 | 244 | 256 | 223 | 218 | 234 | 202 | 222 | 269 | 288 |
| Digital sales | | | | | 137 | 335 | 434 | 599 | 656 | 713 | 768 | 865 | 997 | 1,103 | 1,145 |
| Physical sales | 2,701 | 2,752 | 2,839 | 2,859 | 2,585 | 2,484 | 2,159 | 2,040 | 1,763 | 1,524 | 1,342 | 970 | 900 | 822 | 767 |

**Figure 5.17** The revenue mix (excluding publishing) of Warner Music Group, 2001–2015
Source: After Warner Music Group (2001–2015)

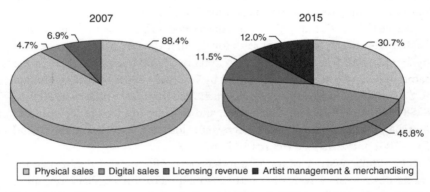

**Figure 5.18** The revenue mix (excluding publishing) of Warner Music Group, 2007 and 2015
Source: After Warner Music Group (2007, 2015)

Maverick Records – a joint venture with Madonna and her manager – from 50 per cent to 80 per cent. Two years later the rest of Maverick Records was bought and Madonna signed to concert promoter Live Nation. Also in 2004, WMG bought Ryko Corporation for $67.5 million. In 2007 and 2010 hard rock and heavy metal label Roadrunner Records was bought for $106 million. WMG also acquired a 50 per cent stake in Frank Sinatra Enterprises for $50 million, and last but not least Parlophone Music Group, along with EMI and Virgin Classics, Chrysalis/Ensign and several EMI country branches, were bought from Universal Music Group for $740 million.[7] In addition, WMG's parent company invested $239 million into French music-streaming service Deezer in 2012 and 2016.[8]

While the recording catalogue and artist management functions were strengthened, WMG drastically reduced CD manufacturing and physical distribution capacities. WEA Manufacturing Inc. in the US and Warner Music Manufacturing Europe, as well as Warner's physical distribution operations of WEA Corp., were sold along with Ivy Hill Corporation (a CD and DVD packaging company) and Giant Merchandising to Cinram International for $1,050 million in 2003 (Warner Music Group 2005: 10). The restructuring and the decreasing production costs from digitization have helped to increase annual profits (OIBDA) from $189 million in 2003 to $340 million in 2014 (Warner Music Group 2005: 28 and 2014: 48).

Warner Music Group has diversified its recorded music business through 360 deals into artist management and has acquired several record companies to expand its master recording catalogue. At the same time CD manufacturing and distribution capacities have been outsourced to save production costs. Indirectly WMG is also involved in digital music distribution through Access Industry's investment in Deezer. Hence, this music major in the digital age is more than just a record company: it is a full service provider for artists and a licensing platform for recording master rights.

## Notes

1. See www.soundout.com (retrieved 19 February 2017).
2. BusinessWire, "The Nielsen Company & Billboard's 2011 Music Industry Report", 5 January 2012, www.businesswire.com/news/home/20120105005547/en/Nielsen-Company-Billboard%E2%80%99s-2011-Music-Industry-Report (retrieved 1 February 2016).
3. See www.merlinnetwork.org (retrieved 19 February 2017).
4. Phonographic Performance Limited (PPL), "Company History", www.ppluk.com/About-Us/Who-We-Are/Company-history/ (retrieved 22 February 2016).
5. Music Business Worldwide, "Deezer Absorbs €100m Investment from Orange and Access Industries", 20 January 2016, www.musicbusinessworldwide.com/deezer-absorbs-e100m-investment-from-orange-and-access-industries/ (retrieved 6 February 2016).

6.  See http://y.qq.com/ (retrieved 19 February 2017).
7.  Billboard.biz, "Warner Music Group Closes on Acquisition of Parlophone Label Group", 1 July 2013, www.billboard.com/biz/articles/news/global/1568720/warner-music-group-closes-on-acquisition-of-parlophone-label-group (retrieved 19 February 2016).
8.  See note 5, above.

# 6
# LIVE MUSIC

## The function of the live music market

Apart from the artists, the main players in the live music business are (1) music promoters and festival organizers, (2) concert venue operators, (3) music agents and bookers, (4) support service providers and (5) ticketing companies. Thus, the live music business is based on a division of labour with many different occupational roles.

## Music promoters and festival organizers

### Promoters
Music promoters organize concerts, tours and festivals at their own risk and expense by selling tickets. The promoter conceptualizes a musical event or a concert tour and, to this end, contracts the artists. A tour manager and crew attend to and support the artists while they are travelling and performing. Before staging the music event, the promoter is in charge of event publicity and public relations and seeks to support the sales of tickets in order to cover the costs already incurred. The promoter will inform the public about the event through an advertising campaign comprising posters, flyers, mailings, radio and television adverts, and social media networking, as well as by arranging interviews for the artists with journalists, and even press conferences. However, if the pre-sales of tickets indicate an insufficient demand for the event, the promoter will cancel it and has to bear the costs already incurred.

We can roughly distinguish between (1) small local promoters who organize concerts in small venues such as bars and music clubs, (2) regional promoters organizing concerts in medium-sized venues and (3) national promoters who arrange several concert dates and put together national and international tours. Concert promotion involves a high level of risk. The promoters have to spend money up front and cannot guarantee that a sufficient number of tickets will be sold to cover the costs. The larger the capacity of the venue and the greater the number of shows, the higher the risk for the promoter. Therefore, national promoters spread the risk by coupling concert dates of an artist for a tour to cross-collateralize possible losses from one concert with possible gains from others.[1] However, the business model of extremely high guaranteed payments and cross-collateralized concert tours reduces the profitability of the music promotion business on the one hand, but on the other exploits economies of scale with decreasing costs per unit, as fixed costs are spread out over more units of output (see Figure 6.1).

Economies of scale are an entrance barrier for smaller concert promoters in the live music market as they have to bear high fixed costs without the possibility to cross-collateralize the losses. This encourages a concentration of large regional and national promotion companies, resulting in the emergence of Live Nation.[2] Live Nation Entertainment has become the undisputed market leader in the US and in the international music promotion

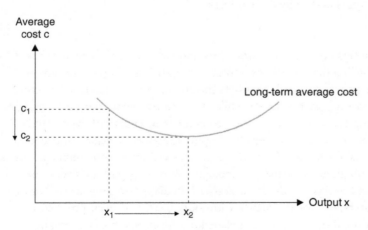

**Figure 6.1** The concept of economies of scale
Source: After Varian (2010: 379)

business. Whereas the top ten promoters accounted for 44 per cent of all concert tickets sold in 1996, Live Nation and Anschutz Entertainment Group (AEG) accounted for 77 per cent of the sales of the top 25 US promoters in 2009 (Hull *et al.* 2011: 155).

*Festival organizers*

A specialized field of concert promotion is the music festival. The modern concept is rooted in the Bayreuther Festspiele, which were established by opera composer Richard Wagner in 1876 with financial support of King Ludwig II of Bavaria. In the early twentieth century several classical music festivals emerged: Ravinia Festival in Illinois (1904), Glastonbury in the UK (1914) and the Salzburg Festival in Austria (1920). The first jazz festival was established by Elaine and Louis Lorillard in Newport, Rhode Island in 1954, and this became the role model for folk and blues festivals as well as the Monterey pop festival, which was held for the first time in 1967.

Music festivals became important platforms for talent-scouting. Jimi Hendrix, Janis Joplin, Canned Heat, Otis Redding and Steve Miller launched their careers at the Monterey festivals, and most of the acts performing at Monterey received their first record contract there (Tschmuck 2012: 154).

Music festivals can have a significant economic impact on the local economy. A UK for Music study of 2011 highlights that attendance by 7.7 million music festival tourists in the UK generated a spending of £1,400 million on tickets, catering, accommodation and transportation in 2009 (cited in O'Reilly *et al.* 2013: 213). The festival market has boomed in recent years. In the UK, the number of music festivals in all genres increased by 38 per cent from 2000 to 2007, with growth then slowing because of the global financial crisis of 2007/08 (O'Reilly *et al.* 2013: 212).

Concert venue operators

The promoter has to enter into an agreement with the concert and festival venue. Usually the promoter pays a rental fee – either as a fixed amount or as a percentage of ticket sales – and agrees to the services provided by the venue. In a so-called "four walls" deal, the venue provides nothing more than the facility, but it is common for concert venues to also provide supporting services such as an in-house stage crew, electricians and lighting, audio engineering, cloakroom attendants, cleaning personnel, ticketing, security and so on (see Hull *et al.* 2011: 157).

Apart from rental fees, venues also earn ancillary income from parking fees, as well as from selling food and beverages. Usually artists and promoters have no share in ancillary revenue, unless the promoter owns the venue. Live Nation owns and operates several large concert venues in North America and Europe: the traditional Fillmore theatres, the House of Blues chain of live music concert halls and restaurants, the famous Roseland Ballroom in New York, the historic Riverside Fox Theatre in California, as well as the Heineken Music Hall and Ziggo Dom in Amsterdam, the O2 Apollo Theatre in Manchester and the Reading and Leeds Festival sites. The number of amphitheatres and arenas with a capacity of 5,000 to 30,000 seats that Live Nation owned, leased, operated and booked exclusively rose from 40 in 2005 to 62 in 2015. The number of Live Nation theatres increased from 19 to 72 in the same period. Live Nation also owned and leased five festival sites in 2015 compared to two in 2005 and won the exclusive booking rights to stage concerts in the London Olympic Stadium and in the surrounding park in 2013 (Live Nation 2015: 6–7) (see Table 6.1).

Live Nation clearly states in its annual report that the purchase of concert venues helps them to "pursue our strategy to develop additional ancillary revenue streams around the ticket purchase" (Live Nation 2016: 3). Thus, the

**Table 6.1** Concert venues owned, leased, operated and exclusively booked by Live Nation, 2005 and 2015

| Concert venues | 2005 | 2015 | Change |
|---|---|---|---|
| Stadiums (capacity: more than 30,000 seats) | – | 1 | +100.0% |
| Amphitheatres, arenas (capacity: 5,000–30,000 seats) | 40 | 62 | +55.0% |
| Theatres (incl. House of Blues) (capacity: 1,000–6,500 seats) | 19 | 72 | +278.9% |
| Music Clubs (capacity: less than 1,000 seats) | 8 | 27 | +237.5% |
| Festival sites | 2 | 5 | +150.0% |
| Total | 69 | 167 | +142.0% |

Source: After Annual Reports by Live Nation 2005 and 2015

international live music business has shifted from selling concert tickets to other revenue streams such as sponsoring, merchandising and ancillary services.

## Music agents and bookers

Music agents are the middle persons between artists and their management on one side and promoters on the other. Their task is to find employment opportunities for the artists. In the live music business, agents book concert and tour dates for their clients and support the artists with travelling and accommodation arrangements. The local agents, who book lesser-known and new artists into music clubs, bars, parties and local events in cities or rural areas, need to book a lot of acts to earn a living since they cannot charge a substantial commission from one client. The commission fee ranges from 10 to 20 per cent of the artist's gross payments. Regional agents book larger clubs and theatres in municipal areas as well as small tours, and try to secure their acts as openers for well-known artists. "The dream of the regional agent is to hook up with some rising artist who becomes a star and who will take the agent along" (Hull *et al.* 2011: 151). The big players in the agency business are national and international talent agencies.

Although the Pollstar Booking Agency Directory of 2017[3] lists about 600 talent agencies in the US, the agency market is highly concentrated, with the top five agencies accounting for almost half of major concert ticket sales (Hull *et al.* 2011: 151). Three big agencies dominate the booking market: Creative Artists Agency, William Morris Endeavor and United Talent Agency. Other large agencies are Paradigm Talent Agency, The Gersh Agency, ICM Partners and Agency for the Performing Arts (APA).

The oldest talent agency in the US is the William Morris Agency (WMA), which was founded in New York City in 1898 by the German-Jewish immigrant Zelman Moses, who adopted the English name William Morris. Initially William Morris booked performers for vaudeville theatres, but changed his focus to the emerging Hollywood film industry, representing artists such as Al Jolson, Charlie Chaplin and the Marx Brothers. In 1965 WMA became a central player in the rock music business by booking the Rolling Stones and the Byrds in the US and representing Sonny & Cher as well as the Beach Boys. WMA also set up an office in Nashville to become a powerhouse for country musicians (Rose 1996). In 2009 WMA merged with Endeavor, another large US talent agency with a focus on television stars. William Morris Endeavor (WME) now represents artists across all entertainment sectors – movies, television, music, theatre, publishing and even the National Football League.[4]

The Creative Artists Agency (CAA) was founded by former employees of the William Morris Agency in 1975. The Jackson 5 were among its first signed artists. Although it is primarily known for its representation of Hollywood stars it maintains a strong roster of musicians (Griffin & Masters 1997). Currently CAA represents One Direction, Iggy Azalea, Lady Gaga, Iron Maiden, Stevie Wonder, Sting, James Morrison and Robin Thicke.[5]

The United Talent Agency (UTA) is the result of the merger in 1991 of the Bauer-Benedek Agency and Leading Artists Agency, both of which were initially engaged in book publishing. However, UTA expanded its activities to film and television, theatre, broadcasting news and video games, as well as music. UTA represents several pop/rock stars such as Mariah Carey, Deep Purple, Norah Jones, Kanye West and Flo Rida, as well as classical violinist David Garrett.[6]

## Support services and ticketing

The live music business needs support services that are either provided by the venue operator or subcontracted by the promoter. Support services include logistics and transportation, technician services, sound engineering, video production, costume design and wardrobe, stage design and event conceptualization, pyrotechnics, merchandising, catering and ticketing services (for details see Rutter 2011: 64–7).

Ticketing is one of the core business functions in the live music industry. Initially tickets were sold at the live music venues, but with the emergence of a pre-sale system, companies specializing in ticketing were able to enter the business. One of the early computer-based pre-sale ticketing providers was Ticketmaster, which was founded by a group of university graduates in 1974/75. In 1982 the company's counsel Frederic Rosen decided to buy Ticketmaster with the help of financial backing from the Pritzker family, who became majority owners of Ticketmaster (Budnick & Baron 2011: 81). Ticketmaster challenged the market leader Ticketron by paying advances against proceeds to the venue owners and promoters instead of charging ticketing fees. On the one hand, the upfront payments made it easier for the promoters to budget and to meet the demands of the bookers; on the other hand, they became dependent on the cash injections from Ticketmaster. However, Ticketmaster went a step further by providing marketing, advertising and promotion for the events (Budnick & Baron 2011: 78). In the following years, Ticketmaster grew to become the undisputed leader in the ticketing business in the US, even acquiring its main competitor Ticketron in 1991 (Budnick & Baron 2011: 89). In 2010 Ticketmaster was the world's largest ticketing company and merged with the world's largest concert promoter Live Nation.[7]

With the advent of the Internet, online ticketing services were launched. Most services operated as ticketing resale platforms, which were initially assessed as a "black market". However, the secondary ticketing market rapidly evolved and soon established ticketing companies such as Ticketmaster started operating online, including running secondary ticketing websites (Budnick & Baron 2011: 287–96). Despite the emergence of online ticketing, the ticketing market remains highly concentrated and dominated by a few large companies in the national markets: Live Nation/Ticketmaster in both the US and the UK and CTS Eventim in Germany.

### The market and industry structure of live music

The live music market

Chapter 2 highlighted that live music events and recorded music are complementary goods, whereas Krueger (2005) argues that digitization has weakened the link between concert ticket and record sales. Thus, concerts are no longer seen as promotional tools for selling recorded music, but instead serve as a main income source for artists. The Billboard Money Makers List shows that all top ten artists earned more than 80 per cent of their total income from touring in 2014. Taylor Swift, who has headed the list in the past two years, ranked only fifteenth in 2014 because even though she had the top-selling album of the year, she did not tour.

The statistics of the German association for the promotion business (Bundesverband der Veranstaltungswirtschaft) also confirm the increasing economic relevance of the live music business (see Figure 6.2).

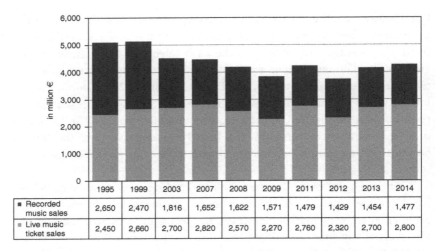

| | 1995 | 1999 | 2003 | 2007 | 2008 | 2009 | 2011 | 2012 | 2013 | 2014 |
|---|---|---|---|---|---|---|---|---|---|---|
| ■ Recorded music sales | 2,650 | 2,470 | 1,816 | 1,652 | 1,622 | 1,571 | 1,479 | 1,429 | 1,454 | 1,477 |
| ▪ Live music ticket sales | 2,450 | 2,660 | 2,700 | 2,820 | 2,570 | 2,270 | 2,760 | 2,320 | 2,700 | 2,800 |

**Figure 6.2** The German market for live music and the recorded music market in comparison, 1995–2014
Source: After GfK (2014: 6) and IFPI Germany (1999–2014)

The share of the live music market in Germany was 48 per cent in 1995 and in 2014 rose to 65 per cent of the combined revenue from ticket and recorded music sales. Declining recorded music sales as well as increasing concert ticket sales explain the higher sales share of the live music market.

Although ticket sales in Germany decreased by 18 per cent from 2007 to 2012 as a result of the global economic downturn, sales recovered in the following years and peaked in 2014 at €2,800 million. The German live music sector had 32,629 employees in 2014 and generated a gross value added (GVA) of €1,040 million – compared to 19,866 employees and €880 million GVA in the recorded music sector. Music promoters contributed €251 million in GVA, music agencies/bookers €77 million, production service providers €132 million, concert venue operators €164 million, concert, opera and musical theatres €391 million and ticketing agencies €26 million (Seufert *et al.*, 2015: 38–9, 46–7).

According to UK for Music, the UK live music sector had 25,100 employees and contributed £924 million gross value added (GVA) to the British economy in 2014. The GVA of the UK live music sector has increased by 50 per cent since 2012, and is the fastest-growing sector of the UK music industry. The live music sector in the UK is, therefore, economically more relevant than the

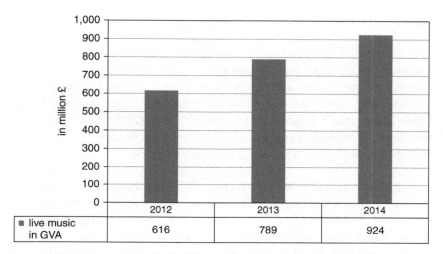

| | 2012 | 2013 | 2014 |
|---|---|---|---|
| ■ live music in GVA | 616 | 789 | 924 |

**Figure 6.3** The gross value added of the UK live music sector, 2012–2014
Source: After UK for Music 2013, 2014

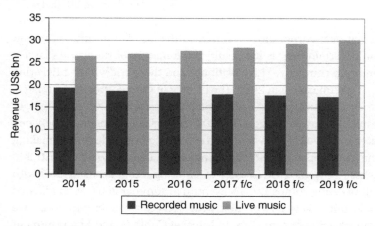

**Figure 6.4** Global live and recorded music revenue, 2014–2019 (projected)
Source: PwC (2015)

combined recorded music and music producers' and recording studios sectors – £731 million in GVA (UK for Music 2014: 13; 2015: 4) (see Figure 6.3).

Global data on the live music market indicate that the trend of a growing live music revenue will continue, whereas recorded music sales will decrease further.

Industry structure

The global live music market is dominated by a few large companies that cover almost all aspects of the live music business – artist agencies, concert promotion, supporting services and even ticketing. Historically, the live music business was not – unlike the recorded music industry – a tight oligopoly but a locally and regionally fragmented market. Frith *et al.* (2010) have shown that the UK music promotion business was initially organized locally in the period after the Second World War, and identify three periods:

> The first period of 1955–1969 is characterized by the absence of corporations and ancillary industries and presence of entrepreneur concert promoters; … The second period of 1969–1996 is characterized by record labels subsidizing tours to promote record sales; … The third and final period of 1996–2009 is characterized by … the rise of multi-national corporations entering the live music market.
>
> (Frith *et al.* 2010: 4)

The "multi-national corporation" referred to is Live Nation Entertainment. Live Nation Entertainment is the result of the merger of the world's largest music promotion company – Live Nation – and the world's largest ticketing company – Ticketmaster – in 2010. The history of both corporations reflects the fundamental change of the live music business since 2000.[8] The merger was the result of a power struggle. In 2008 the exclusive agreement between Ticketmaster and Live Nation was due to expire and both sides began making strategic moves to improve their bargaining power. Live Nation demonstrated its willingness to bypass Ticketmaster by entering into a licensing deal with the German ticketing company CTS Eventim in summer 2007, and indicated that it would not renew its contract with Ticketmaster. In addition, Live Nation acquired a 50 per cent stake in Michael Cohl's Grand Entertainment ($123 million in stock and $10 million in cash), the music club chain House of Blues ($350 million) and a majority stake in Coran Capshaw's MusicToday (Budnick & Baron 2011: 308). However, Ticketmaster fought back by buying Irving Azoff's Front Line Management Group – one of the world's largest artist agencies – having outbid Live Nation, which was also interested in entering the artist management business. Having lost the Front Line Management deal, Live Nation developed a new business model: the unified rights deals or 360 degree deals.[9] In October 2007 Live Nation announced a ten-year, $120 million deal with Madonna, which included everything from touring, merchandise, fan clubs, studio albums, sponsorships and branding. Further 360 deals were signed: a twelve-year deal with U2 for $100 million in March 2008 (including touring, merchandise, image licensing, website and fan club rights); a ten-year deal with Jay Z for $150 million in April 2008 (including touring, recordings, publishing, management and record label businesses); a ten-year deal with Shakira for $70 million in July 2008 (including touring, recordings and merchandise); a three-album and touring deal with Nickelback for an assumed $50–70 million (Budnick & Baron 2011: 309–10).

However, the financial markets were anything but convinced about Live Nation's new business model, which was incorporated as Artist Nation within the Live Nation empire. Between the Madonna and U2 deals, Live Nation's share price plummeted by 50 per cent. Since Live Nation did not want to become a record label, it stopped signing new 360 deals (Budnick & Baron 2011: 312). In addition to its 360 deal troubles, Live Nation was struck by another disaster: CTS Eventim's ticketing system crashed at the end of January 2009, when the tickets for the Phish reunion tour were put on sale. It became clear that Live Nation was not able to compete with Ticketmaster and it was no surprise when both companies announced a $2,500 million merger as an all-stock deal on 10 February 2009 (Budnick & Baron 2011: 314).

This mega-merger uniting the world's largest concert promotion company with the world's leading ticketing company, which also owned a significant artist management agency, was the object of anti-trust investigations by the US Justice Department in two congressional hearings. The hearings revealed that both companies controlled a remarkably high market share in their specific markets. Jam Productions co-founder Jerry Mickelson testified that Live Nation controlled 75 amphitheatres, making it nearly impossible for competitors to enter the market successfully. Ticketmaster's CEO Irving Azoff admitted in the hearings that his company had provided ticketing services to 87 of the top 100 concert venues in 2007 and to 84 in 2008 (Budnick & Baron 2011: 321). These figures underline the threat of a vertical monopoly in the live entertainment business through the merger of Ticketmaster and Live Nation. Both companies argued the merger was brought about because of the poor economic environment, which made it necessary for them to join forces.

Live Nation's CEO Michael Rapino pointed out in the hearings that they lost $70 million on their 1,000 concerts in 50 amphitheatres and blamed it on the artists' managers, who demanded unreasonably high up-front payments and a 90 per cent stake in the ticket sales, forcing Live Nation to earn the money back through sales of ancillaries – food, drinks, parking, and so on. Rapino calculated that his company made an average of $12–15 per person from ancillaries, but only an average of $4 per person on every $100 from ticket sales (Budnick & Baron 2011: 321).

In the end, the authorities approved the Ticketmaster–Live Nation merger in January 2010, although they imposed several conditions. Ticketmaster was required to license a copy of its software to the world's second-largest concert promotion company, AEG, to enable it to launch its own ticketing system. Ticketmaster also had to divest itself of the ticketing company Paciolan, which it had acquired in 2008. Ticketmaster and Live Nation were also forbidden to take action against any venue owner who used another ticketing or promotion service. Finally, firewalls had to be installed to protect confidential competitor data from the company's promotion and management business.

The Ticketmaster–Live Nation merger marks the beginning of a new era in the music business, with all activities within the industry now being integrated, including live music events, venue operations, ticketing services, sponsorship and advertising sales, and artist management and services (Live Nation 2015: 4).

Live Nation describes its business in its 2015 annual report as follows:

> We believe we are the largest producer of live music concerts in the world, based on total fans that attend Live Nation events as compared to events of other promoters, connecting nearly 59 million fans to almost 23,000 events for over 2,700 artists in 2014. Live Nation owns, operates, has exclusive booking rights for or has an equity interest in 158 venues, including House of Blues music venues and prestigious locations such as The Fillmore in San Francisco, the Hollywood Palladium, the Ziggo Dome in Amsterdam and 3Arena in Ireland.
>
> (Live Nation 2015: 2)

Therefore, Live Nation Entertainment operates in four different business segments (Live Nation 2015: 28–9):

1. The concerts segment, which involves the global promotion of live music events in owned or operated venues as well as in rented third-party venues. This segment covers the management of music venues and the production of music festivals such as the Lollapalooza festivals around the world.
2. The ticketing segment, which sells tickets for Live Nation events and for other clients by charging a processing fee.
3. The Artist Nation segment, which provides management services to music artists in exchange for a commission on the earnings of these artists. It also creates and sells merchandise articles for music artists at live performances, to retailers and directly to consumers on the Internet.
4. The sponsorship and advertising segment, which creates and maintains relationships with sponsors and branding partners.

Prior to 2012, Live Nation also operated an e-commerce segment that included acquired online ticketing platforms and the online media research company BigChampagne, which it bought in 2011. However, the e-commerce segment was dissolved in 2012 and its operations were divided among the ticketing and sponsorship and advertising segments (Live Nation 2012: 5).

An analysis of Live Nation's annual reports highlights impressive statistics. In 2015 Live Nation recorded 7,700 full-time employees (Live Nation 2016: 8) and promoted 25,519 music events – concerts, festivals and concert tours – attracting 63.5 million visitors worldwide. Since Live Nation was spun off from Clear Channel as a stock company in 2005, the number of promoted music events has tripled and attendance nearly doubled (Live Nation 2006: 50; 2016: 31) (see Figure 6.5).

The financial results of Live Nation only partly reflect this positive trend, however. Although revenues have grown by 147 per cent to $7,200 million in 2015, total expenses have increased at nearly the same rate – 141 per cent. Since the merger with Ticketmaster in 2010, Live Nation has reported annual net losses, even though these have decreased to $15.8 million in 2015. The financial picture becomes brighter if operating income is considered. Live Nation reported an operating gain of $131.4 million for 2015, after losses in 2010 and 2012. However, the concerts segment did not contribute to the operating gain. In each year since the merger, Live Nation's concerts segment has shown an operative loss – for example $190.5 million in 2014 and $105.3 million in 2015. The cost of revenue in the concerts segment has been more or less stable at a high level of 85 per cent since 2010. This can be explained by

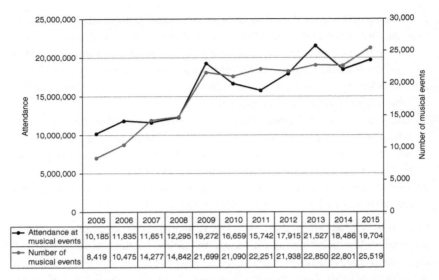

| | 2005 | 2006 | 2007 | 2008 | 2009 | 2010 | 2011 | 2012 | 2013 | 2014 | 2015 |
|---|---|---|---|---|---|---|---|---|---|---|---|
| Attendance at musical events | 10,185 | 11,835 | 11,651 | 12,295 | 19,272 | 16,659 | 15,742 | 17,915 | 21,527 | 18,486 | 19,704 |
| Number of musical events | 8,419 | 10,475 | 14,277 | 14,842 | 21,699 | 21,090 | 22,251 | 21,938 | 22,850 | 22,801 | 25,519 |

**Figure 6.5** Number of Live Nation music events and attendance figures, 2005–2015
Source: After Live Nation (2006–2016)

razor-thin profit margins in the live music business, as Live Nation's CEO pointed out in the Congressional Hearings on the Live Nation–Ticketmaster merger. As we have seen, Live Nation has to pay advances of 90 per cent of ticket sales to the artists. Hence, Live Nation has to earn this money back from ancillaries (Budnick & Baron 2011: 321).

Live Nation's operating gain arises, therefore, from both the ticketing segment and the sponsoring and advertising segment, with costs of revenue being slightly below 50 per cent and 13 to 18 per cent, respectively. In contrast, the Artist Nation segment, which includes the agency business and expanded rights deals, has shown operating losses since 2010 with a cost of revenue of about 55 to 65 per cent depending on the financial year (see Figures 6.6, 6.7 and 6.8).

This analysis of Live Nation's financial reports highlights a mixed picture. Live Nation's core business segment – concert promotion and touring – contributes annual operating losses to the company's performance, whereas sponsoring and advertising, as well as ticketing, account for an operative gain in the consolidated company. Unlike these segments, Artist Nation is a loss-generating business segment, which might indicate a strategic failure

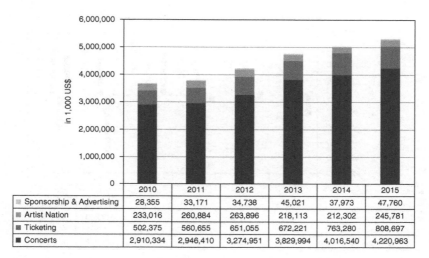

| | 2010 | 2011 | 2012 | 2013 | 2014 | 2015 |
|---|---|---|---|---|---|---|
| Sponsorship & Advertising | 28,355 | 33,171 | 34,738 | 45,021 | 37,973 | 47,760 |
| Artist Nation | 233,016 | 260,884 | 263,896 | 218,113 | 212,302 | 245,781 |
| Ticketing | 502,375 | 560,655 | 651,055 | 672,221 | 763,280 | 808,697 |
| Concerts | 2,910,334 | 2,946,410 | 3,274,951 | 3,829,994 | 4,016,540 | 4,220,963 |

**Figure 6.6** Live Nation's revenues by business segments, 2010–2015
Source: After Live Nation (2001–2016)

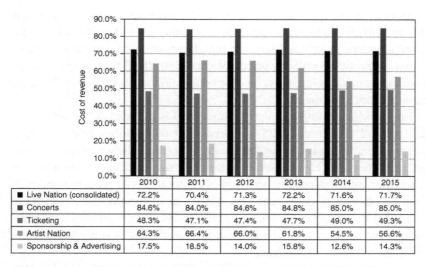

| | 2010 | 2011 | 2012 | 2013 | 2014 | 2015 |
|---|---|---|---|---|---|---|
| Live Nation (consolidated) | 72.2% | 70.4% | 71.3% | 72.2% | 71.6% | 71.7% |
| Concerts | 84.6% | 84.0% | 84.6% | 84.8% | 85.0% | 85.0% |
| Ticketing | 48.3% | 47.1% | 47.4% | 47.7% | 49.0% | 49.3% |
| Artist Nation | 64.3% | 66.4% | 66.0% | 61.8% | 54.5% | 56.6% |
| Sponsorship & Advertising | 17.5% | 18.5% | 14.0% | 15.8% | 12.6% | 14.3% |

**Figure 6.7** Live Nation's cost of revenue by business segments, 2010–2015
Source: After Live Nation (2011–2016)

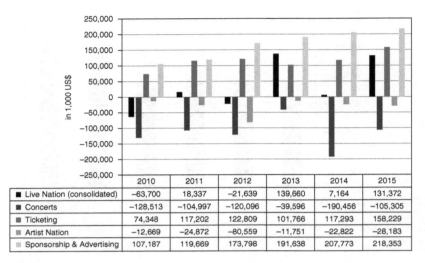

| | 2010 | 2011 | 2012 | 2013 | 2014 | 2015 |
|---|---|---|---|---|---|---|
| ■ Live Nation (consolidated) | −63,700 | 18,337 | −21,639 | 139,660 | 7,164 | 131,372 |
| ■ Concerts | −128,513 | −104,997 | −120,096 | −39,596 | −190,456 | −105,305 |
| ■ Ticketing | 74,348 | 117,202 | 122,809 | 101,766 | 117,293 | 158,229 |
| ■ Artist Nation | −12,669 | −24,872 | −80,559 | −11,751 | −22,822 | −28,183 |
| ▨ Sponsorship & Advertising | 107,187 | 119,669 | 173,798 | 191,638 | 207,773 | 218,353 |

**Figure 6.8** Live Nation's operating income by business segments, 2010–2015
Source: After Live Nation (2011–2016)

in promoting 360 deals in the past. Live Nation's figures also highlight that the international live music business is a highly contested market despite its oligopolistic structure. Thus, the big players compete for market shares instead of profit-maximizing prices. Nevertheless, the live music market has become the primary income source for performing artists by demanding high advances and sales shares.

The Anschutz Entertainment Group (AEG) is the world's second-largest promoter of live music. AEG is a subsidy of the privately held Anschutz Corporation, which is why no financial results are publicly available. Similar to Live Nation, AEG is a large music promoter owning and operating several entertainment venues such as the Staples Center in Los Angeles, the StubHub Center in Carson, California and the O2 arenas in London and Berlin. AEG also has a ticketing portal that was sold by Live Nation owing to the obligations imposed on it by the US anti-trust authority in the course of the Ticketmaster–Live Nation merger.

Most of the national live music markets reflect an oligopolistic global market structure. In North America, Live Nation and AEG are the undisputed market leaders. Notable smaller competitors are Another Planet Entertainment, Jam Productions, Ltd., Bowery Presents and I.M.P., in addition to many smaller regional companies and various casinos (Live Nation 2016: 8). In the UK, just a few relevant promoters such as MCD Productions and SJM Concerts dominate the market alongside Live Nation and AEG. In Germany, Live Nation competes with a handful of middle-sized promoters such as CTS Eventim and Deutsche Entertainment AG. Other smaller promoters operate on a local and regional basis and are focused on specific music genres such as jazz, classical music or EDM. The live music market remains highly concentrated and dominated by a few influential players.

## Notes

1. For the history of the new live music business model, see Chapter 1: The growing importance of the live music business in the music industry.
2. See Chapter 1: The growing importance of the live music business in the music industry.
3. Pollstar, "Booking Agency Directory 2017", https://store.pollstar.com/p-430-booking-agency-directory-2017-edition.aspx (retrieved 20 February 2017).
4. See www.wmeentertainment.com/ (retrieved 19 February 2017).
5. Creative Artists Agency (CAA), "Artist Roster", www.caatouring.com/Public/Artist Roster.aspx (retrieved 8 March 2016).
6. United Talent Agency (UTA), "Artist Roster", https://music.utatouring.com/full-roster/ (retrieved 8 March 2016).
7. See Chapter 1: The growing importance of the live music business in the music industry.
8. *Ibid.*
9. The blueprint was Robbie Williams' 360 deal with EMI in 2002. See Chapter 5: The A & R function.

# 7

# SECONDARY MUSIC MARKETS

Beyond publishing, recording and live performance, music is economically relevant in secondary markets as an important input factor. Music is integral content in radio and television broadcasting, in television films and motion pictures, as well as in games and advertisements. Music licensing links the primary music markets to the secondary ones. This chapter focuses on the relevant secondary music markets and sheds light on the prevailing business models. Moreover, as branding, sponsoring and merchandising are relatively new income sources for musicians, it is useful to analyse these aspects of the music business, too.

## Radio broadcasting

As highlighted in Chapter 1, radio played the major role in music distribution from the 1930s to the mid-1950s. At the time, the music industry was primarily a broadcasting industry that considered record selling merely as a side business. In the US, the business model was based on advertising income that financed live radio music shows with popular dance music orchestras – think of the infamous *Camel Caravan Show* with Benny Goodman and His Orchestra sponsored by the tobacco giant Reynolds from 1936 to 1939 (Tschmuck 2012: 93–4).

However, radio broadcasting lost its influence on the music industry with the advent of commercial television in the 1950s and 1960s, as a result of which advertising revenue was reallocated from radio to television. Nevertheless, radio became an important platform where record labels could promote their new releases. Indeed, even today radio airplay is still the most important tool for selling music in physical and digital formats.

The introduction in 1953 of the top 40 radio format by radio stations owner Todd Storz inaugurated a new era (Shaw 1974: 66). Until the early 1950s, AM radio programmes consisted of pre-scheduled and advert-sponsored blocks including radio dramas, shows and music. Storz and his programme director Bill Stewart observed that the more people heard a song from the jukebox, the more probable it was that they would buy a record.[1] Thus, Storz programmed his radio stations like jukeboxes, playing the 40 most popular songs of the hit parade all day long, which provided a conducive environment for advertising. The top 40 format was a considerable economic success and became a blueprint for other radio stations within and outside the US. The top 40 format later changed to contemporary hit radio (CHR) and other radio formats such as album-oriented radio (AOR), middle-of-the-road radio (MOR) and adult contemporary (AC), and eventually format radio emerged even for classical music and oldies.

With the invention of format radio, the decision-making process of music programming shifted from radio DJs to programme committees and programme directors. Record labels again tried to influence the programming of radio stations by employing independent music promoters. Krasilovsky *et al.* (2007: 383) estimate that payments to independent promoters could range "from $200 to $300,000 per promoted recorded song on a formula that averaged $500 to $2,000 each time the recorded song was added to the repeat promotional play list of a designated station". No wonder such a practice also created a fertile ground for payola (see Chapter 5). In 2002 New York District Attorney Eliot Spitzer and his team revealed that the majors had made payola deals with several large commercial radio chains, and since the evidence was overwhelming, Sony-BMG agreed to pay a fine of $10 million in 2005. In 2006 Universal Music Group, Warner Music Group and EMI also settled out of court for $12 million, $5 million and $3.75 million, respectively (Krasilovsky *et al.* 2007: 384).

Nevertheless, payola remains a serious threat. When the Telecommunications Act of 1996 lifted the regulation stipulating that a single company could not own more than 40 radio stations in the US, the radio market became highly concentrated. After a process of consolidation, four radio stations ended up controlling access to more than 60 per cent of the CHR market (Krasilovsky *et al.* 2007: 385). The reduction in the number of radio networks made payola more attractive. In 2007 the Federal Communication Commission (FCC) won a lawsuit against the four largest US radio station owners. CBS Radio, Clear Channel, Citadel and Entercom had to pay a total penalty of $12.5 million for payola violations (Krasilovsky *et al.* 2007: 385).

Collecting societies license the use of music to radio stations. For example, the US collecting society ASCAP provides "access to over 10 million musical works from over 575,000 ASCAP songwriters, composers and publishers as well as works from over 90 affiliated societies from all over the world".[2] Fees are calculated either on a blanket licence basis as a percentage of a radio station's revenue or on a programme period basis. A blanket licence allows radio stations to use music without the need to provide music usage information, whereas the programme period calculation method requires a station to produce music usage information to calculate fees. The fees are negotiated between the collecting societies and the Radio Music License Committee (RMLC), which represents all commercial FCC-licensed radio stations.[3] In the 1970s, however, a group of radio stations with a religious format refused to pay the RMLC fees and demanded lower fees, arguing that their programmes did not primarily rely on copyrighted music. After unfruitful negotiations, the religious radio stations established the National Religious Broadcasters Music License Committee (NRBMLC) to enforce a lower fee even by litigation. Eventually the NRBMLC succeeded and had negotiated the first special license with BMI by the mid-1980s. ASCAP subsequently also joined the agreement to provide a Local Commercial Radio Station License with lower licence fees for nearly 600 religiously oriented radio stations.[4] In addition to commercial radio stations, non-commercial radio services (college radio, university radio and non-educational non-commercial radio) also have to license music use from collecting societies, but they do so at a lower rate set by the Copyright Royalty Board (CRB).

ASCAP collected $173.6 million of licensing fees from terrestrial and satellite radio broadcasters in 2015, which is an increase of 3.7 per cent on 2014. However, the revenue from radio licensing has remained more or less stable over the past four years (see Figure 7.1).

Revenues from licensing music to radio stations contributed 17.3 per cent to ASCAP's total receipts in 2015, making it the third most important revenue source after licensing fees from cable and terrestrial television and ASCAP's foreign collections (see Figure 7.2).

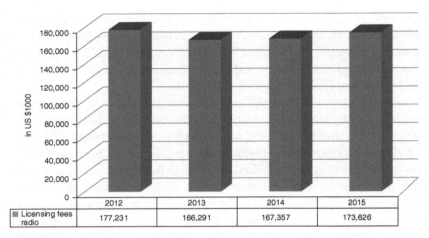

**Figure 7.1** ASCAP's revenue from licensing radio stations, 2012–2015
Source: ASCAP (2013–2016)

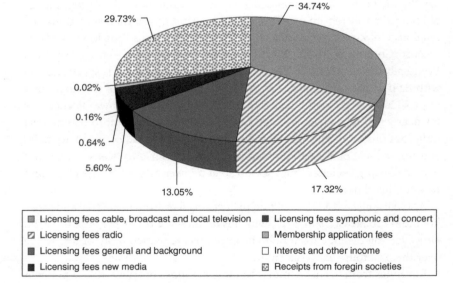

**Figure 7.2** The revenue sources of ASCAP in 2015
Source: After ASCAP (2016)

**Table 7.1** Rights administration by PRS for Music, MCPS and PPL

| Rights required for | To broadcast | To copy | To broadcast | To copy |
|---|---|---|---|---|
| Musical work | PRS for Music | MCPS | PRS for Music | MCPS |
| Sound recording | PPL | PPL | MCPS | MCPS |

Source: After: www.prsformusic.com/users/broadcastandonline/Radio/Pages/RadioLicensingFAQs.aspx (retrieved 15 May 2016)

In Europe, music licensing to radio stations works differently. Europe is dominated by public broadcasters that are financed either by government, by obligatory broadcasting fees or by a mix of advertising income and state funds/obligatory fees. Thus, unlike in the US, European radio licensing is not a purely market-driven process, since it includes a regulatory and state-interventionist component. The public broadcasters, such as the BBC in the UK and the RAI in Italy, are powerful participants in the national European music markets.

Nevertheless, both public and private radio stations have to license music from their national collecting societies. Unlike in the US, European radio stations have to obtain not just the right to broadcast and copy a musical work from a Performance Rights Organization (PRO) and Mechanical Rights Organization (MRO), but also the sound recording right from a neighbouring rights organization.[5] Thus, a UK radio station needs a music licence from the Performing Rights Society (PRS for Music) to broadcast a musical work, and a mechanical license from the Mechanical-Copyright Protection Society (MCPS) to copy a musical work for internal usage and to broadcast and copy sound recordings, as well as a licence from Phonographic Performance Limited (PPL) to broadcast and copy a sound recording. PRS for Music and MCPS collect the licensing fees on behalf of their authors and publishers. PPL distributes the collected fees to the record companies and performers (see Table 7.1).

Since PPL does not report separate numbers for radio royalties, the following figures are limited to data from PRS for Music. In 2014 PRS for Music collected £49 million from public and private radio stations in the UK. The revenue level of radio royalties has remained more or less stable for the past few years. Compared to other revenue categories, radio royalties are less important with a revenue share of 7.4 per cent in 2014 (see Figures 7.3 and 7.4).

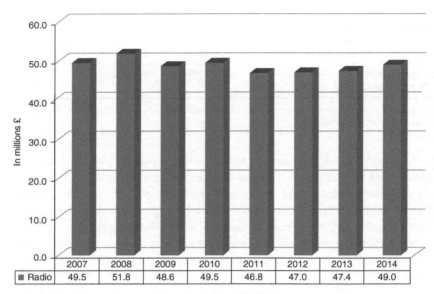

**Figure 7.3** PRS for Music radio royalties revenue, 2007–2014
Source: After PRS for Music (2008–2015)

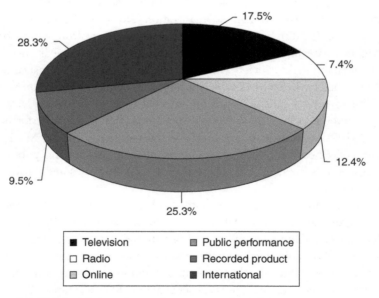

**Figure 7.4** PRS for Music radio royalties revenue share, 2014
Source: After PRS for Music (2015)

## Television and music television

Music plays also an important role in television. Music is essential in television films, drama series and documentaries, as well as in music format shows (e.g. *X Factor*, *Pop Idol*). Depending on the context, either music is specifically composed for television or pre-existing music is licensed for use on television.

Television programmes are usually produced by a production company. In the US, most of the production companies are affiliated to the major Hollywood studios such as Warner Bros., Disney, Paramount, Sony/Columbia, DreamWorks and so on. In Europe, independent production companies are usually commissioned by both public and private stations to produce music for films, series and documentaries.

In both cases, the production companies have to include a considerable amount of money for music in their production budgets. Brabec and Brabec (2004: 122) offer the following rule of thumb for the US: "If a show is a 1-hour series or a 2-hour movie of the week, the initial rough music budget would be $20,000 to $25,000 for the series episode and $40,000 to $50,000 for the movie of the week. For a mini-series, the per-hour budget would probably be projected somewhat higher." If the music is an original composition, the music budget usually includes payment to the composer, sound engineers and musicians, as well as the cost to rent the studio and instruments; if pre-existing music is used, the music budget includes synchronization fees.

## Produced music

If music is originated for a television project, the production company will commission a composer. In a television underscore contract, the composer commits to create the background score for a series or television film and the composition fee will depend on whether the music is composed for background usage only or also as title music. The fee also depends on whether music is composed for a pilot or for all episodes of a series (Brabec & Brabec 2004: 126–9).

In the US, compositions for television are usually "work for hire", which means that the production company becomes the owner of the work and of all related rights by buying out the creator. In this case the creator has to negotiate a share from both the performing royalties and all earnings derived from licensing beyond broadcasting. In Europe, the situation is different as the composer remains the author of the work and is, therefore, entitled to royalty payments from a collecting society separate from a contracted revenue share.

### Synchronization licences for pre-existing music

If pre-existing music is used in television shows and documentaries, television stations must obtain a synchronization licence – a synch licence – directly from the rights owner (publisher and/or author). The synch licence allows television stations to combine music with other content. Since specialized television production companies produce television films, series and documentaries, they are the licensees of synch licences and the television stations buy the final product.

Synchronization fees depend on whether music is used in free television, in pay/subscription television or in basic cable television. "The standard synchronisation fees charged by music publishers [in the US] usually range from $1,500 to over $3,000 for the use of a song in a television series for unlimited television distribution of the program for 5 to 6 years throughout the world" (Brabec & Brabec 2004: 138). The fees are higher for pay television and can range from $2,500 to $3,500, whereas synch fees for cable television are in the range of those charged for free television (Brabec & Brabec 2004: 139–40). It also makes a difference whether a song is sung by a character on camera ($3,000) or is used as theme music ($1,200) or as background music to a scene ($1,300) (Brabec & Brabec 2004: 144). If a master recording is used, the synchronization fee paid to the record company is considerably higher in the US. The reason for higher "master fees" is the lack of performance royalties for neighbouring rights in the US (Brabec & Brabec 2004: 139).

### Performance fees

The use of music in television also leads to the payment of performance fees. Collecting societies' pay-outs from licensing music performance rights to television stations and cable networks are considerably higher than radio fees. ASCAP collected $348.1 million of performance fees from the television sector, compared to $173.6 million from radio stations. Thus, licensing fees from

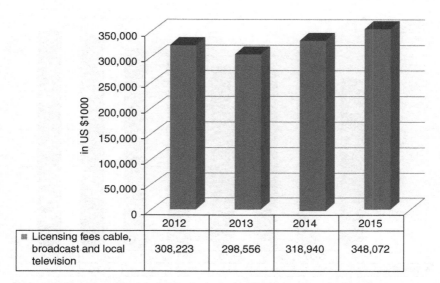

**Figure 7.5** ASCAP's revenue from licensing television stations, 2012–2015
Source: After ASCAP (2013–2016)

television and cable are the most important revenue source for ASCAP with a share of 34.7 per cent. Indeed, their economic relevance increased by 12.9 per cent from 2012 to 2015 (see Figure 7.5).

The figures for the UK's PRS for Music also confirm the economic significance of licensing music performance rights to television stations. After years of growth, television fees accounted for 17.5 per cent of total performance and mechanical rights income in 2014 and PRS for Music's income from television licensing fees has increased by 29 per cent from 2007 to 2014 (see Figure 7.6).

Music usage on television has become a highly significant revenue source for authors, music publishers, record companies and performers. The revenue originates not only from television usage but also from licensing income beyond broadcasting and synchronization. Music exposure on television helps to sell recorded music and generates income from home videos, sheet music sales and commercials.

## Music television

In 1981 a new age of music consumption emerged with MTV, a joint venture between Warner Communication, RCA's Communications Satellite

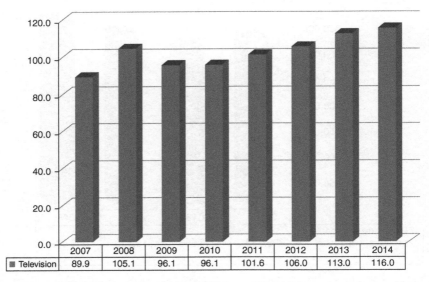

**Figure 7.6** PRS for Music television royalties revenue, 2007–2014
Source: After PRS for Music (2008–2015)

Corporation and IT&T. MTV was eventually sold to Viacom, and other music television stations such as Viva and VH1 were established (Tschmuck 2012: 167). MTV changed the rules of music marketing. It became obligatory to produce a more or less sophisticated music video to promote a new music release. This significantly increased the production costs in the recorded music industry with some music video productions costing $300,000, most notably Michael Jackson's *Thriller*, which was shot by Hollywood director John Landis (Garofalo 1997: 363).

However, with the advent of the Internet the popularity of music television rapidly decreased. MTV was relaunched as a youth television channel re-airing programmes from other Viacom-owned channels and has lost its relevance for showing music videos.

The video-sharing platform YouTube has replaced MTV as the most popular hub for music video consumption. YouTube, founded in 2005 (and sold a year later for $1,650 million to Google) (Tschmuck 2012: 191) is a user-generated platform and has attracted controversy over the copyright-infringing practices of users who upload content without the permission of the rights holders. Therefore, YouTube now operates Content ID technology to identify copyrighted material and enable rights holders either to enforce the removal of the video or to sell advertising around it.[6] Rights holders have also complained about low royalty payments, which are calculated on the advertising income a YouTube video generates. As a consequence, YouTube launched the Partner Program in 2007, which allows video uploaders to share in the advertising revenue (50–55 per cent) produced by the video.[7] Nevertheless, authors and publishers remain unhappy with YouTube's payments and continue to demand a higher share of YouTube's revenue.[8] Besides YouTube, several video-hosting services exist, but only a few focus on music, including Vevo – a joint venture between Universal Music Group, Sony Music Entertainment and Abu Dhabi Media – which is hosted by YouTube. Other video music services are Tape TV, a video platform based in Ireland that shows only music videos, and QQ Video, the most popular video-hosting site in China.

## Motion pictures

The music and film industry have been closely related since their emergence around 1900. Edison was not only the inventor of the phonograph, which laid the grounds for the modern music industry but also a pioneer in the infant film industry. In France, the Pathé Brothers were not only the first people to import talking machines to Europe and to become a major record producer, but also contributed patents to the emerging film industry to become the world's largest film equipment and film production company around 1900.

Music has played an integral part in movies from the start. Initially, a pianist played music to cover the noise made by the film projector; later, film producers realized the emotional effect of underscore music and commissioned composers to write the soundtrack for feature films (Wierzbicki 2009: 13). In the first half of the 1920s it was common for full-scale orchestras to accompany movie screenings in large motion picture theatres (Wierzbicki 2009: 48–50).

The music and film industry coalesced with the advent of sound films in 1926/27 with film production companies investing in music publishers and recording companies. After the Second World War, all major Hollywood studios had their own recorded music branches to promote movie soundtracks: Warner Bros. Records, Paramount Records, United Artists Records, 20th Century Fox Records and MGM Records (Tschmuck 2012: 134).

Synergies of the music and film industry reached a new level when disco music producer Robert Stigwood introduced the concept of cross-marketing with *Saturday Night Fever*. The music was used to promote the film and vice versa. The first single – "Stayin' Alive" – was released months before the soundtrack album and film were released, and was used in all film trailers. Two additional singles from the movie soundtrack followed before Christmas 1977, when the film and the soundtrack album were simultaneously released. Thirty million copies of the soundtrack album were sold worldwide within a few weeks and the film earned $130 million at the box office (Sanjek & Sanjek 1991: 235).

Music in motion pictures is without any doubt of huge economic significance to the music business. As with television productions, music can be composed specifically for motion pictures or pre-existing music can be licensed to be used in a film. A music publisher has to be approached by a film producer to license a song for a movie and the synchronization fees charged can range from $15,000 for low-budget independent productions to $60,000 for a major production, and even more for potential blockbusters (Brabec & Brabec 2004: 175). If an original sound recording is used, the film producer also has to pay for a master licence ($15,000 to $70,000) to the record company. Both licences include the right to show the film in cinemas and to include the song in trailers, previews and advertisements of the motion picture, as well as to distribute the film to terrestrial, cable and satellite television stations for the entire copyright term. Performance and broadcasting rights are usually excluded from the deal (Brabec & Brabec 2004: 177).

In the case of music originally produced for a motion picture, we have to distinguish between specific songs written for a movie and the background music score. Whereas film songwriting contracts are usually non-exclusive, background music composers work on an exclusive basis. In both cases, however, US film producers employ the composers/songwriters under a work-for-hire agreement. Thus, the film production company owns the song and pays a non-recoupable writing fee ranging from $1,500 for the lyrics of a song up to $300,000 if the songwriter is a famous performing artist. In addition, the songwriter is paid a guarantee of future income in the form of royalties – usually 50 per cent of mechanical revenue from recorded music sales, 50 per cent of synchronization royalties and a negotiated rate for sheet music sales (Brabec & Brabec 2004: 192). As previously mentioned, another scenario, more common in Europe, is for a film producer to enter into a standard publishing contract with a songwriter, who remains the copyright owner. In this case, the film producer pays the usual advances, which are fully recoupable from the publishing royalties.

The composition of background music scores is dominated by a handful of specialized composers, some of them gaining stardom, such as John Williams (*Star Wars, Superman, Harry Potter, Indiana Jones*), Henry Mancini (*The Pink Panther, Breakfast at Tiffany's, Charade*), Bill Conti (*Rocky, The Karate Kid, The Thomas Crown Affair*), Ennio Morricone (*Once Upon a Time in the West, The Untouchables, The Hateful Eight*) and Jerry Goldsmith (*Rambo, Chinatown, Total Recall, Basic Instinct*). Background music composers are hired:

> to compose all of the background music (in some cases, individual songs) for the film as well as to arrange and orchestrate the score; to conduct an orchestra to record the work; to produce, supervise and edit the recording of the score; and to deliver the final, fully edited and mixed master recording in accordance with the film's postproduction schedule.
>
> (Brabec & Brabec 2004: 208)

Depending on the past success of the composer, composing fees have ranged from $20,000 to $1 million – and even more for a well-known composer (Brabec & Brabec 2004: 209).

These figures suggest that a film music budget for major film studios can far exceed the million-dollar threshold, especially if the production company commissions a famous background music composer and uses popular preexisting songs in the movie. However, film music can generate considerable additional income from the sale of soundtrack albums, licensing the movie for home video and for television broadcast, earning publishing fees from collecting societies and licensing film music use in commercials.

## Commercials

The music industry and the advertising industry were already closely linked in the infant years of both industries. Manufacturers of branded goods used sheet music as an advertising platform (Wang 2013) and later big companies sponsored radio broadcasts.[9]

Thus, commercials on radio, television and the Internet are intimately connected with music. A manufacturer of branded goods will usually commission an advertising agency to create a campaign and that agency is usually tasked with finding suitable music for a jingle. Large advertising agencies may have in-house music departments with a staff of songwriters and music producers, or they may commission a specialized jingle production company – often associated with sound studios – to produce the required piece of music. According to Brabec and Brabec (2004: 227), the costs of a jingle in a 30 second commercial have ranged from $5,000 to over $50,000. The advertising agency may also choose to contract an independent songwriter to produce a jingle. Depending on the campaign and the songwriter's standing, the writing fees can range from a few hundred to a few thousand dollars. "If the agency is dealing with a superstar such as Britney Spears, Phil Collins, Stevie Wonder or Michael Jackson, however, the total creative fees can easily range from $250,000 to over $4 million if a multiple-year arrangement is involved" (Brabec & Brabec 2004: 227).

Agencies also use pre-existing music for advertising campaigns. Classical pieces of music are preferred since they are in the public domain and free from permission fees. Nevertheless, copyrighted music is also used, especially if the recognition of a song helps to identify a product or brand. Synchronization fees charged by music publishers for a pre-existing song have ranged from $100,000 to $300,000 (Brabec & Brabec 2004: 228). But for the right to use a hit song for one year in a commercial, advertising agencies have typically paid fees of more than $1 million. If a master recording is used for the jingle, the advertising agency also has to approach the record label owning the recording. In most cases a combined fee that can range from $250,000 to over $750,000 has to be paid to the record label and the publisher (Brabec & Brabec 2004: 229).

These figures show that producing a jingle for a commercial can be very costly and the advertising business is therefore an important secondary market for music exploitation. Although no reliable data exists for the advertising music market, it can be assumed that many sound studios, music producers and songwriters earn an essential income from producing jingles, perhaps even more than from selling recorded music.

## Video games

In 2011 the video game music composer Christopher Tin became the first person to win a Grammy for a song – "Baba Yetu", which was part of the video game *Civilization IV* – specifically written for a videogame.[10] The Grammy award acknowledged the important role music plays in video games, as an essential element of a game's dramaturgy. It describes the game's different characters and changes when players reach a new level in the game.

Despite the relevance of music to video games, the percentage of the budget allocated to music is low compared to other aspects of the video game production. Whereas an average production budget for a triple-A video game can be $20 million and more, the expenses for music are usually below 5 per cent of the overall budget. The per game synchronization fees charged by music publishers range from $2,500 for less popular music titles to upwards of $20,000 for a hit song. Because of these high synchronization fees, video games producers commission independent composers in work-for-hire agreements similar to film and television underscore music contracts. The big production companies even employ composers to deliver music for video games (Brabec & Brabec 2004: 421–2).

However, where music constitutes the core of the video game, music-licensing fees can account for a much higher share of the overall production budget since the producer will have to pay hefty licensing fees. Paying such high fees is worth it, however, since music-related video games are often best-sellers. In the early 1990s, *Michael Jackson's Moonwalker* dance game was very popular and the Karaoke game *SingStar* triggered a boom of sing-and-play-along games that culminated in the second half of the 2000s with *Guitar Hero* and *Rock Band*. Some 16.4 million units of *Guitar Hero III: Legends of Rock* have been sold since its release in October 2007, and by April 2016 gamers had bought 61.7 million copies of the different *Guitar Hero* releases, including the band specials with Metallica, Aerosmith and Van Halen. Similarly, the different releases of dance video game *Just Dance* have sold 58.4 million units since its initial release (see Table 7.2).

Clearly, then, video games have become a relevant revenue source for music publishers and composers and function as an important music licensing market.

**Table 7.2** The top five music-related video games, 2005–2016

| | Title | Global sales in million units for all platforms | Publisher |
|---|---|---|---|
| 1 | Guitar Hero – all releases | 61.74 | Activision |
| 2 | Just Dance – all releases | 58.40 | Ubisoft |
| 3 | Rock Band – all releases | 27.96 | MTV Games |
| 4 | SingStar – all releases | 22.09 | Sony Computer Entertainment |
| 5 | Dance Dance Revolution – all releases | 21.68 | Konami Digital Entertainment |

Source: After www.vgchartz.com/gamedb/ (retrieved 30 May 2016)

## Sponsorship and branding

In November 1983 Michael Jackson and Pepsi teamed up to launch a ground-breaking sponsorship campaign that was to change the music business. As we have seen, the sponsoring of bands by manufacturers of branded goods goes back to the jazz bands of the early 1930s. However, Michael Jackson's deal with Pepsi was very different. The $5 million partnership included: the advert "Pepsi: The Choice of a New Generation", which used Jackson's song "Billie Jean" as the jingle; tour sponsorship; Jackson logos on Pepsi cans; co-branded display material for supermarkets; and several PR events with the superstar hosted by Pepsi. The first campaign increased Pepsi's sales to $7,700 million and encouraged the company to strike a second worldwide $10 million deal to support Jackson's release of the *Bad* album and the following world tour in 1987/88.[11] Through the sponsorship deal, the soft drink's brand and the artist's brand became inseparably linked: Pepsi was Michael Jackson and Michael Jackson was Pepsi.

Other superstar artists have followed Michael Jackson's example and entered into sponsoring and brand partnerships with big companies; for example, Volkswagen sponsored the European tours of Pink Floyd (1994), the Rolling Stones (1995) and Bon Jovi (1996) and issued special VW Golf editions bearing the bands' names (Meffert 2013: 713).

Today, music sponsorship is commonplace and the most active sponsors include Anheuser-Busch Beverages, the Pepsi Company, Brown-Forman, Millercoors, Coca Cola and Uber. In North America, sponsorship spending

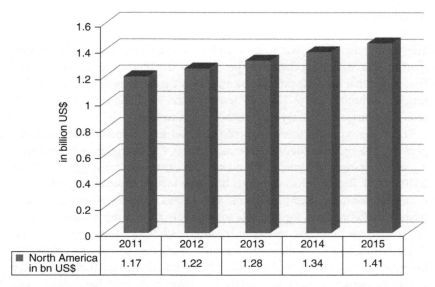

| ■ North America in bn US$ | 2011 | 2012 | 2013 | 2014 | 2015 |
|---|---|---|---|---|---|
| | 1.17 | 1.22 | 1.28 | 1.34 | 1.41 |

**Figure 7.7** Music-related sponsorship spending in North America, 2011–2015
Source: IEGSR (2015)

on tours, venues and music festivals has increased over past years and has resulted in an increase in sponsorship volume of almost 15 per cent to $1,340 million from 2011 to 2014, with further growth expected for 2015 (see Figure 7.7).

Some artists have gone further and market their brands by creating new product lines, especially in the field of fashion and fragrances. In 2005 Beyoncé established the fashion line House of Deréon to market sportswear, handbags, shoes and other apparel under the artist's brand in North America.[12] As a cross-marketing effect, Beyoncé mentions House of Deréon in her songs, for example in "Get Me Bodied" from the *B'Day* album and in "Single Ladies" from the album *I Am … Sasha Fierce* (Tschmuck 2016: 21). Neil Young promoted the Pono music player for a successful crowdfunding campaign.[13] And Dr. Dre was a co-founder of Beats Electronics manufacturing the Beats by Dr. Dre Studio headphones, which was sold along with the Beats music-streaming service to Apple Inc. for $3,200 million in 2014.[14] Thus for well-known artists branding has become a significant revenue source.

## Merchandising

Finally, merchandising has to be mentioned as a relevant secondary music market. Merchandising covers the production, distribution and promotion of fan articles that have the same logo and deliver the same message as a branded article (Tschmuck 2016: 21). The artist's brand is, therefore, monetized by selling T-shirts, caps, scarves and other goods to fans.

There are typically three partners involved in the merchandising business: (1) the rights holder (licenser, e.g. artist), (2) the rights user (licensee, e.g. manufacturer of branded products) and (3) the licensing agency (Korn 2010: 21–3). Rights holders aim at a licensing income from selling merchandising articles using their (artist) brands, whereas rights users seek to accomplish a marketing goal, for example to penetrate an existing market segment and to increase brand awareness and brand sensibility for their own products. The licensing agency mediates the merchandising deal and plays a coordinating role between rights holders and rights users. The merchandising agency covers the design organization and the execution of the merchandising activities, charging a fee for its services (Korn 2010: 22).

Merchandising can generate significant income for artists. Bon Jovi reportedly earned $2 million from merchandising in 2014, which is higher than the band's revenue from music download sales of $300,000.[15] A study of the Future of Music Coalition[16] calculated that 6.6 per cent of a rock band's revenue stems from selling merchandise. Although the average merchandising income for hip hop/rap and country acts, as well as jazz and classical musicians is significantly lower, merchandising does not just generate additional income but also helps to build an artist's brand. And so, merchandising, sponsoring and branding are closely related secondary music markets.

## Notes

1. Legend has it that during a bar visit, Storz and Stewart observed that a waitress, while cleaning up after closing, selected the same song from the jukebox that patrons had repeatedly played (Garofalo 1997: 100).
2. ASCAP, "Licensing types for radio", www.ascap.com/licensing/types/radio (retrieved 15 May 2016).
3. Radio Music License Committee (RMLC), "Licensing History", www.radiomlc.org/ (retrieved 15 May 2016).

4. National Religious Broadcasters Music License Committee (NRBMLC), "Licensing History", www.nrbmlc.com/music-licensing/music-licensing-history/ (retrieved 15 May 2016).
5. In the US, terrestrial radio stations do not have to pay a licensing fee for using sound recordings.
6. The Guardian, "Why Is the Music Industry Battling YouTube and What Happens Next?", 20 May 2016, www.theguardian.com/technology/2016/may/20/music-industry-battling-google-youtube-what-happens-next (retrieved 25 May 2016).
7. See YouTube, "YouTube for Creators", www.youtube.com/yt/creators/benefit-levels.html (retrieved 25 May 2016).
8. Music Business Worldwide, "YouTube Is Paying Less than £0.0009 per Stream to UK Record Labels", 20 May 2016, www.musicbusinessworldwide.com/youtube-is-paying-less-than-0-0009-per-stream-to-uk-record-labels/ (retrieved 25 May 2016).
9. See Chapter 7: Radio broadcasting.
10. See Billboard.biz, "Videogame Composer Christopher Tin Talks Historic Grammy Win", 14 February 2011, www.billboard.com/biz/articles/news/1179275/videogame-composer-christopher-tin-talks-historic-grammy-win (retrieved 30 May 2016).
11. Billboard.biz, "Michael Jackson, Pepsi Made Marketing History", 3 July 2009, www.billboard.com/articles/news/268213/michael-jackson-pepsi-made-marketing-history (retrieved 2 June 2016).
12. See www.lipsy.co.uk/store/brands/house-of-dereon (retrieved 21 February 2017).
13. Billboard.biz, "Neil Young's Pono Raises $6 Million, Third Biggest Kickstarter Ever", 15 April 2014, www.billboard.com/biz/articles/news/digital-and-mobile/6054256/neil-youngs-pono-raises-6-million-third-biggest (retrieved 2 June 2016).
14. Billboard.biz, "Apple Buys Beats in $3 Billion Deal; Iovine, Dr. Dre to Join Tech Giant", 28 May 2014, www.billboard.com/biz/articles/news/digital-and-mobile/6099405/apple-buys-beats-in-3-billion-deal-iovine-dr-dre-to (retrieved 2 June 2016).
15. Billboard.biz, "Music's Top 40 Money Makers 2014: The Rich List", 10 March 2014, www.billboard.com/articles/list/5930326/music-s-top-40-money-makers-2014-the-rich-list (retrieved 2 June 2016).
16. Future of Music Coalition, MIDEM: Bands, Brands and Revenue, 31 January 2012, http://money.futureofmusic.org/the-new-power-trio-bands-brands-and-revenue/ (retrieved 2 June 2016).

# 8

# MUSIC LABOUR MARKETS

If we buy into the Forbes World's Highest Paid Celebrity Top 100 List,[1] musicians were among the best-paid entertainers and athletes in 2015. A third of the top 100 highest paid celebrities were musicians. Pop superstar Taylor Swift headed the Forbes list with annual earnings of $170 million, followed by the boy group One Direction with $110 million. Adele, Madonna and Rihanna followed ranked ninth, twelfth and thirteenth, respectively.

Whereas Forbes compiles all revenue streams, the Billboard Money Makers List focuses on music-related revenues. Taylor Swift once again ranks first with annual earnings of $73.5 million from touring, recorded music sales, streaming and publishing. US country singer Kenny Chesney follows with $39.8 million, ahead of the Rolling Stones and Billy Joel with $39.6 million and $31.7 million, respectively (see Table 8.1).

The Billboard Money Makers List highlights that almost all artists with extraordinarily high earnings – except Adele – were on tour in 2015. Thus, at least two thirds of the music-related revenue derives from the concert business. In most cases, touring accounts for more than 90 per cent of total earnings. If we ignore the case of Adele, who has a special position in the recorded music market, revenues from recorded music sales are modest compared to touring income. In high-charting Taylor Swift's case, for example, her earnings from selling CDs and music downloads amounts to just 10 per cent of her total income. Streaming income is even less relevant for the top 10 superstar artists, accounting for no more than 4 per cent of the artists' revenue mix. Indeed, streaming income is usually lower than music publishing revenue.

**Table 8.1** The Billboard Money Makers List 2015 top ten artists (in US$)

| Artist | Recorded Music Sales | % | Streaming | % | Publishing | % | Touring | % | Total |
|---|---|---|---|---|---|---|---|---|---|
| Taylor Swift | 7,200,000 | 1.1 | 564,000 | 0.8 | 4,100,000 | 6.1 | 61,700,000 | 92.0 | 73,564,000 |
| Kenny Chesney | 1,100,000 | 2.8 | 239,600 | 0.6 | 313,200 | 0.8 | 38,100,000 | 95.8 | 39,752,800 |
| The Rolling Stones | 1,400,000 | 3.5 | 382,600 | 1.0 | 509,100 | 1.3 | 37,300,000 | 94.2 | 39,591,700 |
| Billy Joel | 801,200 | 2.5 | 339,400 | 1.1 | 453,200 | 1.4 | 30,100,000 | 95.0 | 31,693,800 |
| One Direction | 3,100,000 | 12.8 | 891,800 | 3.7 | 652,700 | 2.7 | 19,600,000 | 80.8 | 24,244,500 |
| Grateful Dead | 843,300 | 3.6 | 114,800 | 0.5 | 276,500 | 1.2 | 22,500,000 | 94.8 | 23,734,600 |
| Luke Bryan | 4,000,000 | 17.3 | 511,500 | 2.2 | 694,900 | 3.0 | 17,900,000 | 77.5 | 23,106,400 |
| U2 | 465,800 | 2.1 | 289,400 | 1.3 | 383,800 | 1.8 | 20,600,000 | 94.8 | 21,739,000 |
| Adele | 16,300,000 | 79.6 | 488,000 | 2.4 | 3,700,000 | 18.1 | 0 | 0.0 | 20,488,000 |
| Maroon 5 | 2,700,000 | 14.1 | 796,400 | 4.2 | 2,600,000 | 13.6 | 13,000,000 | 68.1 | 19,096,400 |

Source: www.billboard.com/articles/news/list/7356755/billboard-top-40-money-makers-rich-list (retrieved 27 July 2016)

## Superstar theories

The Forbes and Billboard lists do not reflect the economic reality of professional musicians. The rankings represent an extremely small segment of the artistic labour market – the superstar business. According to Rosen (1981: 845), superstars "earn enormous amounts of money and dominate the activities in which they engage". Adam Smith, the father of modern economics, had already addressed "[t]he exorbitant rewards to players, opera singers, opera dancers, &c." (Smith (1776) 1811: 163) in the late eighteenth century. He explained the superstar phenomenon by pointing to "the rarity and beauty of the talents and the discredit of employing them in this manner". These exorbitant earnings attract more talent than the market can reward, leading to a permanent oversupplied artistic labour market with relatively low average earnings. Smith also points to the mechanism behind the extremely skewed earnings distribution: "In a profession where twenty fail for one that succeeds, that one ought to gain all that should have been gained by the unsuccessful twenty" (Smith (1776) 1811: 161).

Smith had therefore described the winner-takes-all principle that rules modern entertainment markets. Sherwin Rosen (1981) demonstrates in his superstar model that small differences in talent can cause wide earnings differences. Since "lesser talent is often a poor substitute for greater talent" (Rosen 1981: 846), the demand for talent is a convex function: that is, if one person is twice as talented than another, she/he earns more than twice the money than the less talented person earns. Since the talent function is extremely convex, superstar earnings are enormously high compared to artists whose talent is merely average (see Figure 8.1).

However, Rosen (1981: 856) further argues that preferences alone do not explain superstardom, because the emergence of a mass media market has to be considered too. Artists can now reach millions of fans at more or less the same cost as it would take to reach a small audience. Mass media multiplies the earnings effect and creates a highly skewed income distribution.

In "The Economics of Rising Stars", MacDonald (1988) provides a dynamic version of Rosen's model. Since the market entry barriers are low, young, talented musicians overflow the market. At each stage of a gatekeeping process some of them drop out of the race – for example, they may be negatively reviewed or become otherwise frustrated. The process leaves only a small number of successful artists earning the money the drop-outs left in the market.

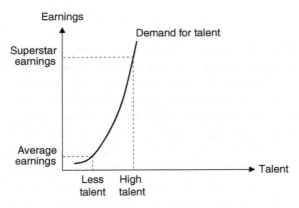

**Figure 8.1** The convex demand function for talent

However, Rosen's superstar model has two problems: (1) it is unrealistic to assume that talent is observable without cost; and (2) there is no measurement for talent. In testing the elasticity of record sales in the US from 1955 to 1987 with regard to voice quality, Hamlen (1991, 1994) finds no evidence that small differences in ability lead to disproportionate levels of success. Thus, Chung and Cox (1994) rejected Rosen's superstar model and empirically demonstrated that even with equal talent, superstardom can emerge. They show that the likelihood that a consumer will buy a CD by a particular artist is correlated to the artist's previous success: the higher the sales for previous CDs were, the higher the likelihood that consumers will buy the artist's new CD. Thus, artistic success follows a stochastic snowballing effect.

In "Stardom and Talent" (1985), Adler provides a model that avoids Rosen's talent assumption. According to Adler, consumers invest time and even money to acquire specialized knowledge about an artist. The more knowledge a fan accumulates, the less likely this fan is to shift her/his attention to other artists because of the time and money (opportunity costs) she/he has already invested in this particular artist. However, fans with accumulated specialized knowledge influence less well-informed consumers by recommending a favoured artist. Similar to a snowball effect, as many people spend money on a particular artist, buying records and concert tickets, resulting in the artist's market dominance. Adler interprets stardom as a "market device to economise on learning costs in activities where 'the more you know the more you enjoy'" (Adler

1985: 208). Owing to the evolution of mass media (records, radio, television), the snowball effect triggered by the accumulation of consumption capital has accelerated, and one can assume that digitization further intensifies the super-star effect rather than distributing income from superstars to less-established artists. Hence Elberse (2013: 11) concludes that "blockbusters will become more – not less – relevant to popular culture and blockbuster strategies will thrive" in the new digital economy. Ordanini and Nunes (2016) find that fewer artists made it to the US single charts after iTunes entered the market in 2003, confirming a stronger superstar-effect resulting from digitization.

## Artistic labour market theories and the music sector

Superstar theories focus on the demand side of the artistic labour market. However, this analysis should not neglect the supply side. The standard labour market model is based on the assumption of a homogeneous work force, where each worker can easily be substituted for another. As the superstar-dom models suggest, however, music labour markets are different. Apart from orchestral and session musicians, labour in the music sector is heterogene-ous. Thus, we can observe not only different talent but also different skills. It is evident that a violinist cannot be substituted by a flautist and vice versa. Musicians invest a lot of time and even money to become highly professional-ized and specialized singers and instrumentalists. The opportunity costs rise with the level of specialization as well as the competition for scarce orchestra jobs. Therefore, it is common for musicians to hold multiple jobs either in music-related fields such as education, booking, artist management and so on, or outside the artistic field as waiters/waitresses and taxi drivers.

Neoclassical labour economics assumes a trade-off between income-generating labour time and leisure: the amount of one's leisure time expands as one's income increases, and vice versa. However, many people working in the music sector are willing to work for low and even no compensation. This fact contradicts the standard labour market models and calls for an alter-native explanation. Throsby (1994) proposes a work preference model for understanding artist labour markets. Since artists have to earn their living, they work for an acceptable income even outside the art sector to "subsidize" their artistic work. "[N]on-arts work is simply a means of enabling as much time as possible to be spent at the (preferred) artistic occupation" (Throsby 2001: 102). In the work preference model, income is "a constraint that takes up labour time the artist would prefer to spend on art work that has cultural value" (Towse 2010: 301). Thus, musicians trade off income from non-music-related occupations with music-related ones. If music provides sufficient earnings, musicians stop driving taxis and so on and devote their work time entirely to music production in the widest sense.

Another characteristic of the artistic labour market is that long-term and salaried employment is an exception. Apart from salaried orchestral musicians and ensemble opera singers, most musicians are self-employed. Labour economics distinguishes between income, which denotes a regular payment to an employee, and earnings including income but also revenue streams from other sources (Towse 2010: 298). Thus, earnings is the more suitable term for musicians who are independent contractors working on a project basis. Musicians even "behave like entrepreneurs managing small businesses and work portfolios and their labor market may be compared to a network of small ad hoc firms trading along matching processes from one project to the other" (Menger 2006: 704). Aronson (1991) therefore assumes that artists' earnings depend on not only their talent and skills but also on their entrepreneurial and managerial abilities.

As a result of the high level of self-employment in the music sector, payment levels differ over time and among musicians. Studies[2] even identify an "earnings penalty", which denotes lower returns from educational investments by artists compared to other occupations (e.g. managers, lawyers, medical doctors, etc.). If there is an "earnings penalty" for artists as most of the studies suggest (Towse 2010: 330), we have to explain why such an earnings gap exists. Santos (1976) suggests that artists are risk-takers, which contrasts with the standard neoclassical model of a risk-averse and profit-maximizing individual. Artists, however, enter the artistic labour market despite the knowledge that they are probably going to face low earnings, uncertain career paths and a high risk of unemployment. They nevertheless hope to succeed by overcoming all obstacles. Another explanation why artists accept an "earnings penalty" is the "psychic income" argument. Artistic occupations offer two types of rewards – monetary and non-monetary. Thus, non-monetary rewards, such as personal autonomy, work variety, low level of routine, creativity, innovativeness and social recognition, compensate artists for earning

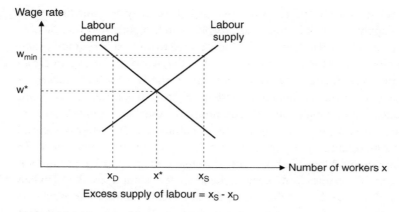

**Figure 8.2** Excess supply of artistic labour markets
Source: After Towse (2010: 294)

a lower income relative to what they could earn in jobs that are less desirable to them (Menger 2006: 777).

However, the peculiarities of the artistic labour market lead to an oversupply or excess supply in the artistic work force. Excess supply means that the quantity supplied exceeds the quantity demanded (Towse 2010: 303) (see Figure 8.2).

Menger (2006: 782–8) suggests further causes of excess supply on the artistic labour market. Innovations extend economies of scale and lower market entry barriers. As a result, more artists enter the labour market, which increases the supply of works. Since "nobody knows" (Caves 2000) who will prevail in the competition for consumers' attention, artists remain in the labour market hoping to gain stardom.

Monopolistic competition among artists is another cause of an excess supply in the artistic workforce. As long as artists are demanded, they benefit from a temporary monopoly. However, artists who are less in demand cannot profit from a unique market position; instead, they try to gain it by investing more time in their productions. As a result, the market is oversupplied. Thus, less-recognized artists have to supply their works at a low price or even at a zero price. "[T]his explains why so many creative artists, though working hard and being fully committed, may suffer from low or even very low income levels" (Menger 2006: 787).

Changing industry and organizational structures may also nurture excess labour supply. Christopherson and Storper (1989) highlighted that flexible specialization in the Hollywood film industry led to more subcontracting and self-employment of former employees in the Hollywood studios. Vertical dis-integration also affected the music industry in the late 1960s. Songwriters and music producers became independent short-term contractors to record companies. Despite higher artistic autonomy, the greater employment insta-bility increased dependence on the record companies. The latter benefitted from the increasing variety of talent supplying more works than before. To overcome the problems with a highly disintegrated and flexible production process, the companies form creative clusters – for example, think of Tin Pan Alley in New York City at the end of the nineteenth century and Nashville today as the centre for country music production. The music clusters attract talented musicians, thus increasing excess supply from which the recorded music companies profit (Menger 2006: 784–6). In short, excess supply is not just a supply-side phenomenon of the artistic labour market; it also enshrines the demand for talent.

In an oversupplied labour market, the need for information about the qual-ity of the workforce is high. Intermediaries such as artist agencies, bookers and artist managers provide this information and match the demand and sup-ply side of the market. They act as "market-makers" (Towse 2010: 304), pro-viding the necessary information about the artist's quality. The fees charged by artist agencies signals quality: the higher the fee charged, the more quality the artist provides. The agencies are interested in raising artist fees since they benefit by earning a percentage (usually 15–20 per cent) of the overall fee paid. The role of "market makers" has become more important in the course of digitization, since the oversupply of labour has increased, thus making the information problem more complex.

## Revenue streams for musicians: the US case

The Artist Revenue Streams project identified 45 revenue streams for US artists.[3] The list covers revenues for songwriters/composers, performers and recording artists, session musicians, music teachers and producers, but it also includes brand-related revenue and music funding (see Table 8.2).

**Table 8.2** Revenue streams for US musicians

| | |
|---|---|
| *Songwriter and composer revenue* | |
| Publisher advance | Bulk payment to songwriter/composer as part of a publishing deal |
| Mechanical royalties | Royalties generated through the reproduction of recordings of works |
| Commissions | A request from an ensemble, presenter, orchestra or other entity for a composer to create an original work for them |
| Public performance (PRO) royalties | Royalties generated when works are played on radio, television, in clubs and restaurants |
| Streaming mechanical royalties | Royalties generated when works are streamed via on-demand services |
| Composing original works for broadcast | A commercial request to compose a jingle, soundtrack, score or other musical work for a film, television or cable show, or for an advertising agency |
| Synch licences | Involves licensing an existing work for use in a movie, documentary, television, video games, the Internet or a commercial |
| Sheet music sales | Revenue generated by the sale or licensed reproduction of works as sheet music |
| Lyric display | Revenue generated by the licensed display of lyrics |
| Ringtones | Revenue generated from licensing works for use as ringtones |
| Songwriter awards program | Awards given by ASCAP and BMI Foundations to writer members of any genre whose performances are primarily in venues outside of broadcast media |
| Publisher settlement | Payment from publishers to writers for litigation settlements |
| *Recording artist revenue* | |
| Record label advance | Paid to recording artist as part of signing a deal |
| Record label support | Money from label for recording or tour support |
| Retail sales | Revenue generated from selling physical recordings in retail stores or via mail-order |
| Digital sales | Revenue generated from selling recordings digitally/online as permanent downloads |
| Sales at shows | Revenue generated from selling recordings at shows/live performances |
| Interactive service payments | Revenue generated when recordings are streamed via on-demand services |
| Digital performance royalties | Revenue generated when sound recordings are played on internet radio, Sirius XM, Pandora |

**Table 8.2** *(cont.)*

*Recording artist revenue (cont.)*

| | |
|---|---|
| Master use synch licences | Involves licensing an existing sound recording for use in a movie, documentary, television, video games, the Internet or a commercial |
| AARC royalties | Collected for digital recording of songs, foreign private copying levies, and foreign record rental royalties, distributed to US artists by Alliance of Artists and Recording Companies (AARC) |
| Neighboring rights royalties | Collected for the foreign performance of recordings |
| Film musicians secondary markets fund | Paid to performers on recordings used in film, television and other secondary uses by the Film Musicians' Secondary Markets Fund |
| Sound recording special payments fund | Paid to performers for the sales of music recorded under the American Federation of Musicians (AFM) collective bargaining agreement by the Sound Recordings Special Payments Fund |
| Screen Actors Guild (SAG) and American Federation of Television and Radio Artists (AFTRA) contingent scale payments | Paid to non-royalty artists when a recording hits certain sales plateaus |
| Label settlements | Payments from labels to recording artists for litigation settlements |

*Performer and session musician revenue*

| | |
|---|---|
| Salary as member of an orchestra or ensemble | Income earned as a salaried member of an orchestra, band or ensemble |
| Shows/performance fees | Revenue generated from playing in a live setting |
| Session musician/sideman fees for studio work | Payments to studio musicians/freelancers/sidemen for work in a recording studio |
| Session musician/sideman fees for live work | Payments to studio musicians/freelancers/sidemen for work in a live setting/on tour |
| Non-featured artist payments | Payments from the AFM and SAG-AFTRA Intellectual Property Rights Distribution Fund, which distributes recording and performance royalties to non-featured artists |

*Teaching and producing*

| | |
|---|---|
| Music teacher | Revenue generated from teaching a musical craft |
| Producer | Payment for producing another artist's work in the studio or in a live setting |
| Honoraria or speaker's fees | Payment for conducting a lecture, workshop or masterclass |

**Table 8.2** *(cont.)*

| *Brand-related revenue* | |
| --- | --- |
| Merchandise sales | Revenue generated from selling branded merchandise (T-shirts, hoodies, posters, etc.) |
| Fan club | Money received directly from fans who are subscribing to a fan club |
| YouTube partner program | Shared advertising revenue, paid to partners by YouTube |
| Advertising revenue | Miscellaneous income generated by website properties (click-thrus, commissions on Amazon sales, etc.) |
| Persona licensing | Payments from a brand that is licensing the artist's name or likeness (video games, comic books) |
| Product endorsements | Payments or free goods from a brand for and artist endorsing or using their product |
| Acting | Payments for appearances in television, commercials, movies |

| *Fan, corporate and foundation funding and other sources* | |
| --- | --- |
| Fan funding | Money directly from fans to support or pre-sell an upcoming recording project or tour on a crowdfunding platform, e.g. Kickstarter, Pledge Music |
| Sponsorship | Corporate support for a tour, or for a band/ensemble |
| Grants | Foundation or public arts grants to support works/projects from foundations, state or federal agencies |
| Arts administrator | Money paid specifically for managing the administrative aspects of a group of which the artist is a member |

Source: After http://money.futureofmusic.org/wordpress/wp-content/uploads/2012/01/revenue-streams-handoutlist.pdf (retrieved 1 August 2016)

In an article based on the Artist Revenue Streams project, DiCola (2013) highlights that on average the largest revenue stream for musicians comes from live performances, which account for 28 per cent of total annual income. Teaching is another important earnings source with a share of 22 per cent. Salaries from orchestras, bands and other ensembles account for 19 per cent and session work for 10 per cent. Less important are revenues from compositions (6 per cent) and sound recordings (6 per cent). The smallest contribution to a musician's annual income comes from merchandising sales (2 per cent). Other revenue sources account for the remaining 7 per cent of the musicians' earnings (see Figure 8.3).

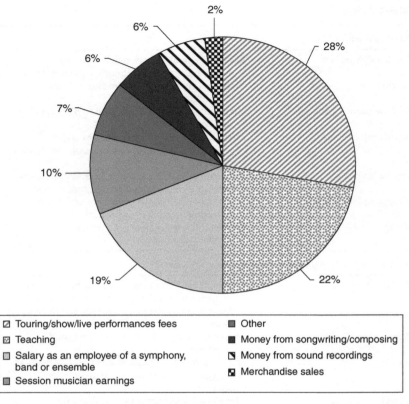

**Figure 8.3** Average share of a musician's income from major music revenue streams
Source: DiCola (2013: 57)

However, a detailed analysis of several income groups reveals remarkable differences. The top income group – earning more than $330,000 from music – reported an annual revenue from compositions of 28 per cent. Therefore, DiCola (2013: 34) concludes: "[T]his simply tells us that composition revenue accompanies success." In contrast, revenue from sound recordings does not exceed 5 per cent for any of the income groups in the top half of the population. For the lowest income group, sound recordings account at least for 9 per cent of the total annual revenue from music. Nevertheless, sound recording revenue does not play an important role for any of the income groups. For the lower income groups session work is more important. However, the most important revenue stream for the lower half of the income groups comes from live performances (see Figure 8.4).

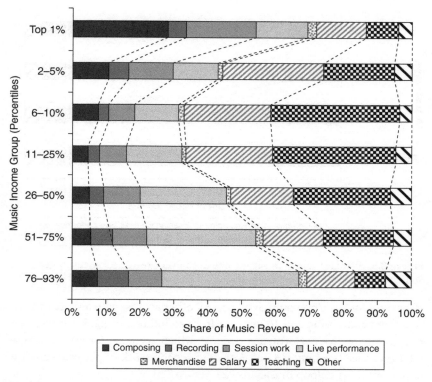

**Figure 8.4** Average share of music income from major revenue streams by income group
Source: DiCola (2013: 57)

The survey also reveals considerable differences in revenue shares by four genre categories: classical, jazz, rock/pop and other genres. Whereas classical musicians make only 10 per cent of their revenue from live performances, they earn 36 per cent instead from salaries and 33 per cent from teaching. Session work is less important for classical musicians with a share of 10 per cent, and revenue from composing and sound recording is more or less irrelevant. Jazz musicians mainly rely on revenue from live performances, which accounts for 37 per cent of their average annual income. A further 15 per cent derives from salaries and 24 per cent from teaching. Similar to classical musicians, jazz musicians earn only a small proportion from composing (4 per cent) and sound recording (3 per cent). These two revenue sources are more

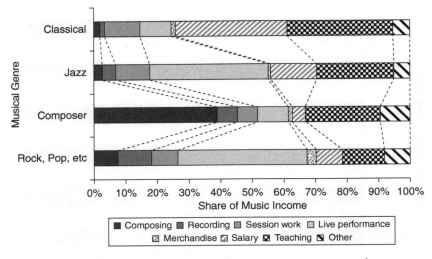

**Figure 8.5** Average share of music income from major revenue sources by genre
Source: DiCola (2013: 57)

important for rock/pop musicians (and all other genres) with a share of 8 per cent from composing and 10 per cent from sound recording. However, they rely heavily on live performance revenue, which accounts for 40 per cent of total revenue. Teaching (13 per cent) and session work (9 per cent) are less important for rock/pop musicians (see Figure 8.5).

The survey also illustrates the differences in the revenue mix by income group and genre. No income group of classical and jazz musicians relies much on composing and sound recording for generating revenue. Only the top income group (first percentile) of jazz musicians relies to some extent on these copyright-related revenue streams, which comprise more than 25 per cent of their total revenues. Session work is only relevant for the highest and lowest income groups of classical musicians, whereas teaching is the predominant revenue source for the middle income groups. With a share of 5–10 per cent, session work is less important for all income groups of jazz musicians. Rock and pop musicians rely more on copyright-related revenue sources than musicians of other genres. The top two income groups earn more than a quarter from composing and sound recording annually. Nevertheless, the relevance of copyright-related income declines with decreasing annual earnings. Likewise, session work is more important for the top two income groups of rock and pop musicians with a share of 25 per cent. The less rock and pop musicians earn annually, the less important is revenue from session work.

Self-defined songwriters and composers have a different mix of revenue streams. Forty per cent of their annual income derives from composing and a quarter comes from teaching. At least 10 per cent of their revenue consists of live performance income and 5 per cent derives from each of sound recording and session work. The top two income groups of composers rely more heavily on their main occupation – composing – than lower income groups: nearly 75 per cent of their income derives from that source. As overall revenue from music decreases, composing fees become less important as a revenue source and account for less than 50 per cent of the annual earnings from music. In turn, teaching becomes more important with as annual earnings decrease.

Digitization has increased diversity in musicians' revenue streams. Thus, DiCola (2013: 43) concludes: "Musicians play multiple roles in their music-related work ... Each musician is like his or her own small business; musicians have to be ready to adjust to different opportunities and changing consumer demand" and "[p]olicymakers should expect musicians to adjust their alloca-tion of time among roles in response to such changes".

If the entire music business shifts away from recorded music sales towards live performance and teaching, then legislators should adjust to such a new situation by supporting the live music business and strengthening the finan-cial basis of orchestras and music ensembles, as well as music education insti-tutions, to improve the economic status of musicians.

## Secondary music labour markets

A study of the German music economy (Seufert *et al.* 2015) counted 127,616 employees in the music sector in 2014, 21.9 per cent or 27,895 of whom were self-employed composers/lyricists and/or interpreters. They contributed 15 per cent of gross value added to the German music econ-omy. The remaining 78.1 per cent (almost 100,000 employees) were not creatives in a narrow sense. The largest group of 32,629 persons (25.6 per cent) were employed in the live music sector. A further 28,506 persons (22.3 per cent) worked in music education (in private music schools and as freelance teachers). The German recorded music industry employed

**Table 8.3** The labour music market in the German music economy, 2014

| Sectors | Total | Self-employed | % | Employed | % | Freelancer | % |
|---|---|---|---|---|---|---|---|
| Live music[1] | 32,629 | 2,988 | 9.2% | 29,641 | 90.8% | 13,031 | 39.9% |
| Music education[2] | 28,506 | 27,629 | 96.9% | 877 | 3.1% | 19,440 | 68.2% |
| Creatives | 27,895 | 22,196 | 79.6% | 5,699 | 20.4% | 8,921 | 32.0% |
| Recorded music | 19,866 | 4,404 | 22.2% | 15,462 | 77.8% | 3,101 | 15.6% |
| Musical instruments | 14,795 | 2,268 | 15.3% | 12,527 | 84.7% | 941 | 6.4% |
| Music publishing | 2,855 | 240 | 8.4% | 2,615 | 91.6% | 372 | 13.0% |
| Collecting societies | 1,070 | 0 | 0.0% | 1,070 | 100.0% | 0 | 0.0% |
| Total | 127,616 | 59,725 | 46.8% | 67,891 | 53.2% | 45,806 | 35.9% |

Source: After Seufert *et al.* (2015: 14–15)

Notes

[1] Employees of publicly funded music theatres and orchestras are not included.

[2] Employees of public music schools and universities/conservatories are not included.

19,866 persons (15.6 per cent) and the musical instruments sector (production and sales) another 14,795 persons (11.6 per cent). The remaining 2,855 (2.2 per cent) and 1,070 (0.8 per cent), respectively, were employed by music publishers and music collecting societies. These figures highlight that the secondary music labour market in Germany was almost 3.6 times larger than the primary labour market of the creatives (authors and interpreters). The secondary labour market's contribution to the gross value added was almost six times higher than that of the primary artistic labour market in Germany (see Table 8.3).

The statistics indicate that a considerable number of the music sector's workers are self-employed. In Germany, the self-employment rate was 46.8 per cent in 2014 and the highest self-employment rate was be found in the private music education sector with 97 per cent,[4] followed by the creatives with almost 80 per cent. The rate of employed persons was highest in the colleting societies (100 per cent), the music publishing sector (91.6 per cent), the musical instruments sector (84.7 per cent) and the recorded music industry (77.8 per cent).

Most employees in the music sector are multi-job-holders. Musicians are often music teachers, producers and bookers, but they also work for recorded music companies, music publishers, promoters and even collecting societies. Thus, the secondary music labour market is highly diversified and fragmented. Besides self-employed label owners, publishers and booking agents, we can also find white-collar employees such as lawyers, accountants, marketing experts and company managers whose skills have hardly any or even no relation to music.

## Notes

1  Forbes, "The Worlds' Highest Paid Celebrities of 2016", 11 July 2016, www.forbes.com/ sites/zackomalleygreenburg/2016/07/11/celeb-100-the-worlds-highest-paid-celebrities-of-2016/#3449c9851fb3 (retrieved 26 July 2016).
2  Alper and Wassell (2006) provide an excellent overview of income studies and they discuss the different findings.
3  Future of Music Coalition, "40 Revenue Streams", http://money.futureofmusic.org/40-revenue-streams/ (retrieved 1 August 2016).
4  The self-employment rate in the music education sector is biased, however, since the authors did not include employees of public music schools and universities/ conservatories.

# ECONOMICS OF THE DIGITAL MUSIC BUSINESS

The digitization of the music business goes back to the introduction to the market of the CD by Philips and Sony in 1982. However, the CD was considered to be only a record format with a larger music storage capacity. Despite the very different production technology involved, the CD did not disrupt the recorded music industry's value-added network. The rapid growth of high speed internet connections and the widespread use of MP3 data compression technology triggered the spread of P2P file-sharing networks and the emergence of the digital music business. In a "war against piracy", the major record companies and music industry bodies around the world sued file-sharing and file-hosting providers and – after some setbacks – eventually succeeded.

However, the emergence of fully licensed and therefore legal digital music services also made file sharing less attractive. After Apple launched its iTunes music download store in 2003, the digital music market evolved. As already highlighted in Chapter 5, digital music sales outperform physical sales in most of the national recorded music markets. However, global digital download sales – single track and album sales – peaked in 2012, whereas streaming revenue continues to grow at a high rate. Thus, the question arises whether music-streaming consumption is cannibalizing download and CD sales.

## The economics of music streaming

With the advent of music streaming, music consumption has shifted from an ownership-based to an access-based business model. This also implies a negative effect – a "cannibalization effect" – of music streaming on recorded music sales. The issue of cannibalization was addressed before the US Copyright Royalty Judges when the US-based music-streaming service Pandora lobbied for lower licensing fees that are payable to copyright holders by presenting a commissioned study by Stephen McBride (2014). The study claimed that plays of an album track on Pandora increase its sales by an average of 2.31 per cent. The study also compared tracks from albums/songs released from major music companies with those from independents. A positive promotional effect of 2.82 per cent was measured for new music from major record companies. The effect is still positive for the majors' catalogue music with an increase of 2.36 per cent. However, the Pandora plays of new tracks released by indie labels showed no significant effect, although Pandora increased the catalogue sales of songs by indie labels by 3.85 per cent. Therefore, McBride concludes: "The Music Sales Experiments confirm that the Pandora radio is promotional of music sales – that is, music sales are higher when music plays on Pandora. ... We also present evidence that the promotional effect is greater for music with greater exposure on Pandora" (McBride 2014: 20).

Independent studies have produced more differentiated results, however. Testing the complementarity of online and offline music consumption, Nguyen, Dejean and Moreau (2014: 328) claim "that streaming has no effect on physical sales of recorded music but does have a positive effect on live music from national or international artists". In contrast, Wlömert and Papies (2015) identified a negative effect of both advert-supported and paid music-streaming consumption on recorded music sales. The adoption of a streaming subscription service such as Spotify reduces recorded music expenditures even more (–24 per cent) than using a free advert-supported service such as YouTube (–11 per cent). These results suggest that consumers rely less on streaming services as a tool for sampling or exploring music that they may later purchase. Rather, on average, the use of streaming services as a substitute for consuming and obtaining music from other channels appears to dominate (Wlömert & Papies 2015: 324).

However, the authors also show that "the adoption of paid streaming services has a significant and substantial positive net effect on revenue", while advert-supported streaming is still negative. Wlömert and Papies (2015: 324–5) therefore conclude: "Streaming services are net positive for the industry. This positive effect, however, only occurs because of the strong positive revenue contribution of paid streaming that offsets the net negative impact of free streaming."

## A typology of music-streaming services

Streaming services differ. To delineate their differences, the following will present a typology of these services. Based on this typology, we will then analyse the business model of personalized streaming services in order to assess their economic potential.

### *Passive internet radios and webcasters*
Internet or web radios broadcast conventional radio programmes online that can be listened to without any interactive and/or personalized features. Most of them are free of charge and thus advert-supported. In Germany, market researcher Goldmedia (2015: 9) counted over 2,442 web radios in 2015 – after a historic peak in 2011 of more than 3,000. Of these, 2,005 are simple online-based radios that broadcast mainly music but also news, sports and other shows such as comedy. In addition, there are about 235 online radio stations operated by FM radios (simulcasters) with an additional 202 online sub-brands (2015: 11). Most of them are advert-supported, but the public radios' online programmes are also fee-funded.

### *Non-interactive personalized web radio*
Non-interactive but personalized web radios such as LastFM and Pandora provide a more innovative concept than conventional online radios. Algorithms help to identify listeners' music tastes to generate playlists, which can be saved and shared with other users. The absence of interactivity is the main distinction from music-streaming services, such as Spotify, that enable a music choice without any restrictions. Hence, full streaming services have to be directly licensed to the owners of the master recordings, whereas for non-interactive webcasters such as US-based Pandora licensing is compulsory and the licensing rate is determined by the Copyright Royalty Board (CRB). Non-interactive services, therefore, are mainly advert-supported with supplementary subscriptions.

### *Interactive personalized web radio*
Interactive streaming services enable users to choose songs without any restrictions from a vast catalogue of several million titles. They offer different models. In the advert-supported version the consumer gets the music for free. This so-called "freemium" model is usually limited in time and bandwidth. On

Spotify, for example, in Germany and Austria, music can be listened to for free only in the first six months of subscribing, after which free music streaming is limited to ten hours per month. Some streaming services such as Apple Music, Amazon Prime and Google Play Music exclusively offer subscription models without any freemium component. Interactive streaming services thus rely on a revenue mix of advertising support and subscription.

### Video-streaming platforms

YouTube is by far the best known and most widely used video-streaming platform. Google Inc. purchased YouTube in November 2006 for $1,650 million. YouTube enables its users to upload their (self-made) videos; thus, YouTube is a so-called user-generated content platform. Music videos are very popular content on the website. YouTube also offers subscription channels to content creators, who benefit not only from monthly fees but also from the revenues of premium advertising. In addition, YouTube also shares the advertising revenue from its freemium model with the right holders. Video-streaming sites such as Vevo and tape.tv operate a different business model, which offers streams of licensed music videos but no user-generated content. Most of them are purely advert-supported.

### Cloud-based music services

Cloud-based music services enable users to upload their music files to a server in the so-called cloud, which allows the music to be streamed from any device. The most popular cloud-based music services are Amazon's Cloud Drive with the Cloud Player, Google's Play Music and Apple's iCloud with iTunes Match. These companies offer a limited free upload capacity, but beyond that users have to pay for further gigabytes.

## Content acquisition model of music-streaming services

The business model of music-streaming services depends on the content acquisition model and the revenue model. For content acquisition, we have to distinguish two different copyrights: (1) the copyright of a musical work created by a composer and/or songwriter (musical copyright = MC) and (2) the copyright for the sound recording (= SR) created by a performer for a record label. A music-streaming service needs both rights and has to approach the different rights holders for licensing. Since the sound recording rights are usually controlled by record labels, Spotify and other similar services have to acquire these rights directly from the record labels. This is always the case for the record majors Universal Music Group, Sony Music Entertainment and Warner Music Group. Indie labels, however, usually do not directly license their sound record catalogues to streaming services, but do so through so-called content aggregators such as The Orchard, Believe Digital and Rebeat, or with the help of a music licensing agency such as MERLIN. In the US, webcasters such as Pandora, Sirius XM and iHeartRadio are treated differently. Since they are not interactive on-demand streaming services, the digital performance rights are licensed from the digital collecting society SoundExchange. The tariffs are determined by the CRB: 50 per cent for the record labels and 45 per cent for the performers. The remaining 5 per cent is distributed by the American Federation of Musicians (AFM) as well as the Screen Actors Guild (SAG) and the American Federation of Television and Radio Artists (AFTRA) to backing singers and studio musicians (see also Figure 5.2).

Streaming services pay upfront or guarantee fees both to the major record labels and also to the indie licensing agency MERLIN to get access to the sound recording catalogues. A leaked Sony–Spotify 2011 contract revealed that the Swedish music-streaming company had to pay advances of $42.5 million to Sony Music over three years. Clause 4(a) of the contract stipulates advance payments of $9 million for the first year, $16 million for the second year and $17.5 million for an optional third year.[1]

Since no streaming service is operating at a profit yet, it is a problem for the majors to license the music catalogues at a market rate. Labels have therefore accepted a sub-market rate in exchange for an equity share in the music-streaming company. It is reported (Hardy 2013: 285) that the three recorded music majors own 18–20 per cent of Spotify. If Spotify is valued at $8,000 million, as speculated in the media,[2] the majors could cash in $2,000 million ($667 million per company) in an initial public offering (IPO) of Spotify. When Beats Music was sold to Apple in 2014, a 13 per cent equity stake of Universal Music's parent company Vivendi was monetized in a payoff of $404 million.[3]

## Revenue model of music-streaming services: Spotify

In January 2016 Spotify's active user base was 100 million,[4] with 36 million paying subscribers in July 2016.[5] In the 2015 financial year, Spotify reported a total revenue of €1,900 million, of which almost 90 per cent (€1,700 million) derives from paid subscriptions and 10 per cent (€200 million) from advertisements[6] (see Figure 9.1).

Despite the impressive revenue growth of almost 80 per cent between 2014 and 2015, total costs and expenses increased by more than 70 per cent to €2,100 million, creating an operating loss of €184.5 million. Thus, the annual loss has further widened by 11.7 per cent compared to 2014[7] (see Figures 9.2 and 9.3).

The main cost drivers are the licensing fees payable to the rights holders. The cost of revenue, which mainly comprises licensing expenses alongside customer services, payment processing and equipment costs, increased by 85.3 per cent to €1,600 million in 2015.[8] Thus, the cost of revenue is 83.5 per cent of Spotify's revenue in 2015, which means that at least 70 per cent of the revenue is used to pay the rights holders, and maybe even more. This has been a stable but still pretty high share for the past three years, but notice that the cost of revenue share was more than 100 per cent in 2010 (see Figure 9.4).

As mentioned before, highly relevant rights holders own 20 per cent of Spotify. So Spotify has little possibility to cut content acquisition costs.

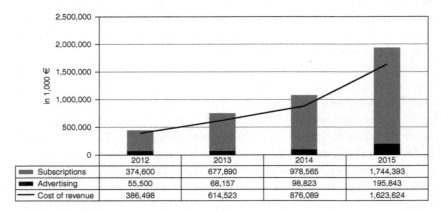

| | 2012 | 2013 | 2014 | 2015 |
|---|---|---|---|---|
| Subscriptions | 374,600 | 677,890 | 978,565 | 1,744,393 |
| Advertising | 55,500 | 68,157 | 98,823 | 195,843 |
| Cost of revenue | 386,498 | 614,523 | 876,089 | 1,623,624 |

**Figure 9.1** Spotify's revenue and cost of revenue, 2012–2015
Source: For 2012–2014, after Music Business Worldwide (2015a); for 2015, after Music Business Worldwide (2016c)

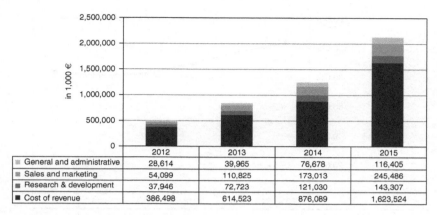

| | 2012 | 2013 | 2014 | 2015 |
|---|---|---|---|---|
| General and administrative | 28,614 | 39,965 | 76,678 | 116,405 |
| Sales and marketing | 54,099 | 110,825 | 173,013 | 245,486 |
| Research & development | 37,946 | 72,723 | 121,030 | 143,307 |
| Cost of revenue | 386,498 | 614,523 | 876,089 | 1,623,524 |

**Figure 9.2** Spotify's expenses, 2012–2015
Source: For 2012–2014, after Music Business Worldwide (2015a); for 2015, after
Music Business Worldwide (2016c)

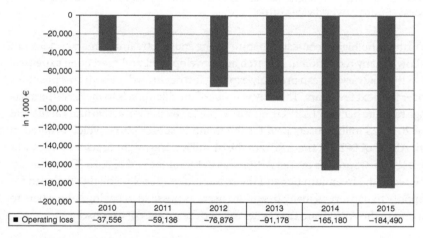

| | 2010 | 2011 | 2012 | 2013 | 2014 | 2015 |
|---|---|---|---|---|---|---|
| Operating loss | −37,556 | −59,136 | −76,876 | −91,178 | −165,180 | −184,490 |

**Figure 9.3** Spotify's operating loss, 2012–2015
Source: For 2012–2014, after Music Business Worldwide (2015a); for 2015, after
Music Business Worldwide (2016c)

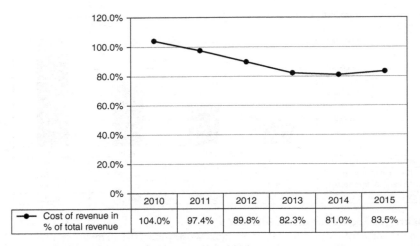

| | 2010 | 2011 | 2012 | 2013 | 2014 | 2015 |
|---|---|---|---|---|---|---|
| Cost of revenue in % of total revenue | 104.0% | 97.4% | 89.8% | 82.3% | 81.0% | 83.5% |

**Figure 9.4** Spotify's cost of revenue, 2012–2015
Source: For 2012–2014, after Music Business Worldwide (2015a); for 2015, after Music Business Worldwide (2016c)

Further, the highly contested nature of the music-streaming market does not allow for any reduction in research and development and marketing expenses. On the contrary, we can probably expect a further growth of both cost positions over the next few years. The only way out of the dilemma is to increase the average revenue per user (ARPU). Spotify reported 89 million active users at the end of 2015; 28 million users paid for the monthly subscription, which resulted in an ARPU of €62.30. The ARPU of the 61 million freemium users, however, was €3.21. Thus, Spotify's overall ARPU was €21.86 at the end of 2015. The value gap between the freemium tier and the subscription model highlights the need for Spotify to convert as many freemium users as possible to paying subscribers to increase the ARPU and to counterbalance the growth of expenses.

### The digital music value-added network

Digitization has not just changed the way music is distributed but has also fundamentally reshaped the value-added network of the music business. Computer- and internet-related companies such as Apple, Amazon and Google have become a highly significant part of the music business by launching music download stores and music-streaming services. Further, companies from other industries that had at best only weak links to the music business use music to sell their products and services: car manufacturers offer their latest models with car radios pre-programmed with music-streaming services; airlines operate music download stores to offer bonuses in their customer relationship programmes if their customers buy music on their portals; supermarkets offer collector cards for downloading the latest hits from music online stores; and coffee house chains such as Starbucks operate their own record labels to increase revenue by selling music.

Thus, digitization has opened up new potentials of added value in the music business that go beyond the usual processes of selling music. As a result, artists have become less dependent on the traditional structures and processes of the music business. It is now common for artists to post their music videos on YouTube, to use Facebook, Instagram and Twitter as direct communication channels with their fans, and even to distribute their music directly through the Internet. Content aggregators such as Believe Digital, The Orchard, Finetunes and Rebeat allow artists and labels to distribute their music to almost all music-streaming and download portals across the world.

Crowdfunding services such as Kickstarter, Sellaband, Starnext, IndieGogo or We-Make-It provide platforms for artists to present and promote an album release, a concert tour, a marketing campaign for a new album and so on, and to collect money from their fans in return for a reward such as concert tickets, CD copies or a private living room concert. Although crowdfunding is not a substitute for the traditional financing model of albums by record labels, it is also a communication tool that allows artists to involve their fans in their projects. Moreover, crowdfunding helps to assess the scope of the fan base with the intent of monetizing it with the help of record labels, publishers, concert promoters, booking agents and other business partners.

Internet-based services allow artists to control all aspects of music production, distribution and marketing. Thus, the value-added network has changed in the course of digitization. In the traditional paradigm, the record was the main revenue source. "Music production and distribution were subordinated to the logic of selling records. PR and marketing aimed at maximising CD sales and even concerts were regarded as promotional tools for record sales. With the aid of the record, music publishers and record labels moved centre stage of the music industry at the latest in the 1950s" (Tschmuck 2016: 15) (see Figure 9.5).

In the traditional value-added network, the record companies and the related music publishers controlled the A & R function, the music production

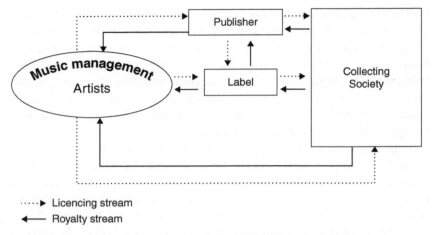

Figure 9.5 The traditional value-added network in the music business
Source: Tschmuck (2016: 15)

process, sound recording studios, record and CD pressing plants, physical distribution networks, the sales and marketing functions, as well as music PR. The artist's main aim was to be signed by a (major) record label. If their records sold well, artists could make a living from recorded music sales and only had to go on tour to promote the latest record release. Creators and interpreters could earn additional income from collecting societies and other forms of music licensing.

In the digital value-added network of the music business, the computer has become the main tool of producing music and many artists can operate their own home recording studios. As highlighted above, artists now have several support services (crowdfunding, digital music distributors, social media channels, etc.) at their disposal, which has helped to emancipate them from the traditional players in the music business and has moved them into the centre of the digital value-added network (see Figure 9.6).

## Disintermediation and intermediation in the digital music business

The digital paradigm shift in the music business has enabled artists to interact directly with their fans. In *Music 2.0*, Gerd Leonhard (2008) predicted a music industry without major record labels and other mediators, allowing

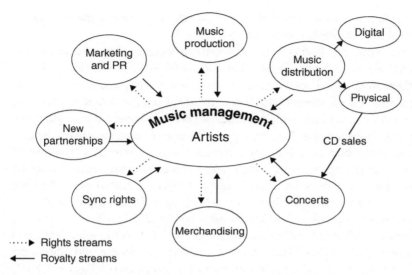

**Figure 9.6** The digital value-added network in the music business
Source: Tschmuck (2016: 16)

artists to connect directly with their fans by operating a do-it-yourself (DIY) approach. This argument refers to the concept of disintermediation, which describes a process of "cutting out the middlemen" in a supply chain (see Gellman 1996: 2). However, "cutting out the middlemen" in the value-added chain has only partly become reality. Bernardo and Martins (2014: 25) argue that in the course of digitization, disintermediation was relevant only in a transitional period, before the emergence of new intermediaries in the digital value-added network. I have highlighted elsewhere (Tschmuck 2012) that in the digital paradigm shift "system-alien" creativity breaks up the established system of production, distribution and reception of music. "[T]echnological possibilities expand, new music practices emerge, the number of actors increases and new business practices form during the period of paradigm change" (Tschmuck 2012: 239). In such a paradigm shift, however, complexity increases, which means that it is not possible to predict which elements will interact and how. This increases uncertainty about the result of actions. Hence, actors seek to reduce uncertainty by preferring specific interactions to non-specific interactions (Tschmuck 2012: 239). By reducing uncertainty, new intermediaries emerge to control a new system of production, distribution and reception of music. Thus, disintermediation in the music business is always followed by intermediation by new actors, a dynamic that defines the music business's digital paradigm.[9]

In the course of digitization, traditional gate-keeping processes have disappeared. Sound recording studios lost control of music production and most of them were closed down. The recorded music majors sold their CD pressing plants and physical distribution networks. Even the A & R function has been outsourced to Shazam, YouTube, Facebook and talent shows. However, the "old" intermediaries have reinvented themselves to get a grip on the new digital music business. The major recorded music companies transformed into copyright aggregators, selling their music back catalogues to digital music providers. Indie labels no longer just sign and record new talent but also offer management services, concert booking and tour support, and social media marketing. Music publishers have redefined themselves as licensing agencies collaborating with collecting societies, such as the joint venture of German BMG Rights Management and GEMA to license and administer online rights for BMG's Anglo-American repertoire across Europe.[10] BMG Rights Management even re-entered the recorded music industry by purchasing Mute Records and the Sanctuary Records Group from Universal Music Group. Concert promoter Live Nation also entered the recorded music business and formed Artist Nation as a subsidiary, providing management services to music artists and selling merchandise articles to fans.

In addition, new intermediaries emerged such as digital music distributors, social media websites and blogs, crowdfunding platforms, search engines, online traders, computer and smartphone manufacturers, data analytics firms, music recognition services, online music management platforms and so on. However, the new intermediaries do not just provide innovative services but also create new dependencies and gatekeeping processes.

## Artepreneurship in the digital music business

As artists moved to the centre of the music business in the course of digitization, they needed increasing expertise in how the music business functions and in self-management. Self-management, however, not only requires knowledge of music business rules and practices, it is also time-consuming. If they can afford it, artists can get support from professional management and/or can use internet-based music management platforms such as PledgeMusic and Revelator. Whereas PledgeMusic[11] is a direct-to-fan music crowdfunding platform, the Israel-based Revelator Limited[12] offers a software solution by integrating sales, marketing, accounting and analytics into a unified system to help artists to run their business. In August 2015 Revelator teamed up with Colu,[13] a cryptocurrency platform like bitcoin, that enables immediate online payments without costly clearance fees. Cryptocurrencies are built on the blockchain technology:

> The blockchain is the technology underpinning bitcoin, a digital currency with a chequered history. It is an example of a "distributed ledger": in essence, a database that is maintained not by a single actor, such as a bank, but collaboratively by a number of participants. Their respective computers regularly agree on how to update the database using a "consensus mechanism", after which the modifications they have settled on are rendered unchangeable with the help of complex cryptography. Once information has been immortalised in this way, it can be used as proof of ownership. The blockchain can also serve as the underpinning for "smart contracts" – programs that automatically execute the promises embedded in a bond, for instance.
>
> (*The Economist* 2016)

The possibility of incorporating smart contracts in cryptocurrencies enables applications in the music business. The music-streaming and download platform PeerTracks invites musicians to sell music over the blockchain-based P2P network MUSE. PeerTrack uses "Note" as a tradable cryptocurrency. "Notes can rise and fall in value depending on that artist's popularity on PeerTracks. The more an artist is streamed, the more music he sells and the more he engages his Note holders, the more each one of his Notes can be worth".[14] The goal is to create a marketplace for "artist coins" that fall and rise with the artist's popularity.

Blockchain technology could provide new value added for the music business. It does not just enable digital payments, but it also significantly lowers transaction costs. Ujomusic, for example, is an open platform using blockchain technology "to create a transparent and decentralised database of rights and rights owners and automates royalty payments using smart contracts and

**Table 9.1** The revenue split for Imogen Heap's "Tiny Human" on ujomusic

| Singer/songwriter | Imogen Heap | 91.25% |
|---|---|---|
| Violin 1 | Stephanie Appelhans | 1.25% |
| Violin 2 | Diego Romano | 1.25% |
| Viola | Yasin Gündisch | 1.25% |
| Cello | Hoang Nguyen | 1.25% |
| Bass trombone | Simon Minshall | 1.25% |
| French horn | David Horwich | 1.25% |
| Mastering | Simon Heyworth | 1.25% |

Source: https://alpha.ujomusic.com/#/imogen_heap/tiny_human/tiny_human

cryptocurrency."[15] A first user of ujomusic is the British singer-songwriter Imogen Heap. In October 2015 she was the first artist to release a song – "Tiny Human" – on the Ethereum blockchain. In a smart contract, Heap defined the revenue split for a song download of $0.60 and a stream of $0.006 (see Table 9.1).

Whenever the song is downloaded or streamed, the smart contract allows for the money to be channelled directly to the artists' virtual wallets without any clearances and reporting. Although blockchain-based applications for the music business are still in their infancy and have to prove their sustainability, there is the potential to strengthen the position of artists in the value-added network.

Artists now have the choice either to enter into a traditional relationship with a recorded music label and music publisher or to collaborate with different partners in the value-added network. Music making has become a 360-degree task that also covers economic and legal aspects beyond the core artistic competencies. Engelmann *et al.* (2012) coined the term "artepreneur" – a person who creates value in the artistic and economic sphere, hoping to launch a sustainable and successful career in the music business.

## Prosumption in the digital music business

Artepreneurship, however, is a transitional phase to a much more fundamental change. Fans are no longer passive music consumers. They write music blogs, use RSS feeds, post self-made music videos on YouTube and are engaged in mixing pre-existing music of their favourite artists. The increasing participation of music fans in music production and distribution indicates a pull music culture in which consumers decide what they want (Winter 2012). The pull culture is more than a simple DIY approach: it is the emergence of a new value-added network of music production, distribution and reception. Alvin Toffler coined the term "prosumption" in his bestseller *The Third Wave* (1980). A prosumer consumes what she/he produces by her/himself and disseminates the creative result to other prosumers. The prosumption process was initially described by Marshall McLuhan and Barrington Nevitt in *Take Today* (1972), where they foresaw that electronic media had the potential to turn consumers into producers, and vice versa.

In the meantime, prosumption has become a reality, as crowdfunding exemplifies. However, crowdfunding is only one aspect of a much broader concept of crowdsourcing. "Crowdsourcing is the act of taking a job traditionally performed by a designated agent (usually an employee) and outsourcing it to an undefined, generally large group of people in the form of an open call" (Howe 2008: 281–2). Crowdsourcing includes crowd creation, crowd wisdom and crowd voting. In crowd creation, the creativity of a large group of people leads to the creation of new content. The user-generated content platform YouTube is a good example of crowd creation in the music sector. In crowd wisdom, the collective intelligence of social networks creates new knowledge, as in the case of Wikipedia, including generating user playlists on music-streaming services. Crowd voting relies on the judgement of internet users to reveal preferences by rating, for example, musical content on webpages.

On the electronic music scene, prosumption is already integral to the creative process. DJs benefit from their fans' creative and financial input. The value-added process in the club scene links the material and the socio-cultural aspects of music production and dissemination (Lange & Bürkner 2010: 61–4). Since the artists rely on live performances of derivate works, they act as prosumers. Reputation and economic value is both created and destroyed by the scene, since fans are directly involved in the value-added processes. Together, artists and fans co-create artistic and economic value by branding, merchandising and licensing synchronization rights. In such a setting, the record is not the final product of a creative process but a business card for an artist. The traditional concept of music as a work is therefore no longer valid. Instead, music has become an endless stream of creation and recreation. The *process* of music making is what is most relevant, not the song as a final product. Thus, music is used and further developed in a prosumption process that exceeds merely passive music consumption.

## Notes

1. The Verge, "This Was Sony Music's Contract with Spotify", 19 May 2015, www.theverge.com/2015/5/19/8621581/sony-music-spotify-contract (retrieved 11 July 2016).
2. Bloomberg, "Spotify Value Tops $8 Billion as Investors Bet on Streaming", 6 October 2015, www.bloomberg.com/news/articles/2015-06-10/spotify-valued-at-8-2-billion-as-teliasonera-buys-stake (retrieved 11 July 2016).
3. Forbes, "Apple Finalizes Beats Deal After Paying Vivendi $404 Million", 2 August 2014, www.forbes.com/sites/amitchowdhry/2014/08/01/apple-finalizes-beats-deal-after-paying-vivendi-404-million/#36c0d2f72162 (retrieved 11 July 2016).
4. Statista.com, "Number of Global Monthly Active Spotify Users from July 2012 to June 2016", www.statista.com/statistics/367739/spotify-global-mau/ (retrieved 13 July 2016).
5. Music Business Worldwide, "Spotify Surpassed 35m Subscribers – And Is Growing Faster than Ever", 7 July 2016, www.musicbusinessworldwide.com/spotify-surpassed-35m-subscribers-growing-faster-ever/ (retrieved 14 July 2016).
6. Music Business Worldwide, "Spotify Revenues Topped $2bn Last Year as Losses Hit $194m", 23 May 2016, www.musicbusinessworldwide.com/spotify-revenues-topped-2bn-last-year-as-losses-hit-194m/ (retrieved 14 July 2016).
7. *Ibid.*
8. *Ibid.*
9. For the concepts of intermediation, disintermediation and reintermediation, see Chircu and Kauffman 1999.
10. GEMA press release, "BMG Rights Management and GEMA Sign Deal for the Licensing of Anglo-American Repertoire Online across Europe", 23 May 2012, www.gema.de/en/aktuelles/bmg_rights_management_and_gema_sign_deal_for_the_licensing_of_anglo_american_repertoire_online_acros-1/ (retrieved 15 July 2016).
11. See www.pledgemusic.com/ (retrieved 19 February 2017).
12. See http://revelator.com/ (retrieved 19 February 2017).
13. See www.colu.com/ (retrieved 19 February 2017).
14. See http://peertracks.com/faq.php (retrieved 25 July 2016).
15. See https://ujomusic.com/ (retrieved 21 February 2017).

# CONCLUSION

Digitization has been revolutionizing the music business since the millennium in the same way that radio did in the 1930s. The change, however, is not just technologically driven, but is also embedded in a socio-cultural paradigm shift that alters the relationship of music business actors and their business practices, as well as aesthetic concepts. The 360-degree management model of artists has replaced the record-centred value-added network, which emerged in the rock 'n' roll revolution of the 1950s. The artist is now in the centre of the value-added network and has the power to decide who to collaborate with. Today, there is no need for artists to give away all their copyrights and enter into exclusive contracts. However, digitization has also lowered the music business's entrance barrier: anyone who makes music can put her/his music videos on YouTube, launch a crowdfunding campaign and use social media sites for self-promotion.

The prophecy of a disintermediation in the music business has not come true. Although "old" intermediaries such as recorded music companies and music publishers have lost some of their control in producing and distributing music, they have established new business models to exploit their massive back catalogues to digital music service providers. Thanks to copyright and related rights, they are gatekeeping the access to music by controlling and even owning music-streaming services. Recorded music companies have outsourced former key functions such as A & R, record manufacturing and distribution to focus on exploiting master rights. Music publishers have enlarged their repertoire by acquiring copyrights and entire music catalogues, and have also entered the recording business and provide management services. The live music business has become dominated by a few concert promoters such as Live Nation, which owns concert sites, ticketing services and artist agencies. Thus, we can observe a convergence of the three music subsectors – publishing, recording and live business – to a single music industry support network for artists.

Along with this change, new market entrants such as Apple, Google and Amazon, as well as telecommunications and internet service providers, highlight an innovative disruption (Christensen 1997) in the music business. These companies have established a new business model of digital music distribution that does not rely on the sale of phonograms, but provides access to music from anywhere and at any time, as long as an internet connection is available. The new market entrants use music as a means to sell electronic devices (Apple), micro-advertisements (Google) and other products with higher profit margins (Amazon). Their music distribution services do not need to break even and, thus, have a comparative advantage over established firms in the music business.

Music has become a by-product of other business models in the digital paradigm shift as in the 1930s, when radio broadcasters absorbed the record companies. It is possible that the internet-related companies will acquire the recorded music majors and avoid paying "excessive" licensing fees for the use of music catalogues. It might be an advantage to own the master and publishing rights to feed their digital distribution channels. We have already seen that Apple Music contracts superstars (e.g. Drake) for exclusive streaming deals, and the Google-owned YouTube platform is developing its own stars – "YouTubers" (e.g. Alexa Goddard aka "AlexaMusicTV" and the Ukrainian pianist Viktoriya Yermolyeva). Presumably, it is only a question of time before the internet giants set about buying in content creation and content marketing.

Meanwhile, the recorded music majors ride the wave of music streaming. They have invested in music-streaming services such as Spotify and Deezer and expect to monetize their engagement with initial public offerings of the services. Although streaming is a very attractive way to consume music – it can be seen as the radio of the twenty-first century – its business model does not seem to be profitable and sustainable. Due to the high licensing fees, the cost of revenue of streaming providers is comparably high and losses have increased from year to year. Thus, music-streaming services operated by Apple, Google and Amazon are in a more comfortable position than Spotify,

Deezer and Tidal, which rely solely on music-streaming revenues. In the near future, we can expect a market consolidation in music-streaming services with mergers, acquisitions and probably bankruptcies. Some smaller companies such as Simfy and Rdio have already been victims of the consolidation process.

What does the rise of music streaming mean for artists? Empirical data show that income from music streaming for artists is low and even superstars cannot afford to live on streaming payouts alone. Nevertheless, music streaming is an important promotional tool for connecting with fans and attracting attention. From an artist's perspective, music streaming is just an additional income source alongside concert ticket sales, teaching, synch rights exploitation and diminishing CD sales. The artists' new income situation corresponds with the 360 degree management model for collaborating with different business partners in order to exploit different revenue sources. In such an environment artists need more skills than just making music at a high technical level. They have to understand the underlying economic principles of the music business and how the music industry works. It is the obligation of music educational institutions to provide such knowledge and skills for a new generation of artepreneurs. I hope this book can contribute to this challenging task.

# GLOSSARY

**360** deal – a type of contract usual in the recorded music business, in which the artist agrees to give the recorded music company a percentage of *all* revenue streams including record sales, touring, sponsoring and merchandising.

**Artists and repertoire** (A & R) is the division of recorded music companies that scouts for new talent and acquires new compositions and lyrics.

**Broadcasting right** is the right of a composer and/or lyricist to allow the broadcast of her/his work on radio, television and cable networks.

**Club good** (toll good) is excludable but non-rivalrous in consumption, for example, a concert, opera and theatre performance.

**Common goods** are non-excludable but rivalrous in consumption, for example fishing grounds and public heritage sites.

**Cross-collateralization** means that non-returnable advances paid by recorded music companies to interpreters can be recouped from the artist's royalties as long as a sound recording has yet to break even. Cross-collateralizing advances is also a practice in music publishing and in the live music business.

**Crowdfunding** is a tool for raising money for projects from a large number of people on the Internet.

**Deadweight loss** is a loss in efficiency that occurs when market equilibrium is not achievable, for example in monopolies.

**Dissemination right** is the right of a composer and/or lyricist to decide whether her/his work embodied in a phonogram can be sold, lent and transferred by any other means to users.

**Download music services** such as iTunes and Amazon Music sell audio files over the Internet to music consumers.

**Externality** arises when an individual engages in an activity that influences the well-being of a third party, but neither pays nor receives compensation for that effect.

**Freemium** is a pricing policy in which goods and services are given away for free in order to generate customer and brand loyalty for further exploitation.

**Graduated response measures** are based on laws to fight illegal file sharing by sending a series of notifications, warning infringers, and eventually cancelling their internet access if they continue their unlawful behaviour.

**Income elasticity of demand** measures the responsiveness of demand for a good to a change in the income of a household demanding that good.

**Information goods** derive their value from the information they contain. Books, CDs, music downloads, newspapers and other media outputs are examples of information goods.

**Loss-leader pricing** is a strategy to sell a product or service at a price below its production cost to stimulate sales of other more profitable products or services.

**Making available right** is the right of a composer and/or lyricist to upload her/his work on the Internet.

**Master recording** is the final product of the music recording process.

**Mechanical right** is the right of a composer and/or lyricist to decide whether her/his work is reproduced/copied and disseminated by a phonogram and other technical devices to the public.

**Mechanical rights organizations** (MROs) collect mechanical royalties on behalf of their members (composers/lyricists and publishers) from third parties (recording companies, broadcasters, etc.) who wish to reproduce a musical work and to disseminate it on a phonogram/technical device to the public.

**Merit goods** make a person better off, but the person does not realise the benefit deriving from consuming the good.

**Monopolistic competition** is a market form with companies selling goods or services that cannot be perfectly substituted, because of differences in perceived quality (e.g. branded goods).

**Monopoly** is a market form with only one company supplying a good or service.

**Moral rights** are rights of creators of copyrighted works. They include the attribution right, the integrity right and the right to publish a work under the author's name.

**Napster** was the first peer-to-peer file-sharing network introduced on the market in 1999. Due to copyright infringement accusations, Napster was shut down in 2002.

**Natural monopoly** is a market form in which high costs and other entrance barriers allow only the largest enterprise to supply the market.

**Neighbouring rights** (also related rights) are rights that are not directly connected with authors but with other parties in the creative process. They cover, for example, the rights of performers, recorded music companies, producers and broadcasters.

**Network externality** arises when the use of a network is of value for all other users in the network.

**Oligopoly** is a market form dominated by a small number of companies supplying a good or service.

**Peer-to-peer** (P2P) file sharing enables internet users to access media files using a software program that searches for other connected computers on the Internet to find the desired content.

**Performance (performing) right** is the right of a composer and/or lyricist to perform her/his work in public (in concerts, bars, restaurants as well as on television, radio and the Internet).

**Performance rights organizations** (PROs) collect performance royalties on behalf of their members (composers/lyricists and publishers) from third parties (promoters, broadcasters, etc.) who want to use music in public.

**Price elasticity of demand** measures the responsiveness of a price change of a good on its demand.

**Public goods** are non-excludable and non-rivalrous in demand. Thus, individuals cannot be effectively excluded from using the good and usage does not reduce availability and benefit to others.

**Publishing right** is the right of a composer and/or lyricist to publish her/his work. Publishing rights are usually assigned to music publishers for further exploitation.

**Related rights** see neighbouring rights.

**Reproduction right** is the right of an author and/or lyricist to copy her/his work using technical devices.

**Synchronization right** is the right of a composer and/or lyricist to couple (synchronize) her/his work with visual media (film, television shows, advertisements, video games, etc.). Synchronization rights are usually assigned to music publishers for further exploitation.

**Trade value** is the value of sales measured in wholesale prices – in contrast to retail value.

**Tragedy of the commons** describes a situation of overuse and deletion of common goods if no clear rules of usage are defined.

**Value added** is the economic contribution of an industry to the GDP. It is calculated as the difference between total sales revenue and the total cost of input factors.

**Work for hire** is a work created by an employee as part of a job in an organization. As a result the employer is the copyright holder in that work.

# REFERENCES

## Printed secondary sources

Aaker, J. L. 1997. "Dimensions of Brand Personality", *Journal of Marketing Research*, 34(3): 347–56.

Adler, M. 1985. "Stardom and Talent", *American Economic Review*, 75: 208–12.

Alper, N. O. & G. H. Wassell. 2006. "Artists' Careers and Their Labour Markets", in V. A. Ginsburgh & D. Throsby (eds), *Handbook of the Economics of Art and Culture*, vol. I. Amsterdam: Elsevier, 813–64.

Andersen, B. & M. Frenz. 2007. "The Impact of Music Downloads and P2P File-Sharing on the Purchase of Music: A Study for Industry Canada". Ottawa: Industry Canada.

Andersen, B. & M. Frenz. 2010. "Don't Blame the P2P File-Sharers: The Impact of Free Music Downloads on the Purchase of Music CDs in Canada", *Journal of Evolutionary Economics*, 20: 715–40.

Aronson, R. L., 1991. *Self-Employment: A Labor Market Perspective*. Ithaca, NY: ILR Press.

ASCAP. 2013 to 2016. Annual Reports. New York.

Baierle, C. 2009. *Der Musikverlag: Geschichte, Aufgaben, Medien und neue Herausforderungen* [Music publishing: history, functions, media and new challenges]. Munich: Musikmarkt-Verlag.

Bernardo, F. & L. G. Martins. 2014. "Disintermediation Effects on Independent Approaches to Music Business", *International Journal of Music Business Research*, 3(2): 7–27.

Blackburn, D. 2004. On-line Piracy and Recorded Music Sales, working paper, Harvard University.

Brabec, J. & T. Brabec. 2004. *Music, Money and Success: The Insider's Guide to Making Money in the Music Industry*, 4th edition. New York: Schirmer.

Buchanan, J. M. 1965. "An Economic Theory of Clubs", *Economica*, New Series, 32(125): 1–14.

Budnick D. & J. Baron, 2011. *Ticketmasters: The Rise of the Concert Industry and How the Public Got Scalped*. New York: ECW Press.

Carey, C., 2007. "Pindar, Place and Performance", in S. Hornblower & C. Morgan (eds), *Pindar's Poetry, Patrons & Festivals*. Oxford: Oxford University Press, 199–210.

Caves, R. E., 2000. *Creative Industries: Contracts between Art and Commerce.* Cambridge, MA: Harvard University Press.

Chapple, S. & R. Garofalo. 1977. *Rock 'n' Roll Is Here to Pay.* Chicago, IL: Nelson-Hall.

Chircu, A. M. & R. J. Kauffman, 1999. "Strategies for Internet Middlemen in the Intermediation/Disintermediation/Reintermediation Cycle", *Electronic Markets: The International Journal of Electronic Commerce and Business Media,* 9(2): 109–17.

Christensen, C. M. 1997. *The Innovator's Dilemma: When New Technologies Cause Great Firms to Fail.* Boston, MA: Harvard Business School Press.

Christopherson, S. & M. Storper. 1989. "The Effects of Flexible Specialisation on Industrial Politics and the Labor Market: The Motion Picture Industry", *Industrial and Labor Relations Review,* 42(3): 331–47.

Chung, K. H. & R. A. K. Cox. 1994. "A Stochastic Model of Superstardom: An Application of the Yule Distribution", *Review of Economics and Statistics,* 76: 771–5.

CISAC. 2010 to 2015. CISAC Global Collections Reports. Neuilly-sur-Seine.

Coase, R. 1937. "The Nature of the Firm", *Economica,* 4(16): 386–405.

Department for Culture, Media and Sport (DCMS). 2015. Creative Industries Economic Estimates (London).

Denisoff, S. R. 1988. *Inside MTV.* New Brunswick: Transaction.

Diamond, P. A. & J. A. Hausman. 1994. "Contingent Valuation: Is Some Number Better than No Number?", *Journal of Economic Perspectives,* 8(4): 45–64.

DiCola, P. 2013. *Money from Music: Survey Evidence on Musicians' Revenue and Lessons about Copyright Incentives,* Northwestern University School of Law, Law and Economics Series No. 13–01.

Döhring, S. 1990. "Dresden and Leipzig: Two Bourgeois Centres", in A. Ringer (ed.), *The Early Romantic Era: Between Revolutions, 1789 and 1848.* Basingstoke: Macmillan Press, 141–59.

Ehrlich, C. 1990. *The Piano: A History,* revised edition. New York: Oxford University Press.

Elberse, A. 2013. *Blockbusters: Why Big Hits – and Big Risks – Are the Future of the Entertainment Business.* London: Faber.

Elias, N. 1983. *The Court Society.* New York: Pantheon.

Elste, M. 1984. "Zwischen Privatheit und Politik: Die Schallplattenindustrie im NS-Staat", [Between privacy and policy: the recorded music industry in the NS state], in H.-W. Heister & H. G. Klein (eds) *Musik und Musikpolitik im faschistischen Deutschland* [Music and music policy in fascist Germany]. Frankfurt: Fischer, 107–44.

Engelmann, M., L. Grünewald & J. Heinrich. 2012. "The New Artepreneur: How Artists Can Thrive on a Networked Music Business", *International Journal of Music Business Research,* 1(2): 32–46.

European Union. 2001. Directive 2001/29/EC of the European Parliament and of the Council of 22 May 2001 on the harmonisation of certain aspects of copyright and related rights in the information society.

Fantel H. 1971. *Johann Strauss: Father and Son and Their Era.* London: Newton and Abbot.

Fetthauer, S. 2000. Deutsche Grammophon: Geschichte eines Schallplattenunternehmens im "Dritten Reich" [Deutsche Grammophon. History of a record company in the "Third Reich"]. Hamburg: von BockelVerlag.

Foster Morell, M. 2010. Governance of online creation communities: Provision of infra-structure for the building of digital commons. PhD dissertation, European University Institute, Florence and Fiesole.

Frith, S., M. Brennan, M. Cloonan & E. Webster. 2010. "Analysing Live Music in the UK: Findings One Year into a Three-Year Research Project", *Journal of the Association for the Study of Popular Music*, 1(1): 1–30.

Garofalo, R. 1997. *Rockin' Out: Popular Music in the USA*. Upper Saddle River, NJ: Prentice Hall.

Gelatt, R. 1955. *The Fabulous Phonograph: From Tinfoil to High Fidelity*. New York: J. B. Lippincott.

Gellman, R. 1996. "Disintermediation and the Internet", *Government Information Quarterly*, 13(1): 1–8.

GfK. 2014. Konsumstudie des Veranstaltungsmarktes 2013 [Music consumption study of the promotion market 2013]. Bundesverband der Veranstaltungswirtschaft and Musikmarkt Magazine.

Goldberg, I. 1930. *The Tin Pan Alley: A Chronicle of American Popular Music*. New York: Day.

Goldmedia. 2015. Webradiomonitor 2015. Online-Audio-Angebotein Deutschland [Web monitor 2015. Online-audio services in Germany], commissioned by Bayrische Landeszentrale für neue Medien and Bundesverband Digitale Wirtschaft (BVDW).

Griffin, N. & K. Masters. 1997. *Hit and Run: How Jon Peters and Peter Guber Took Sony for a Ride in Hollywood*. New York: Simon & Schuster.

Hamlen, W. A. 1991. "Superstardom in Popular Music: Empirical Evidence", *Review of Economics and Statistics*, 73: 729–33.

Hamlen, W. A. 1994. "Variety and Superstardom in Popular Music", *Economic Inquiry*, 32: 395–406.

Hammond, R. G. 2012. *Profit Leak? Pre-Release File Sharing and the Music Industry*, working paper, North Carolina State University, May 2012.

Hardin, G. 1968. "The Tragedy of the Commons", *Science*, 162 (1968): 1243–8.

Hardy, P. 2013. *Download! How the Internet Transformed the Record Business*. London: Omnibus.

Howe, J. 2008. *Crowdsourcing: Why the Power of the Crowd is Driving the Future of Business*. New York: Three Rivers Press.

Hull, G. P., T. Hutchison & R. Strasser. 2011. *The Music Business and Recording Industry: Delivering Music in the 21st Century*, 3rd edition. New York: Routledge.

Hunter, D. 1986. *Music Copyright in Britain to 1800*. London: Music & Letters.

Huygens, A., P. Rutten, S. Huveneers, *et al*. 2009. *Ups and Downs: Economic and Cultural Effects of File Sharing on Music, Film and Games*. TNO report commissioned by the Ministries of Education, Culture and Science, Economic Affairs and Justice of the Netherlands, 18 February 2009.

IFPI (International Federation of the Phonographic Industry), vols 1973 to 2013. *The Recording Industry in Numbers*. London.

IFPI (International Federation of the Phonographic Industry). 2014a. *Investing in Music: How Music Companies Discover, Nurture and Promote Talent*. London.

IFPI (International Federation of the Phonographic Industry). 2014b. *The Recording Industry in Numbers 2014*. London: IFPI.

IFPI (International Federation of the Phonographic Industry). 2015a. *IFPI Digital Music Report 2015*. London.

IFPI (International Federation of the Phonographic Industry). 2015b. *The Recording Industry in Numbers 2015*. London: IFPI.

IFPI (International Federation of the Phonographic Industry). 2016. *Global Music Report 2016*. London.

IFPI Germany. 1999 to 2014. *Musikindustrie in Zahlen 1999 to 2014*. Berlin.

Klembas, R. 2013. Das A & R Management im digitalen Paradigmenwechsel [A & R Management in the Digital Paradigm Shift], PhD thesis, University of Music and Performing Arts, Vienna.

Korn, K. 2010. *Musik Merchandising aus Konsumentenperspektive: Ein Ansatz zur Erklärung des Konsumentenverhaltens bei Fan-Artikeln von Musikacts* [Music merchandising from the consumers' perspective: An approach for explaining consumption behaviour using fan articles on music acts]. Wiesbaden: Gabler.

Kornfeld, B. 2011. *Pop Song Piracy: Disobedient Music Distribution since 1929*, Chicago, IL: University of Chicago Press. Kindle edition.

Kotler, P. T. 2015. *Marketing Management*, 15th edition. Upper Saddle River, NJ: Prentice Hall.

Krasilovsky, W. M., S. Shemel, J. M. Gross, *et al.* 2007. *This Business of Music*, 10th edition. New York: Billboard Books.

Krueger, A. B., 2005. "The Economics of Real Superstars: The Market for Rock Concerts in the Material World", *Journal of Labor Economics*, 23(1): 1–30.

Krugman, P. & R. Wells. 2012. *Microeconomics*, 3rd edition. New York: Worth.

Landes, W. M. and R. A. Posner. 1989. "An Economic Analysis of Copyright Law", *Journal of Legal Studies*, 18(2): 325–63.

Landes, W. M. and R. A. Posner. 2003. *The Economic Structure of Intellectual Property Law*. Cambridge, MA: Harvard University Press.

Lang, Michael, 2009. *The Road to Woodstock*. New York: HarperCollins.

Lange, B. & H.-J. Bürkner. 2010. "Wertschöpfung in der Kreativwirtschaft: Der Fall der elektronischen Klubmusik" [Value added in the creative economy: The case of electronic club music], *Zeitschrift für Wirtschaftsgeographie*, 54(1): 46–68.

Leonhard, G. 2008. *Music 2.0: Essays by Gerd Leonhard*. Media futurist.

Lessig, L. 2001. *The Future of Ideas: The Fate of the Commons in a Connected World*. New York: Random House.

Liebowitz, S. J. 2004. Peer-to-Peer Networks: Creative Destruction or Just Plain Destruction?, working paper, University of Texas at Dallas, School of Management.

Liebowitz, S. J. 2006. "File Sharing: Creative Destruction or Just Plain Destruction?", *Journal of Law and Economics*, 49(1): 1–28.

Liebowitz, S. J. 2008. "Testing File-Sharing's Impact on Music Album Sales in Cities", *Management Science*, 53(4): 852–9.

Live Nation. 2006 to 2016. Annual Reports, New York.

Locke, R. P. 1990. "Paris: Centre of Intellectual Ferment", in A. Ringer (ed.), *The Early Romantic Era: Between Revolutions, 1789 and 1848*. Basingstoke: Macmillan Press, 32–83.

Lyng, R., O. Heinz & M. V. Rothkirch. 2011. *Die neue Praxis im Musikbusiness* [New practices in the music business], 11th edition. Bergkirchen: PPV Medien.

MacDonald, G. M. 1988. "The Economics of Rising Stars", *American Economic Review*, 78: 155–67.

Mankiw, G. N. 2014. *Principles of Microeconomics*, 7th edition. Stanford, CA: Cengage.

Martland, P. 1997. *Since Records Began: EMI – The First 100 Years*. London: The EMI Group.

McBride, S. 2014. Written direct testimony in the matter of determination of rates and terms for digital performance in sound recordings and ephemeral recordings before the United States Copyright Royalty Judges, 7 October 2014.

McKenzie, J. 2009. "Illegal Music Downloading and Its Impact on Legitimate Sales: Australian Empirical Evidence", *Australian Economic Papers*, 48(4): 296–307.

McLuhan, M. & N. Barrington, 1972. *Take Today: The Executive as Dropout*. New York: Harcourt Brace Jovanovich.

McVeigh, S. 1993. *Concert Life in London from Mozart to Haydn*. Cambridge: Cambridge University Press.

Meffert, H. 2013. *Marketing: Grundlagen marktorientierter Unternehmensführung* [Marketing: Foundations of market-oriented management], 8th edition. Wiesbaden: Gabler.

Menger, P.-M. 2006. "Artistic Labor Markets: Contingent Work, Excess Supply and Occupational Risk Management", in V. A. Ginsburgh & D. Throsby (eds), *Handbook of the Economics of Art and Culture*, vol. I, Amsterdam: Elsevier, 765–811.

Michel, N. J. 2006. "The Impact of Digital File Sharing on the Music Industry: An Empirical Analysis", *Topics in Economic Analysis & Policy*, 6(1), Article 18.

Musgrave, R. A. 1957. "A Multiple Theory of Budget Determination", *Finanzarchiv*, 17: 333–43.

Musgrave, R. A & P. B. Musgrave. 1989. *Public Finance in Theory and Practice*, 5th edition. New York: McGraw-Hill.

Neumeier, M. 2004. *The Dictionary of Brand*. AIGA Center for Brand Experience.

Nguyen, G. D., S. Dejean & F. Moreau. 2014. "On the Complementarity between Online and Offlinemusic Consumption: The Case of Free Streaming", *Journal of Cultural Economics*, 38: 315–30.

Nielsen, 2005 to 2012. Nielsen Music Industry Year End Reports. New York.

Nielsen, 2014. US Music Year End Report, New York.

Nielsen, 2015. US Music Year End Report, New York.

NMPA, 2002. Survey by the National Music Publishers' Association 1994–2000, Washington, DC.

Noonan, D. 2002. *Contingent Valuation Studies in the Arts and Culture: An Annotated Bibliography*. University of Chicago Cultural Policy Center working paper series, 18 January 2002.

Oberholzer-Gee, F. & K. Strumpf. 2007. "The Effect of File Sharing on Record Sales: An Empirical Analysis", *Journal of Political Economy*, 115(1): 1–42.

O'Hagan, J. 1998. *The State and the Arts*. Cheltenham: Elgar.

Ordanini A. & J. C. Nunes, 2016. "From Fewer Blockbusters by More Superstars to More Blockbusters by Fewer Superstars: How Technological Innovation Has Impacted Convergence on the Music Chart", *International Journal of Research in Marketing*, 33(2): 297–313.

O'Reilly D., G. Larsen & K. Kubacki. 2013. *Music, Markets and Consumption*. Oxford: Goodfellows.

Ostrom, E. 1990. *Governing the Commons: The Evolution of Institutions for Collective Action*. Cambridge: Cambridge University Press.

Peacock, A. T. 1994. "Welfare Economics and Public Subsidies to the Arts", *Journal of Cultural Economics* 18: 151–61, reprinted from *Manchester School of Economics and Social Studies*, December 1969: 323–35.

Peitz, M. & P. Waelbroeck. 2004. "The Effect of Internet Piracy on Music Sales: Cross-Section Evidence", *Review of Economic Research on Copyright Issues*, 1(2): 71–9.

Peterson, R. A. 1990. "Why 1955? Explaining the Advent of Rock Music", *Popular Music*, 9(1): 97–116.

Peterson, R. A. & D. G. Berger. 1975. "Cycles in Symbolic Production: The Case of Popular Music", *American Sociological Review*, 40: 158–73.

Piperno, F. 1984. "Opera Production to 1780", in L. Bianconi & G. Pestelli (eds), *Opera Production and Its Resources*. Chicago, IL: University of Chicago Press, 1–79.

Pitt, I. L. 2010. *Economic Aspects of Music Copyright: Income, Media and Performances.* Heidelberg: Springer.

Pohlmann, H. 1962. *Die Frühgeschichte des musikalischen Urheberrechts (ca. 1400–1800)* [The early history of musical copyright (c.1400–1800)]. Kassel: Bärenreiter.

Pollock, R. 2009. "Forever Minus a Day? Calculating Optimal Copyright Term", *Review of Economic Research on Copyright Issues*, 6(1): 35–60.

PPL, 2008 to 2015. PPL Annual Reviews. London.

PRS for Music, 2008 to 2015. Annual Reports, London.

Rethink Music. 2015. *Fair Music: Transparency and Money Flows in the Music Industry.* Berklee Institute for Creative Entrepreneurship, Boston, MA.

RIAA, 2005 to 2015. RIAA Year End Industry Shipment and Revenue Statistics. Washington, DC.

Riess, C. 1966. *Knauers Weltgeschichte der Schallplatte* [Knauer's world history of the record]. Zurich: Droemer-Knauer.

Rob, R. & J. Waldfogel. 2006. "Piracy on the High C's: Music Downloading, Sales Displacement and Social Welfare in a Sample of College Students", *Journal of Law and Economics*, 49(1): 91–114.

Rose, F. 1996. *The Agency: William Morris and the Hidden History of Show Business.* New York: Harperbusiness.

Rosen, S. 1981. "The Economics of Superstars", *American Economic Review*, 78(5): 845–58.

Rosenman J., J. Roberts & R. Pilpel 1999. *Young Men With Unlimited Capital: The Story of Woodstock*, 3rd edition. Western Ontario: Scrivenery Press.

Rutter, P. 2011. *The Music Industry Handbook.* Cheltenham: Elgar.

Ryan, J. 1985. *The Production of Culture in the Music Industry: The ASCAP-BMI Controversy.* New York: University Press of America.

Sachs, J. 1990. "London: The Professionalization of Music", in A. Ringer (ed.), *The Early Romantic Era: Between Revolutions: 1789 and 1848.* Basingstoke: Macmillan Press, 201–35.

Samuelson, P. A. 1954. "The Pure Theory of Public Expenditure", *Review of Economics and Statistics*, 36(4): 387–9.

Sanjek, R. & D. Sanjek. 1991. *American Popular Music Business in the 20th Century.* New York: Oxford University Press.

Santos, F. P. 1976. "Risk, Uncertainty and the Performing Arts", in M. Blaug (ed.), *The Economics of Arts.* Boulder, CO: Westview.

Scherer, F. M. 2004. *Quarter Notes and Banknotes: The Economics of Music Composition in the Eighteenth and Nineteenth Centuries.* Princeton, NJ: Princeton University Press.

Schoppe, S. 1995. *Moderne Theorie der Unternehmung* [The modern theory of enterprise]. Munich and Vienna: Oldenbourg.

Schulz-Köhn, D. 1940. *Die Schallplatte auf dem Weltmarkt* [The record on the global market]. Berlin: Reher.

Seufert W., R. Schlegel & F. Sattelberger. 2015. *Musikwirtschaft in Deutschland* [Music economy in Germany], commissioned and edited by Bundesverband Musikindustrie, Bundesverband der Veranstaltungswirtschaft, Deutscher Musikverleger-Verband, Europäischer Verband der Veranstaltungs-Centren, GVL, Live-Musik-Kommission, Society of Music Merchants, Verband der Deutschen Konzertdirektoren, VUT. Berlin.

Shapiro, C. & H. R. Varian. 1998. *Information Rules: A Strategic Guide to the Network Economy*. Cambridge, MA: Harvard University Press.

Shaw, A. 1974. *The Rockin' 50s: The Decade that Transformed the Pop Music Scene*. New York: Hawthorne.

Smith, A. (1776) 1811. *An Inquiry into the Nature and Causes of the Wealth of Nations*, in *The Works of Adam Smith, LL.D.*, Vol. II–IV. London: T. Cadell and W. Davies *et al.*; see https://archive.org/details/worksofadamsmith03smitiala.

Somfai, L. 1989. "Haydn at the Esterházy Court", in N. Zaslaw (ed.), *The Classical Era. From the 1740s to the End of the 18th Century*. Basingstoke: Macmillan Press, 268–92.

Sony Corporation. 2012 to 2016. Annual Reports for the Fiscal Years ending 31 March. Tokyo.

Storper, M. & S. Christopherson. 1987. "Flexible Specialization and Regional Industrial Agglomerations: The Case of the US Motion Picture Industry", *Annals of the Association of American Geographers*, 77(1): 104–17.

Suisman, D. 2009. *Selling Sounds: The Commercial Revolution in American Music*. Cambridge, MA: Harvard University Press. Kindle edition.

Tanaka, T. 2004. *Does File Sharing Reduce Music CD Sales? A Case of Japan*, IIR Working Paper WP#05–08. Institute of Innovation Research, Hitotsubashi University Tokyo.

Throsby, D. 1994. "A Work Preference Model of Artists' Behaviour", in A. Peacock & I. Rizzo (eds), *Cultural Economics and Cultural Policies*. Dordrecht: Kluwer, 69–80.

Throsby, D. 2001. *Economics and Culture*. Cambridge: Cambridge University Press.

Toffler, A. 1980. *The Third Wave*. New York: Bantam.

Towse, R. 2010. *A Textbook of Cultural Economics*. Cambridge: Cambridge University Press.

Tschmuck, P. 2001. "The Court's System of Incentives and the Socio-Economic Status of Court Musicians in the Late 16th Century", *Journal of Cultural Economics*, 25(1): 47–62.

Tschmuck, P. 2002. "Creativity without a Copyright: Music Production in Vienna in the Late Eighteenth Century", in R. Towse (ed.), *Copyright in the Cultural Industries*. Cheltenham: Elgar, 210–20.

Tschmuck, P. 2009. "Copyright, Contracts and Music Production", *Information, Communication & Society*, 12(2): 251–65.

Tschmuck, P. 2012. *Creativity and Innovation in the Music Industry*, 2nd edition. Heidelberg: Spinger.

Tschmuck, P. 2016. "From Record Selling to Cultural Entrepreneurship: The Music Economy in the Digital Paradigm Shift", in P. Wikström & R. De Fillippi (eds), *Business Innovation and Disruption in the Music Industry*. Cheltenham: Elgar, 13–32.

UK for Music. 2011. *Destination Music: The Contribution of Music Festivals and Majors Concerts to Tourism in the UK*, London.

UK for Music. 2014. *Measuring Music 2013*. London.

UK for Music. 2015. *Measuring Music 2014*. London.

UNCTAD. 2010. *Creative Economy Report 2010*, Creative Economy: A Feasible Development Option, New York.

US Copyright Board. CRB Decision, 74 F.R. 4529, 26 January 2009.

Varian, H. R. 2010. *Intermediate Microeconomics: A Modern Approach*, 8th edition. New York: Norton.

Vivendi. 2002 to 2015. Annual Reports for Fiscal Year ended 31 December. Paris.

Vivendi. 2016. Financial Report and Audited Consolidated Financial Statements for the Year Ended 31 December 2015, Paris.

Wang, P. 2013. *Musik und Werbung: Wie Werbung und Medien die Entwicklung der Musikindustrie beeinflussen* [Music and commercials: How commercials and media impact the development of the music industry]. Wiesbaden: VS Verlag.

Warner Music Group. 2001 to 2015. Annual Report for the fiscal year ended 30 September. New York.

Wicke, P. 1998. *Von Mozart zu Madonna: Eine Kulturgeschichte der Popmusik* [From Mozart to Madonna: A cultural history of popular music]. Leipzig: Gustav Kiepenheuer Verlag.

Wierzbicki, J. 2009. *Film Music: A History*. New York: Routledge.

Wiesmann, S. 1990. "Vienna: Bastion of Conservatism", in A. Ringer (ed.), *The Early Romantic Era: Between Revolutions, 1789 and 1848*. Basingstoke: Macmillan Press, 84–108.

Williamson, O. E. 1975. *Markets and Hierarchies, Analysis and Antitrust Implications*. New York: The Free Press.

Williamson, O. E. 1979. "Transaction-Cost Economics: The Governance of Contractual Relations", *Journal of Law and Economics*, 22(2): 233–61.

Winter, C. 2012. "How Media Prosumers Contribute to Social Innovation in Today's New Networked Music Culture and Economy", *International Journal of Music Business Research*, 1(2): 46–73.

Wlömert, N. & D. Papies 2015. "On-demand Streaming Services and Music Industry Revenues: Insights from Spotify's Market Entry", *International Journal of Research in Marketing*, 33(2): 314–27.

World Intellectual Property Organization (WIPO). 1961. International Convention for the Protection of Performers, Producers of Phonograms and Broadcasting Organizations ("Rome Convention" of 26 October 1961).

Zentner, A. 2006. "Measuring the Effect of File Sharing on Music Purchases", *Journal of Law and Economics*, 49(1): 63–90.

## Internet sources

Access Industries. n.d. Holdings by Industry. www.accessindustries.com/industry/ (retrieved 21 November 2016).

ASCAP. n.d. "Licensing types for radio", www.ascap.com/licensing/types/radio (retrieved 15 May 2016).

Austrian Copyright Act of 1846 in Primary Sources of Copyright (1450–1900), www.copyrighthistory.org/cam/tools/request/showRecord.php?id=record_d_1846b (retrieved 22 February 2017).

Baden Civil Code of 1809 in Primary Sources on Copyright (1450–1900), www.copyright history.org/cam/tools/request/showRecord.php?id=record_d_1809 (retrieved 22 February 2017).

Billboard.biz. 2009. "Michael Jackson, Pepsi Made Marketing History", 3 July, www.billboard.com/articles/news/268213/michael-jackson-pepsi-made-marketing-history (retrieved 2 June 2016).

Billboard.biz. 2011. "Videogame Composer Christopher Tin Talks Historic Grammy Win", 14 February, www.billboard.com/biz/articles/news/1179275/videogame-composer-christopher-tin-talks-historic-grammy-win (retrieved 30 May 2016).

Billboard.biz. 2013. "Warner Music Group Closes on Acquisition of Parlophone Label Group", 1 July, www.billboard.com/biz/articles/news/global/1568720/warner-music-group-closes-on-acquisition-of-parlophone-label-group (retrieved 19 February 2016).

Billboard.biz. 2014a. "Neil Young's Pono Raises $6 Million, Third Biggest Kickstarter Ever", 15 April, www.billboard.com/biz/articles/news/digital-and-mobile/6054256/neil-youngs-pono-raises-6-million-third-biggest (retrieved 2 June 2016).

Billboard.biz. 2014b. "Apple Buys Beats in $3 Billion Deal: Iovine, Dr. Dre to Join Tech Giant", 28 May, www.billboard.com/biz/articles/news/digital-and-mobile/6099405/apple-buys-beats-in-3-billion-deal-iovine-dr-dre-to (retrieved 2 June 2016).

Billboard.biz. 2014c. "Sony/ATV Launches Pan-European Licensing Venture SOLAR", 25 September, www.billboard.com/articles/business/6259381/sonyatv-launches-pan-european-licensing-venture-solar (retrieved 15 January 2016).

Billboard.biz. 2015. "BMG, GEMA Ink New Pan-European Digital Licensing Deal", 10 June, www.billboard.com/articles/news/6590840/bmg-gema-ink-new-pan-european-digital-licensing-deal (retrieved 15 January 2016).

Billboard.biz. 2016. "Music's top 40 money makers 2014: the rich list", 10 March, www.billboard.com/articles/list/5930326/music-s-top-40-money-makers-2014-the-rich-list (retrieved 2 June 2016).

Blog of Music Business Research. 2015. "Music Streaming Revisited: The Superstars' Music Streaming Income", 13 July, https://musicbusinessresearch.wordpress.com/2015/07/13/music-streaming-revisited-the-superstars-music-streaming-income/ (retrieved 5 November 2015).

Bloomberg. 2015. "Spotify Value Tops $8 Billion as Investors Bet on Streaming", 6 October, www.bloomberg.com/news/articles/2015–06–10/spotify-valued-at-8–2-billion-as-teliasonera-buys-stake (retrieved 11 July 2016).

BusinessWire. 2006, "US Music Purchases Exceed 1 Billion Sales", The Nielsen Company 2006, Year-end music industry report, 4 January 2007, www.businesswire.com/news/home/20070104005813/en/2006-US-Music-Purchases-Exceed-1-Billion (retrieved 5 February 2016).

BusinessWire. 2012. "The Nielsen Company & Billboard's 2011 Music Industry Report", 5 January, www.businesswire.com/news/home/20120105005547/en/Nielsen-Company-Billboard%E2%80%99s-2011-Music-Industry-Report (retrieved February 1, 2016).

Company check. 2015. "Financial accounts of Kobalt Music Publishing", https://company check.co.uk/company/04089275/KOBALT-MUSIC-PUBLISHING-LIMITED/financial-accounts (retrieved 31 January 2016).

Copyright Act for the North German Confederation 1870 and the German Empire 1871 in Primary Sources of Copyright (1450–1900), www.copyrighthistory.org/cam/tools/request/showRecord.php?id=record_d_1870 (retrieved 22 February 2017).

Creative Artists Agency (CAA). n.d. "Artist Roster", www.caatouring.com/Public/ArtistRoster.aspx (retrieved 8 March 2016).

*The Economist.* 2016. "The Blogchain in Finance: The Hype Springs Eternal", 19 May, www.economist.com/news/finance-and-economics/21695068-distributed-ledgers-are-future-their-advent-will-be-slow-hype-springs (retrieved 25 July 2016).

Forbes. 2014. "Apple Finalizes Beats Deal After Paying Vivendi $404 Million", 2 August, www.forbes.com/sites/amitchowdhry/2014/08/01/apple-finalizes-beats-deal-after-paying-vivendi-404-million/#36c0d2f72162 (retrieved 11 July 2016).

Forbes. 2016. "The World's Highest Paid Celebrities of 2016", 11 July, www.forbes.com/sites/zackomalleygreenburg/2016/07/11/celeb-100-the-worlds-highest-paid-celebrities-of-2016/#3449c9851fb3 (retrieved 26 July 26).

French Literary and Artistic Property Act of 1793 in Primary Sources on Copyright (1450–1900), www.copyrighthistory.org/cam/tools/request/showRecord.php?id=record_f_1793 (retrieved 22 February 2017).

Future of Music Coalition. n.d. "40 revenue streams", http://money.futureofmusic.org/40-revenue-streams/ (retrieved 1 August 2016).

Future of Music Coalition. 2012. "MIDEM: Bands, Brands and Revenue", 31 January, http://money.futureofmusic.org/the-new-power-trio-bands-brands-and-revenue/ (retrieved 2 June 2016).

GEMA press release. 2012. "BMG Rights Management and GEMA sign deal for the licensing of Anglo-American repertoire online across Europe", 23 May, www.gema.de/en/aktuelles/bmg_rights_management_and_gema_sign_deal_for_the_licensing_of_anglo_american_repertoire_online_acros-1/ (retrieved 15 July 2016).

*The Guardian.* 2016. "Why Is the Music Industry Battling YouTube and What Happens Next?", 20 May, www.theguardian.com/technology/2016/may/20/music-industry-battling-google-youtube-what-happens-next (retrieved 25 May 2016).

*The Hollywood Reporter.* 2012. "BMG Buys Virgin, Famous Music Catalog From Sony/ATV", 21 December, www.hollywoodreporter.com/news/bmg-buys-virgin-famous-music-406080 (retrieved 31 January 2016).

IEGSR. 2015. "Sponsorship Spending on Music to Total $1.4 Billion In 2015", 8 September, www.sponsorship.com/iegsr/2015/09/08/Sponsorship-Spending-On-Music-To-Total-$1-4-Billio.aspx (retrieved 21 February 2017).

Milsom, J. n.d. "Minnesinger", in *The Oxford Companion to Music Online*.

Milsom, J. n.d. "Troubadours", in *The Oxford Companion to Music Online*.

Music & Copyright. 2016. "WMG makes biggest recorded music market share gains of 2015; indies cement publishing lead", music & copyright blog, 28 April, https://musicandcopyright.wordpress.com/2016/04/28/wmg-makes-biggest-recorded-music-market-share-gains-of-2015-indies-cement-publishing-lead/ (retrieved 2 May 2016).

Music Business Worldwide. 2015a. "How Spotify Can Become Profitable", 11 May, www.musicbusinessworldwide.com/how-can-spotify-become-profitable/ (retrieved 14 July 2016).

Music Business Worldwide. 2015b. "Kobalt Launches a Collection Society – and Invites Publishers to Join", 8 June, www.musicbusinessworldwide.com/kobalt-launches-collection-society-invites-publishers-join/ (retrieved 31 January 2016).

Music Business Worldwide. 2015c. "$25 Billion: The Best Number to Happen to the Global Music Business in a Very Long Time", 10 December, www.musicbusinessworldwide.com/25-billion-the-best-number-to-happen-to-the-music-business/ (retrieved 19 January 2016).

Music Business Worldwide. 2016a. "Deezer absorbs €100m investment from Orange and Access Industries", 20 January, www.musicbusinessworldwide.com/deezer-absorbs-e100m-investment-from-orange-and-access-industries/ (retrieved 6 February 2016).

Music Business Worldwide. 2016b. "YouTube is paying less than £0.0009 per stream to UK record labels", 20 May, www.musicbusinessworldwide.com/youtube-is-paying-less-than-0-0009-per-stream-to-uk-record-labels/ (retrieved 25 May 2016).

Music Business Worldwide. 2016c. "Spotify revenues topped $2bn last year as losses hit $194m", 23 May, www.musicbusinessworldwide.com/spotify-revenues-topped-2bn-last-year-as-losses-hit-194m/ (retrieved 14 July 2016).

Music Business Worldwide. 2016d. "Spotify surpassed 35m subscribers – And is growing faster than ever", 7 July, www.musicbusinessworldwide.com/spotify-surpassed-35m-subscribers-growing-faster-ever/ (retrieved 14 July 2016).

National Religious Broadcasters Music License Committee (NRBMLC). n.d. "Licensing history", www.nrbmlc.com/music-licensing/music-licensing-history/ (retrieved 15 May 2016).

Oxford Music Online. n.d. "Music industry", www.oxfordmusiconline.com/subscriber/article/grove/music/A2262804 (retrieved 15 August 2016).

Page, C. n.d. "Medieval", in *Grove Music Online*.

Page, W. 2015. "$25 Billion: The Best Number to Happen to the Global Music Business in a Very Long Time", Music Business Worldwide, 10 December, www.musicbusinessworldwide.com/25-billion-the-best-number-to-happen-to-the-music-business/ (retrieved 19 January 2016).

Phonographic Performance Limited (PPL). n.d. "Company history", www.ppluk.com/About-Us/Who-We-Are/Company-history/ (retrieved 22 February 2016).

Pollstar. 2017. "Booking Agency Directory 2017", https://store.pollstar.com/p-430-booking-agency-directory-2017-edition.aspx (retrieved 22 February 2017).

PRS/MCPS. n.d. "Our history", www.prsformusic.com/aboutus/ourorganisation/our history/Pages/timeline.aspx (retrieved 5 November 2015).

Prussian Copyright Act of 1837 in Primary Sources on Copyright (1450–1900), www.copyrighthistory.org/cam/tools/request/showRecord.php?id=record_d_1837a (retrieved 22 February 2017).

PwC. 2015. "Music: Key Insights at a Glance", www.pwc.com/gx/en/global-entertainment-media-outlook/assets/2015/music-key-insights-1-growth-rates-of-recorded-and-live-music.pdf (retrieved 21 February 2017).

Radio Music License Committee (RMLC). n.d. "Licensing history", www.radiomlc.org/ (retrieved 15 May 2016).

Reuters. 2009. "KKR, Bertelsmann plan music venture", 7 July, www.reuters.com/article/bertelsmann-idUSN0735018520090708 (retrieved 31 January 2016).

SACEM. n.d. "History", https://societe.sacem.fr/en/history (retrieved 5 November 2015).

Saxon Copyright Act of 1844 in Primary Sources of Copyright (1450–1900), www.copyright history.org/cam/tools/request/showRecord.php?id=record_d_1844 (retrieved 22 February 2017).

Schmidt, C. B. n.d. "Il pomo d'oro", in *The New Grove Dictionary of Opera Online*.

Sony Corporation, n.d. Labels. www.sonymusic.com/labels/ (retrieved 21 November 2016).

Statista.com. n.d. "Number of Global Monthly Active Spotify Users from July 2012 to June 2016", www.statista.com/statistics/367739/spotify-global-mau/ (retrieved 13 July 2016).

United Talent Agency (UTA). n.d. "Artist roster", https://music.utatouring.com/full-roster/ (retrieved 8 March 2016).

The Verge. 2015. "This was Sony Music's Contract with Spotify", 19 May, www.theverge.com/2015/5/19/8621581/sony-music-spotify-contract (retrieved 11 July 2016).

Vivendi. 2016b. Simplified Organisation Chart. www.vivendi.com/investment-analysts/key-figures-and-simplified-organization-chart/ (retrieved 21 November 2016).

Wikipedia. n.d. "Creative Commons License", https://en.wikipedia.org/wiki/Creative_Commons_license (retrieved 2 December 2015).

Wikipedia. n.d. "List of video hosting" services, https://en.wikipedia.org/wiki/List_of_video_hosting_services (retrieved 25 May 2016).

Wikipedia. n.d. "Music industry", https://en.wikipedia.org/wiki/Music_industry (retrieved 15 August 2016).

YouTube. n.d. "YouTube for Creators", www.youtube.com/yt/creators/benefit-levels.html (retrieved 25 May 2016).

# TABLES AND FIGURES

## Tables

## Figures

# INDEX